Silvia Schultermandl

Transnational Matrilineage

Contributions to Transnational Feminism

edited by

Erin Kenny
(Drury University, MO)
and
Silvia Schultermandl
(University of Graz, Austria)

Volume 1

LIT

Silvia Schultermandl

Transnational Matrilineage

Mother–Daughter Conflicts in Asian American Literature

LIT

Gedruckt mit Unterstützung des Bundesministeriums
für Wissenschaft und Forschung in Wien

Das Land Steiermark

→ Wissenschaft

Bibliographic information published by the Deutsche Nationalbibliothek
The Deutsche Nationalbibliothek lists this publication in the Deutsche Nationalbibliografie; detailed bibliographic data are available in the Internet at http://dnb.d-nb.de.

ISBN 978-3-7000-0823-1 (Austria)
ISBN 978-3-8258-1262-1 (Germany)

A catalogue record for this book is available from the British Library

Krotenthallergasse 10/8
A-1080 Wien
Tel. +43 (0) 1-409 56 61
Fax +43 (0) 1-409 56 97
e-Mail: wien@lit-verlag.at
http://www.lit-verlag.at

LIT VERLAG Dr. W. Hopf
Berlin 2009
Fresnostr. 2
D-48159 Münster
Tel. +49 (0) 2 51-620 32 22
Fax +49 (0) 2 51-922 60 99
e-Mail: lit@lit-verlag.de
http://www.lit-verlag.de

Distribution:

In Germany: LIT Verlag Fresnostr. 2, D-48159 Münster
Tel. +49 (0) 2 51-620 32 22, Fax +49 (0) 2 51-922 60 99, e-Mail: vertrieb@lit-verlag.de

In Austria: Medienlogistik Pichler-ÖBZ GmbH & Co KG
IZ-NÖ, Süd, Straße 1, Objekt 34, A-2355 Wiener Neudorf
Tel. +43 (0) 22 36-63 53 52 90, Fax +43 (0) 22 36-63 53 52 43, e-Mail: mlo@medien-logistik.at

In Switzerland: B + M Buch- und Medienvertriebs AG
Hochstr. 357, CH-8200 Schaffhausen
Tel. +41 (0) 52-643 54 85, Fax +41 (0) 52-643 54 35, e-Mail: order@buch-medien.ch

Distributed in the UK by: Global Book Marketing, 99B Wallis Rd, London, E9 5LN
Phone: +44 (0) 20 8533 5800 – Fax: +44 (0) 1600 775 663
http://www.centralbooks.co.uk/html

Distributed in North America by:

Transaction Publishers
New Brunswick (U.S.A.) and London (U.K.)

Transaction Publishers
Rutgers University
35 Berrue Circle
Piscataway, NJ 08854

Phone: +1 (732) 445 - 2280
Fax: + 1 (732) 445 - 3138
for orders (U. S. only):
toll free (888) 999 - 6778
e-mail: orders@transactionpub.com

In loving memory of my grandmother,
Antonia Pirc.
You died before I fully
understood where your stories came from.

TABLE OF CONTENTS

ACKNOWLEDGEMENTS

There are so many people I want to thank.

First and foremost my colleagues in the American Studies Department at the University of Graz: when I took my job in 2007 I thought I was coming to the department with a finished manuscript. Our conservations over the past year helped me reshape it in ways that were incredibly beneficial. I am indepted to the Austrian Ministery of Education for a scholarship that allowed me to conduct research at Rutgers University in the fall of 2005, a time and place where I had the privilege of meeting in person some of the scholars whose works have shaped my reading of Asian American literature and inspired my own work.

Transnational Matrilineage is the first book in the series Contributions to Transnational Feminism. I want to thank LIT Verlag for giving me the opportunity to establish this new venue, Richard Kisling in their Vienna office for his help with all matters that pertain to the production of this book, and Erin Kenny, my co-editor of the series, for embarking with me on this exciting project. I am also grateful to my colleagues from the Center for the Study of the Americas at the University of Graz for their good cheers and encouragement to start this book series.

This book grew out of my dissertation on mother-daughter relationships in Asian American and Caribbean American literatures and my continuous interest in the literary representation of matrilineage. I would like to thank the editors and readers of the following publishing venues for their comments and feedback on projects that I do are not reprinted in this book but that nevertheless helped me understand the complexity of matrilineage: *Studies in American Indian Literature* (SAIL), *Bilingual Review/ la revista bilingue*, and *Journal of the Association for the Research in Mothering* (JARM). All but one chapters of this book are original and appear here for the first time. A different version of Chapter Five appeared under the title "Writing Rape, Trauma, and Transnationality onto the Female Body: Matrilineal Em-body-ment in Nora Okja Keller's *Comfort Woman*" in *Meridians: Feminism, Race, Transnationalism.*

Thank you to Indiana University Press for granting me permission to reprint it here.

I consider myself fortunate to have received tremendous help in fleshing out my thoughts about matrilineage in Asian American literature by a circle of colleagues and friends who patiently read sections, chapters, and first drafts of the entire book: Cara Cilano, Rocío Davis, Lan Dong, Walter Hölbling, Klara Szmanko, Nicoleta Alexoae Zagni. Finally, I am especially grateful to Jessica Weintraub for her keen eye, critical feedback and cheerful comments ("This paragraph rocks!"). You told me what I needed to hear, both to work on the structure of my line of argumentation and on my strength to complete this project.

Without the support of my families, both Müller and Schultermandl, I could not have made it. Thank you for your patience with me when I was brooding over chapter outlines, bibliographies and drafts of the index while you guys where out playing.

My biggest thank you goes to my husband, Andreas Müller, whose continuous love and support over the years has helped me achieve so much.

INTRODUCTION

Reading Transnationality in Asian American Literature

In *Charlie Chan is Dead: An Anthology of Contemporary Asian American Fiction* (1993), Jessica Hagedorn raises an interesting question about the term that defines the literary production by writers of Asian American heritage: "Asian American literature? Too confining a term, maybe. World literature? Absolutely" (xxx). Hagedorn proposes that, given the cultural multiplicity and diversity of Asian American writers and their ethnic origins, what has been defined as Asian American literature deserves be read under a much more global scope, hence as world literature. In her 1993 essay "Assaying the Gold: Or, Contesting the Ground of Asian American Literature," Shirley Geok-lin Lim postulates in similar terms as Hagedorn that the term "Asian American" is "already collapsing under the weight of its own contradictions" (162). Lim's statement questions the applicability of a single umbrella term to adequately define a field that is so diverse that Hagedorn proposes the term world literature as only viable umbrella term for the literary production of Asian Americans. Lim thereby raises issues about the viability of Asian American criticism and the inherent multiplicity such a term might occult. More importantly, Lim's speculation is part of a general skepticism in multiethnic studies, such as with regards to the question of how and in what context to read multi-ethnic American identities.

This opening up of Asian American literature to global perspectives exposes Asian American writers to a set of new reading practices, different ones from the tendency of reading for depictions of "minority issues" such as racism, sexism, classism and heterosexisim. In line with Diana Fuss's assertion in her book, *Essentially Speaking: Feminism, Nature and Difference* (1989), that "there is no 'natural' way to read a text: ways of reading are historically specific and culturally variable, and reading positions are always constricted, assigned, or mapped" (35), reading Asian American literature as world literature allows critics to look at Asian American writers for references to global issues rather than issues that strictly denote the experience of Asian American diaspora and ethnic identity in the U.S., the space within American culture that Asian American communities have shaped and occupied.

Transnational Matrilineage: Mother-Daughter Conflicts in Asian American Literature reads depictions of mother-daughter relationships by contemporary Asian American female authors in the attempt to unveil possible strategies of building and communicating transnational feminist solidarity. I am particularly interested in how contemporary Asian American writers portray second-generation Asian American women who look at their family's histories through their confronatations with their own mothers. I propose the term "transnational matrilineage" to express two aspects that occur repeatedly throughout the subgenre of mother-daughter literature. On the one hand, the term *transnational* refers to the distance and sense of disconnectedness the daughter protagonists feel as they investigate their matrilineal heritage, most specifically their mothers, from within an American perspective. *Transnational* also refers to the gaps and breaks in the line of cultural inheritance and the sense of disconnectedness from this heritage that the daughters feel. On the other hand, the term matrilineage not only defines the difficult relationships these protagonists have with their mothers and their ultimate need to overcome these difficulties, it is also a metaphor that addresses the daughter protagonists' struggles with their families' histories – histories they misinterpret, are unfamiliar with, or even downright reject – as possible incentive for transnational feminist solidarity. Ultimately, my line of argumentation rests on the observation that the building of a transnational solidarity between mothers and daughters relies on two aspects: the daughter's ambivalence about the mother and her realization that reconciling with her matrilineal heritage is vital to bringing closure to her quest for identity.

In reading Asian American women writers' portrayals of Asian American daughters who confront their Asian heritage through conflicts with their mothers, this project adopts prevalent concerns in transnational feminist theory that deal with the perception, representation, and most importantly, construction of images of the Asian 'Other' in Asian American literature. It takes the focus away from how Asian American writers counter one-dimensional representations of Asian American people and communities in mainstream American culture and takes it to a close look at the transnational conversations between Asian and Asian American women that many authors embed into their depictions of mother-daughter cnflicts. In order to do so, my present project takes cues from the general consensus in transnational feminist theory and practice that revisionist practices are needed in order to expose the hegemonic traditions of Western feminism. Focusing on the specific locations from which feminists from around the globe articulate their concerns by adopting the discourses that they know work for them in a particular context, by scholars of transnational feminist theory have uncovered the power structure within feminist theory and practice and have devised new strategies with which to enable feminist solidarities across race, class, gender, and sexuality. Such strategies also offer new insights into literary texts by Asian American writers and help reshape the discourses about the convergence of ideology and aesthetics in experimental texts such as Kingston's *The Woman Warrior: Memoirs of a Girlhood Among Ghosts* (1976), Amy Tan's *The Joy Luck Club* (1989) and *The Bonesetter's Daughter* (2001), and Mei Ng's *Eating Chinese Food Naked* (1998). It also allows me to look at the transnational conversations in which recent novels such as Nora Okja Keller's *Comfort Woman* (1997) and Vineeta Vijayaraghavan's *Motherland* (2001) participate.

When these writers appropriate experiences of Asian women, they do so from an outside position in so far as their understandings of Asian cultures are not inherited, but relearned and renegotiated from within American culture.[1] I feel the need to emphasize this point in order to highlight the notion that Asian American authors write within specific cultures and thus do not, as some critics have argued, offer authentic insights into Asian American culture at large. I am also emphasizing this notion of writing within a specific culture as a caveat against reading practices that look for depictions of immigration and socialization as a main theme in all Asian American literary productions and that all Asian American writers can be read as "'windows' into the presumed alterity of other cultures" (Amireh and Majaj 2). While some Asian American writers are themselves immigrants, the ways in which the authors that I consider in this study write about mother-daughter relationships do not depict immigration *per se*, but are located in a post-immigration, transnational context. In this light, it is important to remember the authors' specific politics of location. In Adrienne Rich's sense, the term politics of location recognizes that as much as white women are marginal in the face of white, male supremacist ideologies, white women themselves also marginalize non-white women in the work force and in the context of reproductive rights issues, for instance.[2] In transnational feminist theory and practice, this notion of the (white) critic's politics of location is essential in so far as it "investigates the productive tension between temporal

---

[1] This sentence strongly echoes Tzvetan Todorov's observations in "'Race,' Writing, and Culture" (1986).

[2] See, for instance, "Notes Toward the Politics of Location." *Feminist Theory Reader: Local and Global Perspectives* (447-59). Several of Rich's essays published in *Blood, Bread and Poetry: Selected Prose, 1979-1985* (New York: W. W. Norton, 1986) address the issue of a politics of location of feminist critics.

and special theories of subjectivity," which helps "delineate" the postmodern, feminist rhetoric (Kaplan 138).

Asian American literature offers many examples for this postmodern feminist rhetoric by means of characterizing the mother-daughter relationship as a quintessential location of feminist identity politics. When daughter-protagonists in contemporary Asian American literature look at their mothers and at their Asian ancestry, they look for cues about their own, often contradictory, identity locations as minority women in the U.S. It is this turn to the mother in Asian American literature invites approaches from feminist theory and inter-cultural studies. Both fileds characterize identity as constructed, or learned, rather than inherited. In *Feminist Studies / Textual Studies* (1986), Teresa de Lauretis specifies the paradigm of contemporary feminist discourses:

> What is emerging in feminist writings is, instead, the concept of a multiple, shifting and often self-contradictory identity, a subject that is not divided in, but rather at odds with language; an identity made up of heterogeneous and heteronomous representations of gender, race, and class, and often indeed across languages and cultures; an identity that one decides to reclaim from a history of multiple assimilations, and that one insists on as a strategy (9).

In de Lauretis's terms, identity is "not the goal but rather the point of departure of the process by which one begins to know that and how the personal is political, that and how the subject is specifically and materially en-gendered in its social conditions and possibilities of existence" (9). From a different critical background, Stuart Hall offers a similar definition of identity in the context of culture, diaspora, and community. In his essay "Cultural Diaspora and Identity," for instance, Hall writes: "Perhaps instead of thinking of identity as already accomplished fact, which the new cultural practices they represent, we should think, instead, of identity as a 'production,' which is never complete, always in process, and always constituted within, not outside, representation" (Rutherford 222).

This understanding of identity as a constantly shifting process also manifests itself in the literary strategies that Asian American literature perfoms in order to examine and re-vision the trope of the mother-daughter conflict. Taking cues from Anita Diamant's imperative in her novel *The Red Tent* (1997) that "If you want to understand any woman you must first ask her about her mother and then listen carefully" (3), this project listens to the various positionings that feminist writers and authors have assigned to depictions of mother-daughter relationships.

Asian American Literary Scholarship: The Emergence of a Field

Coincidentally or not, the text that has probably shaped the field of Asian American literary studies the most depicts a complex mother-daughter relationship. The publication of Maxine Hong Kingston's memoir *The Woman Warrior* in 1976 launched a renaissance[3] of Asian American literature and informed two distinctly different trends in Asian American literary scholarship. On the one hand, critics reviewed, and continue to read, Kingston's memoir as ethnographic allegory of Chinese culture in the U.S. Especially because of Kingston's use of an autobiographical genre, critics have looked at Kingston's depiction of the Stockton Chinatown and of the Chinese American family for cues about "how culture operates" (Fischer 195) or as "mediation between cultures" and "handbooks of socialization into the codes of Americanness (Sollors 1986, 7). Many critics have vehemently resisted such classification of Asian American literature's authentic insight into Asian American communities. Elaine Kim, for instance, delineates the various misconceptualizations that result from the practice of reading Asian American realities through literature, as she argues in an essay of the same title (1990). As far as Kingston's work in particular is concerned, Sau-ling C. Wong's essay "Autobiography as Guided Chinatown Tour?: Maxine Hong Kingston's *The Woman Warrior* and the Chinese-American Autobiographical Controversy," points out the limitations of such readings that overshadowed the reception of Asian American literature early on. On the other hand, and this may be connected to the authority that critics have instilled in Kingston as a voice of the "Chinese American people," nationalist criticism, especially by male critics such as Frank Chin, Jeffery Paul Chan, Lawson Fusao Inada, and Shawn Wong, has called Kingston's literary agency and cultural authenticity into question. Whereas ethnographic readings of Asian American literature associate authors with their respective Asian backgrounds, nationalist criticism emphasizes the deviation of certain Asian American authors and their texts from traditional Asian literary forms and thus

---

[3] There is vast list of publications that precede Kingston's memoir are; cf. Amy Ling 1999 essay. Some of the better known early publications of Asian American literature include Carlos Bulosan's *America Is in the Heart* (1943), Jade Snow Wong's *Fifth Chinese Daughter* (1945), Monica Sone's *Nisei Daughter* (1953), and Chuang Hua's *Crossings* (1968).

questions their authenticity, for instance, by publicly labeling them as "fake" writers.[4]

Although ethnographic and nationalist readings of Asian American literature argue two completely different positions, they both emerge from the general tendency of highlighting the typically Asian in Asian American literature. This "tendency to de-Americanize" Asian American literature, argues Sau-ling C. Wong (1993, 9), is particularly problematic given the special outsider status of Asian American as "direct transplants from Asia or as custodians of an esoteric subculture" (9). Instead, Wong proposes a reading practice that surmounts exoticization of Asian American texts and their authors and that emphasizes the American context from which Asian *American* writers operate.

In "Re-Viewing Asian American Literary Studies," King-Kok Cheung asserts that "whereas identity politics – with its stress on cultural nationalism and American nativity – governed earlier theoretical and critical formulations, the stress is now on heterogeneity and diaspora" (1997, 1). Elaine Kim's scholarship is a great example of this movement. While her groundbreaking study of the social contexts of Asian American literature of the 19th- and early 20th-century sought to "trace the topography and rich textures of the Asian American experience as it is expressed in Asian American literature" (1982, xi) and to read Asian American literature as a response to the xenophobic stereotypes of "Orientals" that cast Asian Americans as "perpetual foreigners" (Cheung 1997, 5) to mainstream American culture, her later scholarship has focused on the "diasporic shift," that is, on the complex experience of hybridity, in Asian American literature (1992, xiii). This second category of scholarship which investigates the in-between position of Asian American writers is something of a "between worlds approach." Amy Ling's book *Between Worlds: Women Writers of Chinese Ancestry* (1990), for instance examines the "double consciousness" of Chinese American writers as they describe their rootedness in Chinese culture and their entrance into American culture. Ling's reading adopts Elaine Showalter's rhetoric of a "double-voiced discourse" that "always embodies the social, literary, and cultural heritages of both the muted and the dominant" (201) points out the interconnected marginality of Chinese women writers' ethnic and gender consciousness.

Although this approach addresses the complex experience of immigration, diaspora, and hybridity, it also tends to operate with a clear-cut center/margin division that places Anglo-American culture and feminism at the center and the

---

[4] Wendy Ho's chapter "Outlaw Brotherhood: Cultural Nationalism and the Politics of Mother-Daughter Discourse" provides a useful overview of nationalist criticism of Kingston and Tan (85-116).

feminist theory and practice of Asian Americans at the margin. The only existing full-length study in Asian American mother-daughter writing to date, Wendy Ho's *In her Mother's House: The Politics of Asian American Mother-Daughter Writing* (1999), uses this approach to emphasize the social, political, and cultural locations from which contemporary Asian American women write. At the same time, when Helena Grice's argues in "Asian American Feminisms: Developments, Dialogues, Departures" that Asian American feminist scholarship is concerned with "theorizing the gender-ethnicity nexus" (2000, 7), she does so by emphasizing the specific locations in response to U.S. culture studies that the various movements in Asian American studies participated in and not necessarily by foregrounding a transnational heuristic which might allow us to renegotiate the representational logic of Asian American culture altogether. Such a practice, however, is important because it is part of the multi-layered traditions that shaped the discussions of the role of literature specifically in the representation or performance of Asian American identities and communities.

While many critics of Asian American studies agree that their academic field has always been transnational in scope,[5] critics in the past two decades have increasingly recognized the imperative of reading Asian American literature largely from a transnational angle, thereby emphasizing the different locations and the associated discourses of power and privilege in which Asian American studies takes place. Most recently, Lim, Blair, Sohn and Valentino's book, *Transnational Asian American Literatures: Sites and Transits* (2006), considers "the complex, dialogical national and transnational formulations of Asian American imaginations" (2) while refusing to reject the U.S. as primary location of Asian American thought (1). Unlike the "Claiming America" discourse of early Asian American studies promoted by cultural nationalists, *Transnational Asian American Literatures* adopts a transnational scope in its investigation of the current body of Asian American scholarship and thus purports a definition of Asian American literature that "can no longer be viewed as merely a minor ethnic province of a domestic American canon" (22). Instead, the editors and contributing authors of *Transnational Asian American Literatures* emphasize the multiple dynamics at play in Asian American cultural production, dynamics that result in

> the diasporic, mobile, transmigratory nature of Asian American experience, a history characterized by disparate migratory threads, unsettled and unsettling histories churnmed by multiple and different Asian ethnic immigrant groups each with a different language and cultural

---

[5] Christopher Lee therefore speaks of a "renewed turn to the transnational at the moment" (24).

> stock, different value and belief systems, and different notions of literary aesthetics, albeit most largely mediated through the English language. (1)

Reading the definition of Asian American culture and the ubiquitous reference to difference that Lim and her coeditors propose, one cannot help but notice the similarities to Lisa Lowe's groundbreaking essay "Heterogeneity, Hybridity, Multiplicity: Marking Asian American Differences" of some fifteen years prior. Lowe argues that "what is referred to as 'Asian American' is clearly a heterogeneous entity" (27). The complexity of this entity, however, becomes evident from Lowe's unequivocal definition of the field. On the one hand, Lowe points out the importance of "identity politics" in order to facilitate "a concept of political unity that enables diverse Asian groups to understand our unequal circumstances and histories as being related" (30). On the other hand, however, Lowe cautions that "essentializing Asian American identity and suppressing our differences – of national origin, generation, gender, party, class – risks particular dangers: [...] it inadvertently supports the racist discourse that constructs Asians as homogenous group, that implies we are 'all alike' and conform to 'types'" (30).

A similar attention to multiplicity can be noted about Sau-ling C. Wong's concept of "denationalization," a concept which, like Lowe's, foregrounds the inherently diasporic nature of Asian American identity. Wong's term refers to three major changes in Asian American studies: first, the subsiding of "cultural nationalist" discourses for the sake of "a complication of identity politics" and the exploration of "other axes or organization and mobilization including class, gender and sexuality" (1); second, a "relaxation of the distinction between what is Asian American and what is 'Asian,' and between Asian American studies and Asian studies" (1); and third, a "diasporic perspective" that stands in clear opposition to the "domestic perspective" (2) of the "claiming America" trope of the late 1970s and early 1980s. Wong critiques this move toward "denationalization" for its "decontextualization" and its inability to sufficiently encompass the historical development of global movements at large (14).

What becomes evident from Wong's discussion of "denationalization" is the ambivalence toward criticism that stresses discourses of subjectivity exclusively. While Wong, and to a certain extent Lowe, recognize the general necessity to politicize Asian American cultural productions through identity politics, some critics reject the idea of a politicized experience all together. Shari Stone-Mediatore, for instance, offers a poststructuralist critique of experience which points out the dangers of over-emphasizing experience in empiricist narratives of female agency (111-16). In *Imagine Otherwise: On Asian Americanist Critique* (2003), Kandice Chuh even goes so far as to suggest that the current condition of Asian American studies calls for a "subjectless discourse" in order to "create the conceptual space to prioritize difference by foregrounding the discursive constructedness of subjectivity" (9). Chuh identifies one of the pitfalls of contemporary Asian American studies to be too invested in the politicization of Asian American experience, thereby ultimately producing essentialist discourses that operate along principles of particularism and exclusivism rather than offering a candid investigation of the social parameters that inform Asian American cultural productions both in the U.S. and worldwide.

In their collection of essays, *Postcolonial Theory and the United States: Race, Ethnicity, and Literature* (2000), Amritjit Singh and Peter Schmidt note a "postcolonial awareness" in contemporary discourses on ethnic American literatures. Singh and Schmidt define this postcolonial awareness through its "alertness to issues of otherness and creolization and transnational contexts – pointing to a confluence of ideas and paradigms between postcolonial studies and ethnic U.S. studies" (17). A similar awareness is central in contemporary transnational feminism, such as in scholars' commitment to dismantling the discursive positions that American literary and cultural productions assign to the "third world." First and foremost, Chandra Talpade Mohanty's essay "Under Western Eyes: Feminist Scholarship and Colonial Discourses" detects a promotion of one-dimensional images of third world women in Western feminist discourses: "Universal images of the Third World woman (the veiled woman, chaste virgin, etc.), images constructed from adding the 'Third World difference' to 'sexual difference,' are predicated upon (and hence obviously bring into sharper focus) assumptions about Western women as secular, liberated, and having control over their own lives" (Mohanty 2003, 42). In *The World Next Door: South Asian American Literature and the Idea of America* (2004), Rajini Srikanth introduces the notion of a transnational sensibility as a critical practice that helps avoid essentialist conceptualizations of cultural difference. Srikanth's discussion of the depictions of American culture in South Asian American emphasizes the "implications of such a transnational sensibility for issues of belonging and citizenship" (49). Like Srikanth's study does with regards to identity and belonging in a specific regional context, my present project seeks to investigate the implications of a transnational sensibility in the specific inter-personal relationship that frames depictions of the mother-daughter conflict in Asian American literature.

Defining the Asian American through Literature

Asian American literature has been a steady companion in and key informant to the paradigmatic shifts that occurred in the field of Asian American studies over time, and the paradigmatic shifts that occurred in ethnic American studies at large. With the increasing move away from nationalist or essentialist approaches to Asian American writers and their texts and towards a more multilateral appreciation of the multiple discourses that inform the scholarship of Asian American literary productions, "reading transnationally" has invigorated the field of Asian American studies with new possibilities for critical alliances. Perhaps the most animated discussions that contributed to a reconceptualization of Asian American writers and texts in the larger context of American literature pertain to the function that critics have seen Asian American literature play. I am talking here not so much of the discursive practice a text performs in the sense of Pierre Bourdieu's assertion that "the structure of the work" is a "prerequisite for the fulfilling of its function, if it has one" (118). Instead, I am interested in the ways critics have appropriated Asian American literature as illustrative evidence of the various trends in ethnic American studies in general and Asian American studies in particular. To read Asian American literature as ethnographic evidence of the material and historical realities of Asian American individuals and/or communities only addresses the social and political phenomena, and does so often at the expense of the literary and aesthetic aspects of a text. But precisely because Asian American literature, like many other traditions of ethnic American literature, does invite both of these approaches, the questions of which approach trumps the other in which specific academic context is an important one to keep in mind.

Some critics have favored readings that emphasize the writers' locations within American culture and their distance from their respective Asian heritages. Amy Tan has made it clear recently that she writes from an American perspective: "I am an American writer. I am Chinese by racial heritage. I am Chinese-American by family and social upbringing. But I believe that what I write is American fiction by virtue of the fact that I live in this country and my emotional sensibilities, assumptions, and obsessions are legally American" (2003, 310). As problematic as Tan's statement is in that it conflates national identity with cultural identity, it also makes a strong point about the rootedness of American-born writers of Asian heritage within the literary and cultural tradition of the U.S. This rootedness in American culture, and the underlying diasporic distance of Asian American writers from their Asian heritages, is an important point to keep in mind when analyzing the discursive strategies of Asian American authors. In her book, *Assimilating Asians: Gendered Strate-*

gies of Authorship in Asian America (2000), Patricia P. Chu reads Asian American literature for visible cues about "how authors' choices are shaped by the discursive fields they enter, the audience they hope to reach, and the genres they adopt and adapt" (11). The focus on American culture is dominant in Chu's analysis of Asian American writers and their appropriation of the genre of the *bildungsroman*. The texts she investigates "claim Americanness for Asian American subjects" and "construct accounts of Asian ethnicity that complicate, even as they support, the primary claim of Americanness representing Asian Americans as grounded in highly specific histories in America" (4).

With focus on Asian American writers' adaptation to and adoption of an "American" point of view, Sau-ling C. Wong's essay "Sugar Sisterhood," for instance, detects a discursive distance between the American daughters and their Asian ancestry in Amy Tan's *The Loy Luck Club*. Tan's strategy of locating China in the past and American culture in the present runs the risk of orientalizing China as the quintessentially exotic and backward 'Other' to modern American society. Wong suggests that the Americanized daughter in *The Joy Luck Club* "serves as a convenient, unobtrusive stand-in for the mainstream reading public" (197). Chu's and Wong's studies point out very effectively that, given the Americanization of Asian American writers, there are bound to be misrepresentations of Asia if authentic impressions of Asian is what critics are readers are looking for in the individual texts. More importantly, the binary oppositions on which such assertion about American or Asian identity rests operate with notions of purity and syncretism, what Françoise Lionnet and Shumei Shih's project *Minor Transnationalism* (2005) see evidenced in "politics of retrieval" and "politics of inclusion and exclusion" (9) and thus inevitably preclude non-essentialist approaches to Asian American literature.

What contemporary Asian American literary scholarship, including the projects of Wong and Chu, forcefully exemplifies is that America and Asia are far from being culturally pure or homogenous entities, or that they exist in isolation. Instead, Asian American studies evidences a demand for and a supply of a variety of the kinds of "flexible strategies" that Viet Thanh Nguyen locates at the center of anti-essentialist authorial agency as discussed in *Race and Resistance: Literature and Politics in Asian America* (2002, 4). In other words, the field of Asian American studies not only refutes essentialism, but also goes beyond the boundaries of the hyphenated entities implied in the semantics of the terms that designate the two fields themselves. Arjun Appadurai delineates the limitations of such practices that theorize Asian American identity strictly along the concept of hyphenation:

> The formula of hyphenation (as in Italian-Americans, Asian-Americans, and African-Americans) is reaching the point of

> saturation, and the right-hand side of the hyphen can barely contain the unruliness of the left-hand side. [...] The politics of ethnic identity in the U.S. is inseparably linked to the global spread of originally local national identities. For every nation-state that has exported significant numbers of its population to the United States as refugees, tourists, or students, there is now a decolonized transnation, which retains a special ideological link to a putative place or origin but is otherwise a thoroughly diasporic collectivity. No existing conception of Americanness can contain this large variety of transnations (424).

Appadurai's turn to a transnational practice of identity politics epitomizes the sensibility that contemporary scholarship needs to exhibit in order not to categorize Asian American literature as an essential "Other" within the American literary canon.

While the materialist and ideological aspects of Asian American literature have been under particular scrutiny in Asian American studies, more and more scholars now turn to the literary and aesthetic aspects. In the introduction to *Literary Gestures: The Aesthetic in Asian American Writing* (2006), Sue-Im Lee proposes a critique of Asian American literature that investigates "the complementary possibilities of a historically and materially engaged analysis that also recognizes the aesthetic as a rich culture variable" (1). Lee and her co-editor Rocío G. Davis underline the "constructed dimensions" of Asian American writing based on their understanding that literature is a *discursive* practice[6] rather than an ethnographic one (2). Deeply aware that the very genesis of Asian American literary studies, like many other ethnic American literary traditions, relied heavily on the emphasis on the historical and material realities of texts by an ethnic group who remained excluded from dominant literary presence for a long time, Lee sees the potential for a new Asian American critique in a balanced approach that ties together the universal criteria of New Criticism with the particular realities of Asian American literature. That such a balance is rather difficult to achieve is a sentiment that Rajini Srikanth shares when she contends that literature and ethnography form "an uneasy alliance" (2001, xvii). But it is precisely this willingness to explore the deeper potential within this uneasy alliance in Asian American literary scholarships that is needed in order to liberate Asian American literature from the question of authenticity.

---

[6] Lee cites George Levine's assertion in his book *Aesthetics and Ideology* (1994) that literature is "a definable category of discourse" (Davis and Lee 3).

This new interest in the performance of Asian American identity through literary texts also generated new discourses about the location of Asian American writers within the American literary tradition. In the introduction to *Form and Transformation in Asian American Literature* (2006), Zhou Xiaojing observes that the classification of Asian American literature has for the most part occurred along the binary opposition of whether individual texts "demonstrate complicity with or resistance to hegemonic ideologies of assimilation" (2) without looking at how Asian American "authors have resisted, subverted, and reshaped European American literary genres" (2). Such practice, urges Zhou, has inferred to the field of Asian American studies a "category crisis" that results from the extensive subsuming of increasingly experimental texts by Asian American writers under critical practices that cannot cope with such multiplicity and heterogeneity. Such emergence of a category crisis, as Susan Koshy argues in an essay that evokes this concept, reflects the representational practices of Asian American literatures on the level of form as well as of content. In her essay, "The Fictions of Asian American Literature," Koshy convincingly critiques the limiting effects of the ideological practices of canonizing Asian American literature along such parameters as origin or difference. Koshy emphasizes that the field of Asian American literary studies, more than any other discipline in ethnic American studies, is characterized by the status of "about-to-be" (467) since the constant arrival of new immigrant groups from Asia demands a constant expansion of the scope of what classifies as Asian American literature. While this necessary expansion does indeed occur, Koshy cautions that there are inherent hierarchies within the field, hierarchies that position the relevance and outpour of literary scholarship on Chinese American and Japanese American writers, for instance, as more formative and pertinent than scholarship on Filipino American and Cambodian American writers (469). While these hierarchies relate to issues regarding the canonization and anthologization of texts under the rubric of an Asian American literary subcanon, they also speak to a more general question in Asian American studies: who/what is Asian American?

While Koshy approaches this question also from the context of canonicity,[7] it is her investigation of the analytical practices of reading Asian American literature that is interesting in the context of mother-daughter relationships. Of particular interest in her assertion that the different genealogies of the different

[7] See also David Palumbo-Liu (1995); Lisa Lowe (1995); and Rajini Srikanth and Lavina D. Shankar (2000).

"ethnonational"[8] groups in Asian America are reminiscent of the cultural heterogeneity of Asian American communities, the same heterogeneity that many Asian American writers emphasize in their depictions of the differences between mothers and daughters and the resulting issues concerning identification within Asian American literature. In this sense, Koshy reiterates E. San Juan Jr.'s assertion that "Asian Americans as heterogeneous subjects cannot be reduced to a monolithic category" (135). As much as the scope of Asian American studies has been broadened over the past decades, so, too, have definitions of the term Asian American itself undergone multiple shifts in meaning. In a recent essay, Eleanor Ty, for instance, observes that due to the multiple positionings that writers occupy, North Asian American and European ethnic texts can no longer be defined by the intervention of hyphenated identities, especially in the context of writers whose texts are not "primarily concerned with the challenges of assimilation, racial prejudice, or with cultural hybridity" (2002, 239).[9] Reminiscent of Paul Girloy's assertion that hybridity always operates with an implied essentialism, since it "presupposes two anterior purities" (Gilroy 1994, 54), Ty instead offers the term "Asian global narratives," which she defines as "narratives by Asians in the diaspora whose works fall outside of this hyphenated paradigm of Asian plus adopted country" (2002, 242). Ty arranges these Asian global narratives into three different categories: first, works that stress globalization as major point of interest; second, works written by writers of Asian origin which do not offer depictions of the authors' adopted countries; and third, works that do not have anything "Asian" as their subject matter (2002, 240). Going beyond the teleological narrative, these works, continues Ty, "highlight movement, instability, and importance of standpoint or location" (2002, 241).

Why Read Mother-Daughter Conflicts?

Many ethnic American women writers have represented through depictions of mother-daughter relationships cultural agency for their ethnic groups. In reference to Chandra Talpade Mohanty's critique in "Under Western Eyes" that white feminists are prone to over-generalizing and stereotypicizing the woman of color's existence (Mohanty et al. 1991, 51), Wendy Ho detects within contemporary Asian American mother-daughter writing emphatic attempts to

[8] I am borrowing the term "ethnonational" from Wanni W. Anderson and Robert G. Lee's project *Displacements and Diasporas: Asians in the Americas* (2005, 9).

[9] Ty argues a similar point in the collection of essays, *Beyond the Hyphen: Asian North American Identities* (2004), she co-edited with Donald C. Goellnicht.

counter "a tendency to lump all of us as 'Asian women,' 'Third World women,' or 'women of color,' which denies the significance of our experiences and histories" (33). Ho's criticism is based on the premise that motherhood and daughterhood, the most personal of all experiences, do not allow for over-generalizations. Ho suggests the following:

> Many women writers of color sought ways to articulate their specific concerns and contradictions in the telling of their mother-daughter experiences in ways that did not replicate or depend upon white mainstream feminist models and narratives. As much as there were intense conflicts with mothers, they emphasized the mothers' powerful social and emotional presence in nurturing their creativity and in establishing the homeplace as a political space for their subordinated racial-ethnic families. (37)

The discourses and modes of representation that they apply capture the same complexity and ambiguity that are pivotal to the mother-daughter relationships that they depict. The challenge for Asian American women writers is to present the daughters' need for individuality to the same extent as the mothers' need for continuity of herself and of their collective cultural heritage.

There are myriad ways in which mother-daughter relationships feature in Asian American literature, and the texts that I chose to discuss in this project are by no means representative of the large canon of Asian American literature. I thus feel the need to clarify briefly my choice to discuss certain texts and not others. My study focuses on texts whose narrative development proceeds in a *bildungsromanesque* fashion. I therefore leave out entire sub-genres of narrative fiction, including contemporary Asian American "chick-lit" such as Kavita Daswani's *The Village Bride of Beverly Hills* (2005) or Sonja Singh's *Goddess for Hire* (2004).[10] Similarly, I do not devote attention to the representation of mother-daughter relationships in children's literature or adolescent literature such as Cynthia Kahodata's *Kira Kira* (2005) or Linda Sue Park's *Project Mulberry* (2005).[11]

As far as the thematic choices I made are concerned, this project does not discuss texts in which the relationship between mother and daughter appears merely as a subplot, such as in Jumpa Lahiri's novel *The Namesake* (2003), nor does it analyze texts that recover the maternal both as lived experience and as

---

[10] See Pamela Butler and Jiqna Desai's essay "Manolos, Marriage, and Mantras: Chick-Lit Criticism and Transnational Feminism" for a discussion of these texts, among others.

[11] See Dolores de Manual and Rocío G. Davis' special Issue of *Lion and the Unicorn* on *Asian American Children's Literature*.

figural trope in the context of a broad sketching of transnational relationships between Asian and America, such as in Jessica Hagedorn's novel *Dogeaters* (1990) and Shirley Geok-lin Lim's memoir *Among the White Moon Faces* (1997). Moreover, I only look at the conflicts between daughters and their biological mothers. I do not mean to essentialize biological motherhood by leaving out the issues of surrogate motherhood or adoption as depicted in David Ball's *China Run* (2002), Gish Jen's *The Love Wife* (2004), and Aimee Phan's *We Should Never Meet* (2005). On the contrary, I am aware of the fact that the question of adoption plays an important role in contemporary Asian American critique in that it urges us to reconsider East-West relations through discourses pertinent to the domestic realm in similar ways as my project on mother-daughter relationships does.[12] But while a consideration of the transnational practices of Asian American adoption would certainly offer a fruitful discussion of the power relations and ideological conceptualizations of family, I have chosen to analyze in this project only the depictions of the relationships between daughters and their biological mothers and I will not devote any attention to the relationships between daughters and their non-biological mothers. While such texts *do* foreground the daughter's ambivalence about her relationship with her mother, I would argue that the ambivalence they depict emphasizes primarily the fact the daughter is adopted and thus raise different issues about identity and cultural belonging in Asian American communities than the ones that I am interested in.

Because my emphasis is on the conflict between mother and daughter, I have chosen to analyze texts that position mothers and daughters in a distinguishable opposition to each other. This leaves out texts such as Julie Shigekuni's *A Bridge Between Us* (1995), where several generations of women interact, and novels such as Bharati Mukherjee's *Desirable Daughters* (2003) or Gish Jen's *Typical American* (1991) and *Mona in the Promised Land* (1996), novels that do not present a mother-daughter conflict in which the two women maintain polarized positioning.

The narrative texts that this book analyzes, Maxine Hong Kingston's *The Woman Warrior*, Amy Tan's *The Joy Luck* Club and *The Bonesetter's Daughter*, Mei Ng's *Eating Chinese Food Naked*, Nora Okja Keller's *Comfort Woman*, and Vineeta Vijayagharava's *Motherland*, all emphasize the daughter's search for selfhood. While some of the works also portray in equal measures the mother's quest for identity, such as through narratives of the mother's

---

[12] For an excellent discussion of Westerncentric discourses in transnational adoption narratives, see Emily Cheng.

lives in Asia or their experiences of immigration and diaspora, what foregrounds the daughter's perspective is the explicitly transnational negotiation of matrilineage they perform through the daughter's appropriation of her matrilineage. In reflecting on and re-assessing their own childhoods, the daughters in the texts by these Asian American women writers recreate memories and thus attempt self-creation via the narrative process of storytelling. It is this aspect of self-creation through the narrative process that, so I would like to suggest, offers a particularly interesting approach to reading these texts. Hence, I have chosen for my discussion here texts whose narrative focus is on the daughter, partly because the authors themselves have been labeled "daughter-writers" (Grice 2002, 91), and partly because the perspective that these texts convey strongly highlights the American context of the individual narratives, a context which is oftentimes foregrounded through the daughter's side of the story, as it where. Nora Okja Keller, for instance, admits that she first wrote the mother's narrative of her critically acclaimed novel *Comfort Woman*, and later added the daughter's perspective to it because she felt the need for a second narrative strand that would bring the reader "up to date" (Burlingame 2). The texts that I discuss in this study operate with a similar understanding of the daughter's role within the narrative situations of the individual texts.

Transnational frameworks animate my study of Asian American literary texts that depict complex mother-daughter relationships. In particular, the mother-daughter relationship is interesting because it invokes the quintessential feminist ambivalence between self and other, an issue of ample consideration in feminist theory, at the same time as it raises the very questions about identity and representation that the field of Asian American studies confronts. The push and pull factors between independence from and identification with the mother characterize the daughter's complex negotiation of a feminist consciousness between self and 'Other.' In many mother-daughter relationships in Asian American literature, the 'Other' is also marked by distinct cultural differences, which makes the innate ambivalence between mothers and daughters even more complex. More importantly, however, mother-daughter relationships continue to maintain a special, and highly contested, position within Asian American literature. On the one hand, an important number of literary texts that evolve around the issue of mother-daughter conflicts predominates the Asian American literary market, especially by young, female authors. On the other hand, the fact that mother-daughter relationships have been considered by many critics to be emblematic, almost iconic, of Asian American literature has led to avid debates. Some critics have argued that through depictions of mother-daughter relationships, Asian American authors emphasize the generational conflict that is a common trope in American literature in general and ethnic American literature in particular. Critics of that tradition tend to focus on the cultural struggle that they see embodied by the Asian mother and the American daughter, and hence argue, that mother-daughter relationships in Asian American literature provide rich and forceful examples of the social realities of immigrants, namely the impacts of nativism and assimilation. Thus, Walter Shear concludes in reference to Amy Tan's *The Joy Luck Club*, the "mother-daughter tensions are both the articulation of the women's movement and the means of specifying the distinctness of Chinese and Chinese-American culture" (195).

This notion that mothers and daughters consider each other as culturally different may be true of the generational conflicts between mothers and daughters in ethnic American literature in general, since the renegotiation of the cultural identity often happens via an exploration of the daughter's relationship to her mother(s). Perhaps it is because Asian American writers favor daughterly perspectives in their depictions of mother-daughter conflicts (Grice 37) that the ambivalence about embodying the mother's voice is particularly prevalent in the novels' narrative discourse. As Marianne Hirsch points out in her study *The Mother/Daughter Plot: Narrative, Psychoanalysis, Feminism* (1989), the mutilation of the mother's discourse in the family romance is a replication of patriarchal dominance that the daughter applies over her own gender. In reference to psychoanalytic models that describe the social organization of gender, such as Nancy Chodorow's concept of the reproduction of mothering, the daughter's domination of the fictional discourse with the intention of voicing her anger over the mother's over-presence or absence of attention can be read as *reproduction* of patriarchal ideals that stigmatize motherhood in general and the mother as individual in particular (Hirsch 136). Through such discursive 'Othering' of the mother, the daughter becomes complicit with patriarchal domination of women in general and motherhood in particular. This Othering of the mother partly characterizes Asian American literature of matrilineage in that it does not offer the kind of "mother/daughter plot" Marianne Hirsch observes in African American women's writing but employs narrative strategies that illustrate the daughter's ambivalence about her relationship with her mother.[13] By bridging the narrator's agency between individual and collective voice, Asian American mother-daughter writing thus partly "shares a genealogy with mainstream feminism" at the same time as it "departs from it" (Grice 3).

The notion that the mother-daughter conflict in Asian American literature can serve as a metaphor for the formation of Asian American culture has been

---

[13] See Hirsch, *The Mother/Daughter Plot* (177-91); and Marina Heung (1993).

critiqued by numerous scholars. First and foremost, Lisa Lowe astutely counters the practice of reading mother-daughter relationships in Asian American literature as mere instances of the commonplace generational conflict.[14] Such a practice, cautions Lowe in *Immigrant Acts*, relies too heavily on the perception that the relationships between mothers and daughters are essentially "feminized" (78), i.e. that they only address issues related to gender and femininity without accounting for the more universal aspects of heterogeneity in Asian American culture, of which gender is merely one matrix. Therefore, Lowe critiques how mother-daughter relationships have become symbolic of Asian American culture at the expense of acknowledging diversity and plurality in Asian American culture.

I share with Lowe the conviction that to read mother-daughter conflicts primarily as indicative of the generational conflict leads to shorthanded assumptions about Asian American literature as representational of, even derived from, immigrant experiences. The implied dichotomies between nativism and assimilation, while true on a sociological level for Asian immigrant in the U.S., do not apply to Asian American literature at large. First of all, not all of Asian American literature focuses on issues of immigration and disapora, nor are Asian Americans necessarily immigrants. Secondly, to employ the generational conflict metaphorically for an evaluation of Asian American literature reiterates a binary opposition between Asian and American identities. With the mother as a stand-in for Asia and the daughter as a stand-in for America, this binary opposition conjures up ideas of culture that focus on purity and essentialism instead of hybridity and pluralism. It simply disregards the fact that every culture, as Homi K. Bhabha illustrates in *The Location of Culture* (1997), is *sui generis* hybrid. Instead, it locates America and Asia as cultural entities in clear opposition to each other without addressing the complex dynamics that constitute Asian American cultural productions and practices.

Both disclaimers are rooted in recent research that investigates Asian American Studies from a transnational scope. Returning to Shirley Geok-lin Lim and her co-editors' endeavors in *Transnational Asian American Literature: Sites and Transits*, the notion that Asian American cultural productions grow out of and mirror a large variety of geographical, cultural and social locations, and that these locations always brings forth new challenges into discussions of cultural matrixes such as ethnicity, class, gender, sexuality, and age. Therefore, if the mother-daughter conflict can be recovered as a trope in Asian American literature, then only in the form of a trope for the interrelated-

[14] See also the work of Melani McAlister; and of Malinia Johar Schueller.

ness of the different matrixes and the complex cultural appropriations in which it is enmeshed. It can serve as a symbolic manifestation of ambivalence and duality, two aspects that characterize mother-daughter relationships to the same extent as they characterize culture.

To emphasize this interconnectedness is the aim of chapter one of this study, "The Great Unresolved Mystique: Mother-Daughter Relationships in Feminist Literary Theory." In this chapter, I analyze the emergence of the ambivalent relationship between mothers and daughters in Asian American literature both from a psychoanalytical as well as from a cultural perspective. Drawing on the two main theoretical practices within feminist scholarship about mother-daughter relationships, psychoanalytical feminist theory on the one hand and matrilineage as cultural agency on the other, this chapter illustrates that Asian American literature falls in-between these two theoretical discourses. This location of the "in-between" is pivotal in Asian American literature as it echoes contemporary trends to produce Asian American critique in non-essentialist terms. In this vein, one of the main questions that the mothers and daughters face, the controversy over what constitutes female identity, or, more precisely, what demarcates ethnic from female identity, is present throughout my discussions of the individual texts. As the novels and autobiographies discussed in this book exemplify, there is no incentive to believe that mothers and daughters would identify with each other just because they come from the same famly.

The mother-daughter conflict offers a tremendous paradox in the creation and maintenance of transnational feminist solidarity. On the one hand, the mother-daughter relationship constitutes the most imminent possibility for the construction of a feminist bond. On the other hand, however, the very closeness between mother and daughter that might facilitate such formation of a feminist solidarity often leads to conflicts and disputes. This dichotomy, then, houses a wider scope of issues than the commonly employed term "love-hate relationship" implies. Several contemporary Asian American women writers refer to this paradox in their portrayals of mother-daughter relationships where the daughter's constructed self-definition differs from the image of motherhood her mother represents. For instance, Maxine Hong Kingston and Amy Tan often depict daughters who perceive their mothers as backwards and essentially Chinese; the daughters' orientalist and often one-dimensional accounts of their mothers sometimes appear as unchallenged in the text, and thus portray the mothers as institutionalized constructions of old-fashioned Asian women who have trouble assimilating to modern American culture. Such 'othering' of the mother is quite problematic and has contributed to the promoting of images that characterize, in the specific cases of Kingston and Tan, Chinese woman as essentially different from Western women, a rhetoric which refuses to challenge constructed ideals of homogeneity within North American feminist theory and practice. Indeed, Wendy Ho's study *In her Mother's House: The Politics of Asian American Mother-Daughter Writing* (1999) suggests that

> "the Chinese immigrant mothers' experiences in these writers' stories are significantly embedded in Chinese traditions and ways of being and thinking, which have been further dislocated and relocated – culturally, geopolitically, and historically – in the U.S. Sadly, many of the daughters do not understand the value of this legacy: They have lost or devalued the meanings of their mothers' stories in their Anglo-American translations" (41).

Ho's specific observations about Chinese American literature are also applicable to Asian American mother-daughter writing in general.

Twenty-five years span the publication of Kingston's memoir and the *The Bonesetter's Daughter* and *Motherland*, the two most recent books that I analyze. Coincidentally or not, for these novels about the mother-daughter conflict, and several others in the 1980s and 1990s, including Tan's *The Joy Luch Club*, Ng's *Eating Chinese Food Naked*, and Keller's *Comfort Woman*, Kingston's *The Woman Warrior* serves as a mother-text that paved the way for later depictions of an transnational matrilineage between mothers and daughters.[15] Subsequent novels follow the orientation in the elaborate mother-daughter conflict Kingston centers at her memoir and depict the daughter's acquaintance of her collective diasporic memory as inseparable from the daughter's reconciliation with the mother-figure. Maxine remembers this as part of her own identity quest: "Chinese-American, when you try to understand what things in you are Chinese, how do you separate what is peculiar to childhood, to poverty, insanities, one family, your mother who marked your growing up with stories, from what is Chinese?" (5-6). Kingston's memoir, the mother-text which the following generation of Asian American authors and scholars alike consider a definitive moment in Asian American literature in general and Asian American literature of matrilineage in particular, conceptualizes the ambivalent mother-daughter relationship as trope of Asian American literature in search of a self-definition. It is no surprise, then, that *The Woman Warrior* continues to be the

---

[15] In *Between Worlds: Women Writers of Chinese Ancestry*, Amy Ling, for instance, identifies *The Woman Warrior* as one of the texts that triggered her interest in discovering a literary tradition that she can personally identify with (xi).

most widely taught and critically discussed text in ethnic American literatures.[16]

Because of the cultural difference and polarized representation communicated through the mother-daughter relationship, contemporary Asian American women writers amplify the heterogeneity of Asian American communities. They emphasize the distinct differences between first- and second-generation immigrant women and, by so doing, deconstruct notions of a linear, one-dimensional Asian American identity in the contemporary U.S. In this context, the daughters' Americanized perspectives thus lend themselves well for a reading of contemporary Asian American literatures through a transnational feminist lens. At this point, I feel that I need to specify my use of the term Americanized in reference to the daughter protagonists' perspectives and the authors' locations as writers. I am aware of the implied exclusion by referring to the second-generation immigrant daughters and authors as Americanized. I can only reiterate Ien Ang's assertion that the term "Westernized" and its implication that "no matter how long Chinese people have lived in the West, they can only become western*ized*, never pure and simply 'western,'" hints at the possibility of an underlying determination "to keep western culture white" (1994, 15 original emphasis). Similarly, the use of the distinction between first- and second-generation Asian American only partly solves the inherent problematic, since some of the writers I look at in this study were born in Korea or India and came to the U.S. at a very young age. Rather than second-generation immigrant, these writers would classify more as 1.5 generation immigrant, a term Rubén Rumbaut coins to describe the cultural socialization of young refugees who were born abroad and raised in the US. Manisha Roy proposes a useful compromise in her distinction between "Asian(-born)-American mothers and their Asian-American(-born) daughter" (Dasgupta 1998, 97). By means of simplification, I would even go so far as suggesting that Asian *American* daughters and *Asian* American mothers are terms that emphasize the cultural breech within the mother-daughter relationship. However, it is only appropriate in the specific context of Asian American mother-daughter writing where the daughters perceive their mothers as being uncompromisingly Asian and where the mothers perceive their daughters as being entirely American, both, of course, being narrative strategies that manifest the innate difference between the two women.

By analyzing the cultural and social differences between Asian *American* daughters and their *Asian* American mothers, this book applies the framework

[16] In October 2008, the website of the MLA International Bibliography lists 385 entries on *The Woman Warrior*.

of transnational feminism to Asian American representations of Asia with the intention of exploring the possibilities of transnational feminist solidarity. I follow very much Chandra Talpade Mohanty's doctrine in her introduction to *Feminism Without Borders: Decolonizing Theory, Practicing Solidarity* (2003) that "decolonizing feminism involves a careful critique of the ethics and politics of Eurocentrism, and a corresponding analysis of the difficulties and joys of crossing cultural, national, racial, and class boundaries in the search for feminist communities anchored in justice and equality" (11). *Transnational Matrilineage* places itself in this line in that it analyzes the possibilities for a transnational solidarity while considering the obstacles daughters in Asian American literature might confront as they grapple with their Asian heritages.

The individual chapters of this book fall into two categories: in Chapters Two, Three and Four discuss the question of individual identity and the ways in which the daughter's individuality is juxtaposed with multiple communities. These first three chapters elaborate on the discursive constructedness of difference in relation to identity, memory, and home within the complex negotiations of matrilineage that Maxine Hong Kingston, Amy Tan and Mei Ng present, respectively, in their works. In the later chapters, I foreground the discursive construction of community in Asian American literary depictions of mother-daughter relationships. In this light, Chapters Five, Six, and Seven illustrate the various strategies with which Asian American literature addresses the question of community in the face of its own heterogeneity. My discussions of Nora Okja Keller, Amy Tan, and Vineeta Vijayagharavan approach the question of community by analyzing the epistemological overlap of the issues of academic community, literary community, and national community in Asian American literature as well as in transnational feminism.

This book is a very ambitious study: it combines readings of Asian American texts with feminist criticism, postcolonial theory, U.S. culture studies and literary criticism. The myriad of issues implied in the individual texts, however, calls for such a complex scope, one that adds to the existing canon of scholarship on Asian American self-representations the complementary vantage point of Asian American representations of Asia. The urgency for transnational sensibility becomes apparent from Jean Baudrillard's reading of the projection of interpretation: "The deepest avatar of racism is to think that an error about [other] societies is politically or theoretically less serious than the misinterpretation of our own world. Just as a people who oppresses another cannot be free, so a culture that is mistaken about another must be mistaken about itself" (32-33).

CHAPTER ONE

The Great Unresolved Mystique: Mothers-Daughter Relationships in Feminist Literary Theory

> "Only two kinds of daughters. […] Those who are obedient and those who follow their own mind!" Su-yuan Woo in Amy Tan's *The Joy Luck Club*

In a 1981 review essay in *Signs*, Marianne Hirsch argues the following: "Any full length study of the mother-daughter relationship, in whatever field, is by definition both feminist and interdisciplinary" (200). While the fields of study in which mother-daughter relationship features as a prominent trope are diverse and multiple, the specific methodologies with which critics investigate this relationship falls into two main categories: one is psychoanalytical feminism, and the other is matrilineality. Whereas white feminists in the 1970s started out with psychoanalytical interpretations of the mother-daughter dyad that discussed the daughter's quest for individuality, black feminists of the same era emphasized collectivity in their celebrations of motherhood as location of cultural survival in the face of black women's struggle against what was perceived as being a double marginality, i.e. being black and being female. These two traditions of scholarship provide the core vocabulary with which to theorize mother-daughter relationships. Thus also argues Elaine Tuttle Hansen in her book *Mother Without Child: Contemporary Fiction and the Crisis of Motherhood* (1997). Hansen identifies three themes in the literature on mother-daughter relationships: "the story of feminist thinking about motherhood since the early 1960s is told as a drama in three acts: repudiation, recuperation, and the latest and most difficult stage to conceptionalize, an emerging critique of recuperation that coexists with ongoing efforts to deploy recuperative strategies" (5).[17] This chapter seeks to position literary depictions of Asian American mother-daughter relationships within this third stage and by so doing offers a different approach to reading mother-daughter relationships than the essentialist ways which the two aforementioned traditions practiced.

---

[17] Like Hansen, Tess Cosslett distinguishes between "a feminist progress narrative, from matrophobia, to speaking for the mother, to allowing her irreducible difference and mystery" (151)

The Mother-Daughter Dyad in Psychoanalytic Feminism

Scholarship on the mother-daughter dyad in the tradition of psychoanalytic feminism emerged with second wave feminism and its key publications, such as Betty Friedan's *The Feminine Mystique* (1963), Kate Millett's *Sexual Politics* (1970) and Shulamith Firestone's *The Dialectic of Sex* (1970). The field of psychoanalytic feminism seeks to disrupt patriarchal concepts of gender by drawing of psychoanalysis, Marxism, and feminism as its core methodologies. One of the main arguments to incorporate psychoanalysis into feminism has been made by Juliet Mitchell in her groundbreaking book *Psychoanalysis and Feminism: Freud, Reich, Laing and Women* (1974). Mitchell insists that "the way we live as 'ideas' of the necessary laws of human society is not so much conscious as *unconscious* – the particular task of psychoanalysis is to decipher how we acquire our heritage of the ideas and laws of human society within the unconscious mind, or, to put it another way, the unconscious mind *is* the way in which we acquire these laws" (xiv original emphasis). Similarly, Teresa de Lauretis asserts that "Freud [...] does account for the continued existence and functionings of patriarchy as a structure of subjectivity, in the same way as Marx accounts for the socio-economic relations of capital that informs patriarchy in our times" (1984, 165). This ideological trinity of Marxism, psychoanalysis and feminism has largely influenced a re-investigation and reformulation of womanhood within society. The resulting de-constructions of patriarchal ideas of femininity, so in tune with demands for access to equal rights and equal opportunity, also affected women's positions within the family. With the multiple options for women to become more than just 'wife' and 'mother,' the need to define the concept of womanhood separately from motherhood gained topical significance.

One of the key texts of this tradition is Adrienne Rich's *Of Woman Born: Motherhood as Experience and Institution* (1976), a personal account of the author's life as a mother and as a daughter within the realm of the patriarchal white middle-class family. Rich de-mystifies motherhood as patriarchal, and thus restrictive, institution that undermines the possibility for consequential change within society. At the beginning of her groundbreaking book in the field of mother-daughter writing, Rich elaborates on the stereotype "mother" as most determinant constituent of what makes a woman. She starts with a fact which places women and motherhood at the center of life's creation, at least in biological terms, when she postulates that "all human life on the planet is born of woman" (11). Dismantling gender as discursive construct, and with it exposing discourses that shape motherhood, Rich observes that the social vocabulary that describes and ultimately defines women is centered on her biological function: "Woman's status as childbearer has been made into a major fact of her life. Terms like 'barren' or 'childless' have been used to negate any further identity" (11).

Such interference of patriarchy also shapes the social relationships among women, including the mother-daughter relationship. In her chapter "Motherhood and Daughterhood," the "core of [her] book" (218), Rich defines this bond between mother and daughter as already constituted in its prenatal existence: "This cathexis between mother and daughter – essential, distorted, misused – is the great unwritten story. Probably there is nothing in human nature more resonant with charge than the flow of energy between two biologically alike bodies, one of which has lain in the other" (225-26). Rich identifies this "unwritten story" as yet another product of patriarchal domination of female experience and speculates that "[l]ike intense relationships between women in general, the relationship between mother and daughter has been profoundly threatening to men" (226). Thus, Rich concludes that under paternal laws that are reigning over the family, "[t]he loss of the daughter to the mother, the mother to the daughter, is the essential female tragedy. We acknowledge Lear (Father-daughter split), Hamlet (son and mother), and Oedipus (son and mother) as great embodiments of the human tragedy; but there is no presently enduring recognition of mother-daughter passion and rapture" (237). One of the main contributions of Rich's study, the definition of the term "matrophobia" as "the fear not of one's mother or of motherhood but of becoming one's mother," indicates the daughter's limitations and inability to recognize the original "forces acting upon her [mother]" (235, original emphasis). In her matrophobic attitude, argues Rich, the daughter enacts covert self-hatred, but, because it is easier than sorting out her own lot, as it were, imposes her frustration with a sexist society upon her mother (236).

Similar to Rich's account of the mother's role as "our earliest social experience" (12), Nancy Chodorow points out in *The Reproduction of Mothering: Psychoanalysis and the Sociology of Gender* (1978), that mothers contribute through their mothering largely to the "social organization and reproduction of gender" in that they "produce daughters with mothering capacities and the desire to mother" on the one hand, and "sons whose nurturant capacities and needs have been systematically curtailed and repressed" (7). Like other influential works of her era, including Dorothy Dinnerstein's *The Mermaid and the Minotaur: Sexual Arrangements and Human Malaise* (1976), Jean Baker Miller's *Toward a New Psychology of Women* (1976), Jane Flax's "The Conflict Between Nurturance and Autonomy in Mother-Daughter Relationships and Within Feminism" (1978) and Carol Gilligan's *In a Different Voice: Psychological Theory and Women's Development* (1982), Chodorow's psychoanalytic analysis along Freudian lines seeks to trace the origins of difference in male and female personality to the differences in mothering they have seen in the pre-Oedipal phase.[18] Chodorow argues the following:

> Feminine personality comes to be based less on repression of inner objects, and fixed and firm splits in the ego, and more on retention and continuity of external relationships. From the retention of pre-Oedipal attachments to their mothers, growing girls come to define themselves as continuous with others; their experience of self contains more flexible and permeable ego boundaries. Boys come to define themselves as more separate and distinct, with a greater sense of rigid ego boundaries and differentiations. The basic feminine sense of self is connected to the world, the basic masculine sense is separate. (169)

These gender specific personality differences, suggests Chodorow, bear the key to the question why "[w]omen mother" (3), and men do not, a question which addresses the social organization of gender within Western culture at large. Such pre-Oedipal gender differences, emphasizes Chodorow, also constitute the basis for psychoanalytic approaches of the mother-daughter conflict. The paradox is evident: "Turning from mother (and father) represents independence and individuation, progress, activity, and participation in the real world" (82). Yet, a mother tends to experience her "daughter as an extension or double" of herself. In the Oedipal phase of the daughter's identity development, the father, then, becomes a foil for the daughter's separation from the mother. Chodorow argues: "Every step of the way, as the analysts describe it, a girl develops her relationship to her father while looking back at her mother – to see if her mother is envious, to make sure she is in fact separate, to see if she can in this way win her mother, to see if she is really independent" (126). Consequently, the social organization of gender and mothering, as described by Chodorow, inevitably culminate in conflicts that are hurtful to mothers and daughters alike as well as to their alliance against patriarchal domination.

What Rich's and Chodorow's projects have in common is that their emphases on psychoanalysis cannot sufficiently accommodate issues of cultural difference. Their accounts, although insightful in psychoanalytic parameters

---

[18] Pre-Oedipal "denotes the stage of development in which the external object choice is the mother, […] the stage of development in which the importance of the father is not recognized." Consequently, the pre-oedipal attachment to the mother "denotes the character, the quality, and the vicissitudes of the [infant's] instinctual aims directed toward the mother […] prior to the full development of the Oedipus complex" (Eidelberg, 324-25).

and critical of the patriarchal institution that shapes discourses of motherhood, can only partly describe the gender consciousness or the socio-cultural parameters women of color face in the mothering of their daughters. Whereas the biological and emotional mothering capacities, according to Chodorow, "are built into and grow out of the mother-daughter relationship itself" (7), mother-daughter conflicts over different cultural affiliations, for instance, challenge the reproduction of the mother's socio-cultural organization even further. Admitting to limitations of her study's applicability beyond the realms of middle-class Anglo-Saxon *Familienroman,*[19] Adrienne Rich revisits her claims about the mother-daughter relationship in her "Introduction: 1986" for the Tenth Anniversary Edition of her book *Of Woman Born*. There she acknowledges that "[a] consideration of American Indian, African, and Afro-American myth and philosophy might have suggested other patterns" (xxv).[20] In her brief discussion of matrilineage in the literature by contemporary African American, Asian American, Latina American and Native American writers, Rich notes that "the affirmation of the mother-daughter bond is powerfully expressed, not primarily in terms of a dyad but as a facet of a culture of women and a group history that is *not merely personal*" (xxviii, my emphasis). In this new introduction, Rich hints at socio-cultural dimensions of the mother-daughter conflict and the fact that they are underrepresented in the psychoanalytic approach of her book.

Similarly, Chodorow's analysis of the social reproduction of gender addresses mainly white, middle-class families. Critics, such as by Elizabeth Spelman and Elizabeth Abel, denote Chodorow's exclusion of women of color as a typical malfunction of white feminist theory and practice of that era. The formulation of a concept of motherhood that emerges out of the experiences of white middle-class women is a clear indication of white feminist's ethnocentrism which results in the exclusion of non-white women. In families of color, however, the conflicts arising from the psychoanalytical separation during the

[19] Like Rich's *Of Woman Born*, Marianne Hirsch's book *The Mother/Daughter Plot: Narrative, Psychoanalysis, Feminism* focuses on the Freudian *Familienroman* ("family romance") which, as Hirsch herein explains, "is the story we tell ourselves about the social and psychological reality of the family in which we find ourselves and about the patterns of desire that motivate the interaction among its members. The family romance thus combines and reveals as indistinguishable the psychological subjective experience of family and the process of narrative" (1989, 9).

[20] Additional claims in this new introduction are designed to answer the question of how much had changed in terms of motherhood as institution in the ten years after the book was first published. Rich addresses issues of the Women's Liberation movement (e.g. abortion laws) as well as increasingly prevalent concepts of motherhood such as the 'working mother,' the 'single mother,' and the 'lesbian mother.'

daughter's subject formation are not the sole factors complicating the mother-daughter relationship. On the contrary, as Elizabeth Spelman argues in *Inessential Women: Problems of Exclusion in Feminist Thought* (1988), the mother-daughter relationship is largely influenced by the "social and political context" mothers and daughters operate in since "they not only are distinguished from men, but are, along with men of their same cultural background, distinguished from men and women of other cultural backgrounds" (157). Like Spelman, Elizabeth Abel underscores that feminist theory which is based on psychoanalysis exclusively has "lost its material groundings and with them the possibility of interpreting (and thereby promoting) social change" (184). Chodorow herself has reconsidered her initial approach, and admits, like Adrienne Rich did in her "Introduction: 1986," that if she were to write a new *Reproduction of Mothering* she would "examine the link between what seems exclusively gender related and the construction of other aspects of society, politics, and culture" (1981, 514). This generic difference between white and women of color experiences within the family and within white society in general also accounts for the limited applicability of psychoanalytical feminism to the mother-daughter dyads women of color experience.

Matrilineage as Political Front

A general dissatisfaction with psychological feminism caused many critics to turn away from psychoanalytic approaches of the mother-daughter conflict. Paul Smith, for instance, sums up that "[i]t would seem fairly obvious by now that feminism's struggle to infuse into psychoanalytical theory the breath of an efficacious politics has not been a major success. Feminist approaches in recent years [...] have been thwarted by the obstinacy of psychoanalytic universalist theories of subjective construction" (Feldstein and Roof 84-85). Women of color feminists in particular have felt the need to redefine concepts of motherhood that are specifically related to their experiences, experiences that differ drastically from the one's white middle class women have had all through the history of the 'American' family. Because they felt excluded from white definitions of womanhood, women of color feminists have manifested this exclusion in emphasizing concepts of family that are much more representative of their politics and social agendas. With more attention to social, political and cultural dimensions innate to the mother-daughter dyad, contemporary ideas of motherhood and daughterhood emphasize matriarchy and matrilineage.

Inadvertently, the differences in family concepts and their geneses also affect the concepts of motherhood that arise out of the culture-specific experiences of women. In her sociological study of African American, Chinese

American and Mexican American families in the 19th century and women's roles in them, Bonnie Thornton Dill points out the difference in family structures between white and women of color families. Dill argues that white women, although they had "few legal rights as women," were "protected through public forms of patriarchy that acknowledged and supported their family roles as wives, mothers, and daughters because they were vital instruments for building American society" (416). As Dill emphasizes, the middle class socio-economic group divides men and women as confined into either public or private sphere. Contrary to white feminist Marxist critics who strongly lobby for the entrance of women into the public domain, for white women, to sum up Dill's argument, the family, although patriarchally governed, was a secure place of economic, social, and legal representation. In contrast, the experiences of 19th century women of color did not rely on such privilege of a secure domestic domain. Dill explains: "Unlike white women, racial-ethnic women experienced the oppression of a patriarchal society but were denied the protections and buffering of a patriarchal family. Their families suffered as a direct result of the organization of the labor systems in which they participated" (418).

The different approaches to the family in general and the mother-daughter relationships in particular are reminiscent of the dichotomy between white and women of color feminism. Whereas in the writings of white American women the mother-daughter conflict correlates to a large extent with women's resistance to and liberation from patriarchal institutions, women writers of color locate their mother-daughter dyads at the jeopardy of racism and sexism. Under the constraints of double marginality, women of color emphasize as intimate allegiance with their mothers and accept their roles as embodiments of the legacies for which their mothers are fighting. In juxtaposing literary depicts of motherhood across "race," Gloria Wade-Gayles brings to a point the dichotomies in socio-cultural reproduction and re-organization of gender (11-12). As Wade Gayles points out, the relationship between black mothers and daughters differs drastically from the white American mother-daughter dyad. In *Common Differences: Conflicts in Black and White Feminist Perspectives* (1981), a study of African American mothers and daughters, for instance, Gloria Joseph and Jill Lewis note that daughters meet their mothers' struggles with uncompromised respect: "The reason for this [...] seems to be located in the Black daughters' familiarity with the circumstances within which their mothers existed and raised their children and an empathy caused by understanding these situations" (94). Whereas the white mother's struggle is often trivialized and largely misrepresented in the daughter's understanding of their mother-daughter dyad, black daughters seems to be the model for perfect continuity and pro-matrilineal negotiation between individuality and identification.

Struggling for visibility beyond her doubly-marginalized position within the United States, the African American scholars recover a strong matrilineal tradition. In her essay "Black Matrilineage: The Case of Alice Walker and Zora Neale Hurston," Dianne F. Sadoff explains: "Race and class oppression intensify the black woman writer's need to discover an untroubled matrilineal heritage. In celebrating her literary foremothers, however, the contemporary black woman writer covers over more profoundly than does the white writer her ambivalence about matrilineage, her own misreading precursors, and her link to an oral as well as written tradition" (5). The acceptance of matrilineage as political discourse promoting the black woman's emancipation precludes candid depictions of elaborate mother-daughter conflicts are missing from the canon. Sadoff specifies that "the black woman writer will overtly idealize foremothers while disguising anxiety and covertly appropriating concealed rebellious thematic material" (18). E. Frances White paraphrases this uncompromised identification with the mother in the following way: "How dare we admit the psychological battles that need to be fought with the very women who taught us how to survive this racist and sexist world? We would feel like ungrateful traitors" (21).

The literary canon of matrilineage is thriving with voices that celebrate their mothers for the strength and courage they bring forth in the face of double marginality. To name only one in each of the last three decades, influential anthologies include Cherríe Moraga and Gloria Anzaldúa's *This Bridge Called My Back: Writing By Radical Women of Color* (1981), D. Soyini Madison's *The Woman That I Am: The Literature and Culture of Contemporary Women of Color* (1994), and Esmeralda Santiago and Joie Davidow's *Las Mamis: Favorite Latino Author's Remember Their Mothers* (2000). In contrast to white feminist depictions of motherhood as ambivalent influence on the daughter's identity formation, such as in Nancy Friday's *My Mother/My Self: The Daughter's Search for Identity* (1977), the literature of matrilineage supercedes mere analyses of motherhood along psychoanalytic parameters. Instead, the literature of matrilineage engages in a more culturally and socially directed criticism of the aspects of what it means to be a mother and a daughter. In her essay "Maternal Bonds: Recent Literature on Mothering," Alice Adams reviews a number of studies in which "[t]he theme of connection and separation is still apparent [...] but the focus has shifted from the mother-child relationship to the relationship of mothers to society as a whole" (415). Included in Adams' analysis of such discussions outside the psychological frameworks is Suzanna Danuta Walters' *Lives Together/Worlds Apart: Mothers and Daughters in Popular*

Culture (1992), a study which, although it focuses primarily on the Anglo American mother-daughter dyad, Walters elaborates how women writers of color provide "an antidote" (164) to white feminist's preoccupation with Oedipus as they "locate [the mother-daughter] relationship to an extent that mitigates against the purely psychological interpretation" (165).

When Cathy Davidson and E. M. Broner published *The Lost Tradition: Mothers and Daughters in Literature* (1980), the field of matrilineage was relatively unexplored. Mothers and daughters in ethnic families were, as the contributing essay by Natalie Rosinsky suggests, "another minority group," but a minority group under double-constraint: "[m]embers of racial, ethnic, sexual, and economic minority groups, in particular, have delineated their apprehension of the social forces which intervene between mother and daughter. Perhaps because the added oppression of minority group membership exacerbates this often painful relationship, these writers seem particularly aware of its tragic destructiveness" (280). Thus, despite the constraints of double oppression "daughter[s] and mother[s] come to some kind of reconciliation, a recognition of the fact that they are not natural enemies but rather fellow victims" (289). Rosinsky concludes: "It is disheartening to see the pain inflicted upon many women; it is encouraging to realize that individual women can transcend this mutilation to discover the deeper rapport that – along with the suffering – unites them with their mothers" (290).

The juxtaposition of psychoanalytic feminism and socio-cultural approaches of motherhood and daughterhood is central to Marianne Hirsch's *The Mother/Daughter Plot: Narrative, Psychoanalysis, Feminism* (1989). In Hirsch's study, women writers of color seem to provide the exception to the rule that the daughter's discursive dominate when narrating her conflict with her mother. Whereas white women writers are more likely to direct their anger and frustration with patriarchal society discursively against their mothers, black women writers ally with the mother protagonists of their narratives. In her psychoanalytic analysis of feminist fiction from eighteenth century realism through contemporary postmodernism, Hirsch "treat[s] both motherhood and daughterhood as *story* – as narrative representation of social and subjective reality and of literary convention" (10, original emphasis). Several texts of feminist family romances,[21] argues Hirsch, are replications of the pre-Oedipal

---

[21] The feminist family romance, according to Hirsch, perpetuates the "denial of subjectivity to the mothers" in its applications of approaches stemming from oedipal psychology such as "mak[ing] mother-hate the condition of female liberation and self-determination": "So long as mothers remain objects of exploration rather than social, psychological, and linguistic subjects, the hold of tradition cannot be broken, and new

mother-daughter conflict in the face of institutional ideals of motherhood. Hirsch observes that

> the woman as *daughter* [...] occupies the center of the global reconstruction of subjectivity and subject-object relation. The woman as *mother* remains in the position of the other, and the emergence of feminine-daughterly subjectivity rests and depends on that continued and repeated process of *othering* the mother [...]. Daughter and mother are separated and forever trapped by the institution, the function and role of motherhood. They are kept apart by the text's daughterly perspective and signature: the mother is excluded form the discourse by the daughter who owns it. (136-37, original emphasis)

Hirsch finds contrary examples in Alice Walker's short story "Everyday Use" and Toni Morrison's novels *Sula* (1973) and *Beloved* (1987), where the mother/daughter plot is "written in the voice of mothers as well as in that of daughters [and thus] yield[s] a multiple female consciousness" rather than "a 'sustained quest'" (161). What Hirsch postulates here as vision of "ways to 'live afresh'" (ibid.) is a phenomenon commonly found in the literature of matrilineage by African American women writers, not in Anglo American women writers. By relying on an essentialist separation between white and black feminism, Hirsch's presentation of black writers as the quintessential "other" to white feminist thought, was very much the fashion in feminist theory at the time.

Adopting the matrilineal paradigm, the social organization of women of color families and its fundamental differences from white middle class models of motherhood become apparent. Patricia Hill Collins, for instance, argues that the availability of numerous mothers provides daughters in African American families with alternative role models that equally contribute to her sense of social reproduction. In contrast to Nancy Chodorow's model of the reorganization of gender solely based on the mother, such patterns locate the daughter's socialization at the core of Black community and make it the primary task of mothers and "othermothers" alike:

> The presence of othermothers in Black extended families and the modeling symbolized by community othermothers offer powerful support for the task of teaching girls to resist white perceptions of Black womanhood while appearing to conform to them. In contrast to the isolation of middle class

stories cannot be told" (131, 161). See also Jessica Benjamin (1978); and her *The Bonds of Love: Psychoanalysis, Feminism, and the Problem of Domination* (1988).

> white mother/daughter dyads, Black woman-centered extended family networks foster an early identification with a much wider range of models of black womanhood which can lead to a greater sense of empowerment in young Black girls. (173)

The mother's role as bearer of cultural heritage is also central to Ruth Perry and Martine Watson Brownley's *Mothering the Mind: Twelve Studies of Writers and Their Silent Partners* (1984). Perry and Brownley call this process of maternal supervision "mothering the mind," and use this analogy to define the relationships between artists and their metaphorical mother-figures.[22] This concept partly shares Hill Collins' observations about the decentralization of the maternal figure within African American families in so far as the mothering can be performed by any person, not just the biological mother. In the context of African American mother-daughter writing, as Mary Helen Washington argues in her contributing essay "I Sign My Mother's Name," in the writings of Alice Walker, Dorothy West and Paule Marshall "the bond with their mothers is such a fundamental and powerful source of their art that the term 'mothering the mind' might have been coined specifically to define [the] experiences" of these three Black female authors (Perry and Brownley 144).[23] Although the quantity of essays in Perry and Brownley's collection is greatly underrepresentative of women of color experiences, the socio-cultural implications of the underlying concept of their study, *mothering the mind*, allows for an interpretation of mother-daughter relationships situated outside the white middle class feminist malaise.

The mother-daughter conflict in Asian American writers maintains a middle position between the two, largely antagonistic, extremes of white feminism and black feminism. In part, this hybrid location between the two traditions reflects the literary agency Asian American writers applied in order to create visibility for their specific material and historical realities. Sau-ling C. Wong, for instance, asserts that Asian Americans tend to be "regarded as direct transplants from Asia or as custodians of an esoteric subculture" (1993, 9) and that this special kind of xenophobia has urged writers to emphasize their particular location within American culture. In this vein, perhaps the reason why Asian American writers, including Maxine Hong Kingston, Amy Tan, Mei Ng, Nora Okja Keller and Vineeta Vijayarahgavan, reappropriate in equal measures aspects of psychoanalytical feminism and of matrilineality for their specific

---

[22] In the sense of "mothering the mind," Perry and Brownley hold that mothers, lovers, friends, aunts, etc. assume to roles of "mothers" in the artists' lives, for which they often express their gratitude in their dedications, for instance.

[23] See also Dianne F. Sadoff (1985).

literary responses to "the deeply entrenched presumption that Asian Americans are not American" (P. Chu 2000, 4).

In the particular context of immigrant Asian American families, mothers often encourage their daughters to embrace every opportunity American society has to offer and to create better lives than the ones they themselves led in their Asian home-countries. This problematic stems from the close bonding and identification between mother and daughter, which Claudia Kovach Smorada refers to as "side-stepping death":

> When mothers identify too closely with their daughters in a symbiosis that makes the child a potentially perfect version of themselves [...] [t]he recreation, reproduction of self in the daughter allows, among other things, for mothers to side-step death, to achieve a kind of rebirth, at least a chance to fix those elements of themselves they feel are imperfect. (34)

Such ambitions the ethnic mother has for her daughter, argues Thomas J. Ferraro in *Ethnic Passages: Literary Immigrants in Twentieth Century America* (1993), constitutes an additional form of pressure on and oppression of the daughter's individuality. However, the mother's urging contributes to the daughter's confusion about her Asian background. As Ferraro argues, the search for a better life is often the family's main motivation to immigrate to the U.S. in the first place.

The daughters thus receive double messages in their negotiations of the Asian home-cultures: one the one hand, they are encouraged to take advantage of the opportunities American society has to offer, and on the other hand, they are expected to abide by the traditions of their Asian home countries. This cultural difference between mothers and daughters in Asian American families constitutes an additional constraint to the establishing and maintaining of feminist solidarity. Instead of celebrating their matrilineal heritage and the mothers who cultivate it, which is to a large extent the tradition of matrilineal mother-daughter writing, the Asian American writers offer depictions of daughters who grow up disrespecting their mother's efforts of preserving the family's traditions. Eager to assimilate to the dominant Anglo American culture – maybe because of the family's aspiration to the American Dream of success – Asian American daughters interpret any ties to their cultural origins as deficiency in their successful acculturations. In contrast, they perceive such deficiency in their mothers' degrees of assimilation to white American standards e.g. language, customs, lifestyle, etc. In *Negotiating Identity*, a study of Asian American women writing, Helena Grice observes such dilemma in mother-daughter dyads of immigrant Asian women: "As a mediator of the ancestral culture (Chinese or Japanese) the mother figure often represents mother-land" (72). And because the daughter, by assimilating to the dominant culture, often also adopts the prevalent xenophobic attitudes and applies them against her mother in order to distinguish herself from a culture she has grown to disrespect, her search for individuality correlates with her rejection of her matrilineal heritage. This is the quintessential dynamic that precedes the daughter's emotional and cultural alienation from her mother.

Because cultural and emotional alienation from the mother go hand in hand, we need to view the conflicts depicted in contemporary Asian American mother-daughter writing from double angles. In order to do so, I propose the concept of the "Cultural Electra" which combines psychological feminist readings of the mother-daughter conflict and the connectedness of these parameters to the transference of culture between mothers and daughters.

Defining the Cultural Electra

One of the main contributions psychoanalytical feminism draws on is Jung's formulation of an "Electra Complex" as counterpart to the sexually charged distortion of the mother-son relationship Sigmund Freud has coined as "Oedipus Complex." In Jung's definition, the Electra Complex arises out of the triangle of mother-father-daughter in patriarchal families. This Electra Complex goes back to the Greek tragedy of Electra, the daughter whose lack of compassion for the mother's vengeful killing of her husband leads her to plot her mother's death, an act which, in the context of feminist solidarity, is the ultimate crime. In Sophocles' *Electra*, for instance, we encounter a daughter full of aversion against her mother's struggle in fighting patriarchal institutions symbolized by her husband's sacrificial killing of their eldest daughter Iphigenia. In the vengeful killing of Agamemnon, Clytemnestra seeks to retaliate against female powerlessness in a society that denies her the right to decide over the lives of the children she bore. Clytemnestra's confrontation of the mourning and raging Electra urges us to consider the necessity of the daughter's empathy with the mother's struggle for emancipation: "And you should have helped if you had any conscience" (line 706). Yet, Electra's conscience focuses on the father Agamemnon, to whom she devotes her loyalty. The archetypal mother-daughter tragedy of Electra and Clytemnestra constitutes in the daughter's justification of the patriarchal institutions suppressing her mother, her sister, and eventually herself.[24]

---

[24] In *The Mother/Daughter Plot*, Marianne Hirsch points out Electra's reproduction of patriarchal norms when she plots the killing of her mother along sexual divisions of labor i.e. leaves the actual killing up to her brother Orestes (1989 31).

This paradigm translates well into the context of mother-daughter conflicts over cultural affiliations as depicted in numerous texts by contemporary Asian American writers. There, the American culture takes on the place of the father who embodies the oppression and resrtrictions of patriarchal societies. In the neo-colonial context of socio-economic and political disenfranchisement of ethnic minorities in the U.S., issues that feature prominently throughout Asian American literature. In this light, sexism (in the form of patriarchal domination) and racism (in the form of political and social disenfranchisement of immigrant women) correlate, so much so that "the colonial power [...] usurps any role the biological father might play in the child's life" (Simmons 27). The mother's struggle against patriarchy in the classical Greek tragedy of Electra and Clytemnestra shows affinities with the mother's struggle in families of color for her agency in a society which dominates and oppresses ethnic minorities. If a daughter sides with the dominant culture instead of identifying with the matrilineal heritage her mother embodies, she replicates the dynamics of the Electra Complex on a cultural level. This desire to be accepted by the dominant culture becomes especially strong once the daughter herself begins to experience double-marginalization. It is the powerstruggle between mother and daughter, a conflict over the mother's authority the daughter may or may not accept, that leads the daughter to seek allegiance with a stronger ally. Thus, the daughter maintains power over the mother.

The daughter's criticism of her mother's parenting is reminiscent of paternal laws that institutionalize motherhood as execution of patriarchal norms. Here, the parallel to the Greek story of Clytemnestra and Electra becomes evident. By the mere fact that Electra directs her frustration at her mother instead of blaming her father for the absence in the parenting of his children, the daughter underwrites paternal laws that marginalize and oppress women. Similarly, instead of directing her anger against the dominant U.S. society that doubly-suppresses minority women, the Cultural Electra sorts out her un-American mother as sitting target for her own frustration with the double jeopardy she encounters in daily life. After all, as Suzanna Danuta Walters reminds us: "How much easier to struggle against one's mother than against a sexist [and racist] culture that feels overwhelmingly intractable" (233). Thus, the psychoanalytic dimensions of the mother-daughter conflict correlate with the daughter's quest for cultural distinction from her mother.

The cultural distinction from the mother is more important to the daughter than the cultural preservation of her matrilineal heritage. In her discussion of Amy Tan's novel *The Hundred Secret Senses* (1996), Lina Unali refers to the American-born protagonist's voluntary rupture with her Chinese heritage (in this case patrilineal) as "discharge of ethnicity" in the sense that ethnicity is felt "as a burden [...] connected with the undesirable, as a traumatic experience" (135). By the same token, the Cultural Electra attempts to discharge herself of markers of ethnicity she perceives as burdensome in her encounters with white American society. Most specifically, she wants to discharge herself of her mother, the embodiment of ethnicity that links her to a minority culture. Like Anglo-European American society, the Cultural Electra perceives her mother as exotic "Other" in the definition of Edward Said's *Orientalism* (1978).[25] As Sheryl A. Mylan points out in a discussion of the mother-daughter conflict in Kingston's *The Woman Warrior*, Orientalism is also what characterizes the daughter's view of her mother as representative of "all that is baffling and repugnant about [her native] culture" (Brown-Guillory 133).

Yet, the daughter's cultural disassociation is not only hurtful to the continuity of her collective ethnic heritage, it also constitutes major drawbacks for her own identity mapping. By contributing to the reproduction of such cultural ostracism, the Cultural Electra eventually underwrites prevalent policies of double suppression against women of color, including herself. If the murder of Clytemnestra in the Greek mythology, as Luce Irigaray suggests, signifies the "mother's exclusion from culture and the symbolic order" (Hirsch 1989, 30), then the Cultural Electra's reproduction of xenophobic attitudes symbolizes the repression of cultural minorities by the dominant U.S. culture. In this context, Judith Pildes Arcana's transference of the failed mother-daughter relationship onto socio-cultural dimensions underscores the magnitude of the Cultural Electra's breaking with her mother: "The opposition of women has created a breach among us, especially between mothers and daughters. Women cannot respect their mothers in a society that degrades them. Women cannot respect themselves" (1). In her analysis of the classical Greek Electra, Marianne Hirsch maintains that the daughter's planning and plotting of her mother's killing "eliminates the possibility for women to challenge the paternal order and perpetuates a sexual division of labor by which she can act only through the brother" (1989, 31). Thus, on a more universal level of gender organization, the matricide Electra performs equals suicide in so far as she underwrites patriarchal laws that are eventually directed against herself. After all, as Toni Morrison reminds us in her essay "Rootedness: The Ancestor as Foundation": "When you kill the ancestor, you kill yourself" (Madison 497).

---

[25] Although Said coins the term *Orientalism* to describe the Anglo-Franco experience with Islamic and Arabic cultures, namely "the distillation of essential ideas about the Orient – its sensuality, its tendency to despotism, its aberrant mentality, its habits of inaccuracy, its backwardness" (205), the same attitude is common to the culturally estranged daughter vis-à-vis her mother.

The Asian American writers discussed in the subsequent chapters depict daughters who try to liberate themselves from the concepts of womanhood which their mothers embody. When looking at their mothers, they see a cultural 'other' with definitions of womanhood that hardly translate into the American contexts the daughters claim for themselves. Such desperate endeavors to turn themselves less ethnic and their orientalist attitude toward their mothers and other female members of their inherited cultural backgrounds, however, stand in strong opposition to their mothers' fights for the continuity of the cultural legacies they celebrate with ethnic pride. Hence, fierce battles between mothers and daughters arise within the mother-daughter relationship. The more the mothers protest against their daughters' disassociation, the more the daughters want to separate themselves from the image of their naggy, bossy, un-American mothers.

In the following chapters, I will analyze the discursive representation of the struggles that Asian American daughter protagonists confront. I will do so on two accounts. First, I will emphasize the protagonists' positionings and the narrative strategies with which their positions are being configured by looking closely at the stylistic and literary gestures which the individual texts perform. My aim for this analysis of the aesthetic representation of the mother-daughter relationship in Asian American literature is to emphasize the ways in which the individual works illustrate the literary richness of Asian American literature. Second, I will discuss the ways in which the individual works demand of us to rethink through the complex mother-daughter relationships that they depict several prominent tropes in feminist theory. My emphasis in this thematic discussion will be on the cultural encounters that these works locate within the mother-daughter relationship and the ideological underpinnings of transnational feminist theory that resonate within these works. Ultimately, I want to link through my readings of the thematic and aesthetic richness of Asian American literature on mother-daughter relationships to ongoing conversations in transnational feminist theory that recognizes difference as innate component of literary and feminist theories but seeks through careful readings of the representations of difference to uncover the potential for transnational feminist solidarity.

While the author's individual reasons for re-appropriating the mother-daughter relationship are neither the central issue of this book nor of my critical scope for this specific chapter, I wish to argue that an in-depth analysis of the ways in which Asian American literature reflects ongoing discussions of mother-daughter relationships within feminist and literary theory offers a possibility to reposition Asian American literature within the American literary canon. An investigation of the analytical practices that have shaped the scholarship of mother-daughter relationships in Asian American literature also offers incentives about the multiple genealogies of U.S. feminist theory. *Transnational Matrilineage* seeks to animate the critical practice of reading Asian American literature both for its ideological and aesthetic performances by drawing on the methodological interconnectedness of Asian American studies and feminist theory. Since both fields of study are characterized by multiple discourses of critical theory, as the section of the emergence of the filed of Asian American literary criticism in my book's introduction illustrates, this attempt to reposition Asian American writers who depict mother-daughter relationships in their literary works also demands an investigation of the paradigmatic shifts that occurred within feminist literary theory.

From Exclusion, to Essentialism, to Expansion: Toward a Transnational Feminist Solidarity

As the genealogy of the study of mother-daughter relationships in American literature suggests, feminist literary criticism has undergone several paradigmatic shifts since its first emergence in the wake of the civil rights movement and the Women's Liberation movement of the 1960s and 1970s. I esteem it therefore useful for the overall contextualization of my reading practice of contemporary Asian American texts to offer here a rather simplified categorization of three, mostly interconnected, trends in feminist theory that have shaped over the past decades the way that texts by ethnic American women writers were perceived in the larger context of American literature on the one hand and feminist theory on the other.

From a contemporary position, early formulations of a feminist theory and consciousness seem to be concerned primarily with sexual difference. Challenging historical constructions of gender-specific roles and deconstructing the convoluted notion that the biological difference rightfully places men and women in generically different performance groups, feminists beginning in the 1970s read gender against the grain in an array of social domains.[26] These early

[26] French and American feminism equally contributed to the formation of a nowadays well-known canon of second-wave feminist criticism that impacted the Women's Liberation movement in the US of the 1970s: Simone de Beauvoir, *The Second Sex* (1952); Julia Kristeva, "La femme, ce n'est jamais ça" (1974); Luce Irigaray, *Spéculum de l'autre femme* (1974), and Ce sexe qui n'est pass un (1977); Helene Cixous, *La Jeune Née* (1975); Betty Friedan, *The Feminine Mystique* (1963); Mary Ellman, *Thinking About Women* (1968), Kate Millett, *Sexual Politics* (1970); Zillah Eisenstein, ed. *Capitalist Patriarchy and the Case for Socialist Feminism* (1978). For a discussion see Toril Moi, *Sexual/Textual Politics* (1985).

feminist "manifestos" – at times offering discursions into psychoanalysis, at times addressing women's social roles such as the confinement binds them to the household and to the family – speak primarily from and to the white, middle class. Feminist literary criticism of that era, such as Elaine Showalter's *A Literature of Their Own: British Women Novelists from Brontë to Lessing* (1977) and Sandra M. Gilbert and Susan Gubar's *The Madwoman in the Attic: The Woman Writer of the Nineteenth Century Literary Imagination* (1979), do groundbreaking work in the assertion of a female/feminist voice and outlining of a history of feminist literacy. However, these works deal almost exclusively with white, upper-middle class women writers. As a result, definitions of womanhood during this period often occurred at the expense of women who did not fit into the homogenous group identity set by these early trends in second-wave feminism. The absence of specific issues of race, ethnicity, and class from these early feminist discourses is indicative of the limited scope under which mainstream feminist literary theory and feminist practice of the 1970s discussed the constructed images of womanhood. As much as mainstream feminism facilitated a basis for the renegotiation of gender roles within patriarchal societies, its exclusion of non-white and working class women called for expansion of the feminist debate.[27]

The beginning entrance of ethnic women into the feminist debate made apparent the need for more permeable and flexible discourses of feminist theory and practice. Francis Beal's assertion in her essay "Double Jeopardy: To Be Black and Female," which appeared in Robin Morgan's seminal publication, *Sisterhood is Powerful: An Anthology of the Writings from the Women's Liberation Movement* (1970), that feminism is a "white women's movement" brought this demand for a more inclusive feminist discourse to the point (136). Reflecting Sojourner Truth's famous rhetorical question, "Ain't I A Woman" at the Women's Convention in Akron Ohio in 1851, many African American feminist writers and critics have challenged mainstream definitions of womanhood and criticism of the patriarchal family model. For instance, Alice Walker's reception of Virginia Woolf's *A Room of One's Own* (1929), in her essay "In Search of Our Mothers' Gardens," is emblematic of the movement within African American feminists to re-conceptionalize canonical texts of mainstream feminism and re-appropriate them for their culture-specific positions and expressions of gender emancipation both against white and against

---

[27] See, for instance, Elizabeth Fox-Keller and Marianne Hirsch, eds., *Conflicts in Feminism* (1990); Elizabeth Spelman, *Inessential Women: Problems of Exclusion in Feminist Thought* (1988); and Teresa de Lauretis, *Feminist Studies/Critical Studies* (1986).

black sexism, thereby creating agency and making visible the experience and history of oppression of black women.

Due to the lack of visibility, representation and agency of ethnic writers within the feminist debate, non-white feminist scholars and activists started formulating their own locations and movements. There were clearly separate from the "mainstream" of white feminists. Already the terminology that defined these counter-movements betrays with very culture-specific embeddings into the experiences of women from ethnic groups and their different processes of socialization in the U.S. Terms such as "black feminism," "red feminism," and "yellow feminism" are indicative of this recentering of the feminist debate at the core of debates on culture and ethnicity.[28] This counter-movement, characterized by transformation and expansion, introduced the notion of pluralism and multiplicity to a formerly homogeneous feminist theory. However, this focus on essentialism was and continues to be counterproductive to the building of a feminist solidarities within the U.S. academy, where feminist and womanist scholars often positions themselves in opposition to each other. In particular, nationalist and essentialist feminist discourses, despite their important contributions to raising awareness of the specific struggles of marginalized groups, often fail to address the interconnectedness of the specific histories of oppression by foregrounding generic differences that mark the unique experience of the individual groups.

In the context of feminist solidarity, this practice is problematic on various accounts. One the one hand, this emphasis of experience echoes the ethnic nationalism within the U.S. and the related ethnic tensions based on ethnic exclusivity, purity, and supremacy.[29] These essentialist and monolithic definitions of ethnic consciousness imposed a limited possibility for inter-ethnic understanding. By operating with the often-criticized notion that "only biological insiders can understand and explicate the literature of race and ethnicity"

---

[28] bell hooks, *Ain't I a Woman: Black Women and Feminism* (1981), *Talking Back: Thinking Feminist, Thinking Black* (1988); Barbara Christian, Gloria Hull, Patricia Bell Scott, and Barbara Smith, eds., *All The Women are White, All the Blacks are Men, But Some of Us Are Brave: Black Women's Studies* (1982); and most pronouncedly, Alice Walker's definition of term 'womanism' in *In Search of Our Mothers' Gardens: Womanist Prose* (1983). Paula Gunn Allen, *The Sacred Hoop: Recovering the Feminine in American Indian Traditions* (1986). Merle Woo, "Letter to Ma" (1981); Esther Nan-ling Chow, "The Development of Feminist Consciousness Among Asian American Women" (1987).

[29] Chela Sandoval denotes a "supremacist" consciousness with which the oppressed "claim their experience" and, furthermore, "assert that those very differences have provided them access to a superior level than [sic] those currently in power" (1991, 13).

(Sollors 1986, 11), there were, and to a certain extend still are, tendencies of non-mainstream feminism that interpret differences between women as insurmountable obstacle in building a global feminist community. In her essay "Globalizing Feminist Ethics," Alison M. Jaggar contests that rigid boundaries of group identity and hegemonic definitions of community work with the same principles of exclusion as the initial feminist discussions that wrote out non-mainstream women from feminist debates. Jaggar questions: "For instance, if we were to determine that issues that appeared to concern only a single group might be assessed solely by members of that group, so that only prostitutes could evaluate prostitution and only African women could discuss clitoridectomy and infibulation, we would immediately encounter new problems of identity, authorization, and legitimation" (Narayan and Harding 16).

On the other hand, this emphasis on a different location from which ethnic women launch feminist awareness also reinforces the center/margin dichotomy between mainstream and non-mainstream feminists. In fact, this forceful claiming of difference, that it, of a counter-space to make up for the exclusion of ethnic women from mainstream discussions of feminist issues, excludes ethnic women in the U.S. and third world women from the feminist discourses originating at the "center," that is at mainstream feminist theory and practice. What is most counter-productive to the advancement of social issues and the creation of sensibility toward ethnic dilemmas is that this essentialist claiming of difference reinforces stereotypes that the mainstream culture attributes to minority cultures. This claiming of the margin thus also institutionalizes the center-margin division and characterizes ethnic women as essentially different from their white counterparts. As a result, as AnaLouise Keating argues, "the other's oppositional worldview remains locked in a dyadic relationship that inadvertently reinforces existing power structures" (Stanley 23).

Border studies feminism in the U.S. has successfully deconstructed the center/margin division between mainstream and non-mainstream feminist practices. The publication of Cherríe Moraga and Gloria Anzaldúa's anthology *This Bridge Called My Back: Writings by Radical Women of Color* (1981), set a trend in creating feminist alliances among ethnic American women. In *Borderlands/La Frontera: The New Mestiza* (1987), Gloria Anzaldúa defines the complexity of women's experiences of culture, nationality, sexuality, and class by means of representing identity definitions as bordercrossing endeavors. By pointing out the need to abolish rigid definitions of boundaries that distinguish between the diverse parameters that make up a person's identity, Anzaldúa provides a feminist cultural framework that deconstructs the center/margin dichotomy by claiming a location that goes beyond binary oppositions. Anzaldúa calls this the new mestiza consciousness and places it within the realm of a "cosmic race" (99), an identity location that is characterized by inherent internal multiplicity and fragmentation of the self. A similar discourse on internalized borderland experiences can be applied to immigrant and non-immigrant ethnic American writers (Schultermandl 2003). And this notion of mestiza borderlands also gives a sense of the performative potential and literary agency that authors maintain. In *When the Moon Waxes Red* (1991), for instance, Trinh T. Minh-ha's rendition of the ambiguity with which cultural border crossers define their identity locations summarizes well the literary agency many women writers of color in the U.S. claim: "Not quite the Same, not quite the Other, she stands in that undetermined threshold place where she constantly drifts in and out" (74).

The innovative impact of border studies feminism includes a growing tendency within feminist theory and practice to acknowledge the possibility for inter-ethnic and inter-cultural feminist solidarity in ways that premature postulations of "sisterhood," those which cover up for the predominating hegemonic mindset in American feminist theory and practice, failed to establish. Some publications in the tradition of border studies feminism include Chandra Talpade Mohanty, Ann Russo and Lourdes Torres's collection of essays, *Third World Women and the Politics of Feminism* (1991), AnaLouise Keating's *Women Reading Women Writing: Self-Intervention in Paula Gunn Allen, Gloria Anzaldúa, and Audre Lorde* (1996), Sandra Kumamoto Stanley's *Other Sisterhoods: Literary Theory and U.S. Women of Color* (1998). What these scholars share is a deep conviction that, in order to usurp hegemonic feminist theory, women need to build communities in which difference is not so much considered an obstacle for mutual identification but an asset for the development of a multi-lateral consciousness of tolerance and solidarity.

With this emphasis on inter-ethnic feminist solidarity, border studies feminism in the U.S. has created a forum for the discussion of women's location at the crossroads of national and transnational movements. Especially in the past decade, through the espousal of postcolonial theory and through the prolific and groundbreaking works by feminists from postcolonial nation-states, transnational feminism has taken this inter-ethnic debate in the U.S. to a new level and has been breathing new life into the U.S. feminist academia. Some of the most influential publications that attempt an expansion of feminist theory toward a more global heuristic that offers room for the building of a transnational solidarity include: Inderpal Grewal and Caren Kaplan's *Scattered Hegemonies: Postmodernity and Transnational Feminist Practices* (1994), M. Jacqui Alexander and Chandra Talpade Mohanty's *Feminist Genealogies, Colonial Legacies, Democratic Futures* (1997), Caren Kaplan, Norma Alarcón, and Minoo Mallem's *Between Woman and Nation: Nationalism, Transnational*

Feminisms, and the State (1999), Amal Amireh and Lisa Suhair Majaj's *Going Global: The Transnational Reception of Third World Women Writers* (2000), Uma Narayan and Sandra Harding's *Decentering the Center: Philosophy for a Multicultural, Postcolonial, and Feminist World* (2000), Chandra Talpade Mohanty's *Feminism Without Borders: Decolonizing Theory, Practicing Solidarity* (2003), and Inderpal Grewal *Transnational America: Feminisms, Diasporas, Neoliberalisms* (2005). These studies look at feminism under the scope of postcolonial criticism and focus on conveying a multi-cultural, multi-ethnic, and transnational consciousness where difference and diversity do not stand in the way of building feminist alliances. The collections themselves and their multi-national and multi-cultural authorships reflect such heuristics. As Inderpal Grewal and Caren Kaplan assert, transnational feminism houses aspects of "intersections of feminism, colonial and postcolonial discourses, modernism, and postmodern hybridity" (1994, 1). This consciousness of expansion from the local to the global, argues Grewal and Kaplan, is a movement in direct response to globalization: "If the world is currently structured by transnational economic links and cultural asymmetries, locating feminist practices within these structures becomes imperative" (3).

To a similar degree as theoretical feminist scholarship has explored intrinsic relatedness to key issues in the Third Wave of feminism, so, too has feminist pedagogy. While the issue of a transnational feminist pedagogy is an interesting field in itself that cannot be discussed here in detail, I do want to give a brief sense of the publication of a variety of feminist studies readers and anthologies that introduce women's studies in a global context. Some of these anthologies include Anne McClintock, Aamir Mufti, and Ella Shohat's *Dangerous Liaisons: Gender, Nation and Postcolonial Perspectives* (1997), Ella Shohat's *Talking Visions: Multicultural Feminism in a Transnational Age* (2001), Inderpal Grewal and Caren Kaplan's *An Introduction to Women's Studies: Gender in a Transnational World* (2002), and Carole McCann and Seung-Hyung Kim's *Feminist Theory Reader: Local and Global Perspectives* (2003). The individual texts are, as is indicative of transnational feminist heuristics, structured around clusters of issues that allow for multiple readings and that emphasize the similarities and account for the differences between women's experiences of oppression and agency. Race, ethnicity and nationality are, for the most part, no longer the categories around which the individual texts are positioned; however these parameters are crucial factors in interrogating the vantage points from which the individual writers assume agency. Ultimately, the pedagogical aspirations at "'internationalizing' the women's studies curricula" Grewal and Kaplan (2002, xviii), is intricately linked to questions of representation and reflection of the self and of the other in the context of globalization and the increasing contacts of and interactions between peoples and cultures.

Transnational Families

One of the contributions of transnational feminism beyond the debunking of a clear center/margin distinction within American feminist scholarship is the re-investigation of the intimate space that characterized inter-personal relationships, including family life. In the specific context of Asian American studies, representations of Asian American intimate spaces such as family and intra-and inter-racial marriages pose a particularly interesting question in the contextualization of cultural identity within Asian American studies. Lisa Lowe and Susan Koshy, for instance, equally stress patterns of socialization that emerged from the various immigration histories of the individual Asian American communities.[30] Lowe's project about "The Intimacies of Four Continents" recovers the notion of intimacy both in its meaning as geographical and geopolitical interconnectedness of Asian, Europe, Africa and the Americas in the 18th century through the sugar trade and its relevance for the manifestation of ideological phenomena within the intimate space of the family (2006). In her recent book, *Sexual Naturalization: Asian Americans and Miscegenation* (2004), Susan Koshy analyses how anti-miscegenation laws against Asian Americans shaped the impact of race, class and gender in Asian American families. Koshy identifies miscegenation laws as bio-political mechanisms which policed which intimate interactions were available for Asian immigrants in the U.S. and thus infringed upon their citizen rights. Koshy further emphasizes that while anti-miscegenation laws and discourses regulated inter-racial sexual acts between other ethnic minorities as well, they are most virulent in the Cable Act's denaturalization of female citizens as a punishment for what was perceived as their sexual defiance. As Lowe and Koshy illustrate through their discussions of the family realm, such bio-political mechanisms, because they occurred in the home and within the family, illustrate to which extent the domestic space is as much invested with ideological governance as is the public space. And such interconnectedness of the domestic and the public sphere, as Ann Laura Stoler contends in "Intimidations of Empire," largely shaped the historical development of North American societies: "Those tense and tender ties played out in beds, kitchens, nurseries, and schoolrooms were secured and

[30] *Strangers From a Different Shore: A History of Asian Americans*, Ronald Takaki's study of the various Asian American immigration histories, offers a very detailed analysis of the individual genealogies of Asian American communities.

subverted by too much knowledge and movement within and outside what people at particular times considered private or called 'home'" (3).[31]

This recognition of the ways in which ideological phenomena manifest themselves in the intimate realm of family life is pivotal to my reading of the mother-daughter conflict in Asian American literature. Many texts by Asian American writers depict the family as the primary place where people tackle the multiple legacies of immigration, diaspora, and transnationalism. In the texts that I discuss here, these legacies are often constructed along the matrilineal lineages that connect daughters with their mothers and their grandmothers. In Maxine Hong Kingston's memoir *The Woman Warrior: Memoirs of a Girlhood Among Ghosts* (1976), the daughter protagonist confronts such multiple legacies in the stories she tells about her mother's live in China and in the U.S., her aunt's recent immigration, her own childhood memories as a Chinese American girl. In these stories, Maxine investigates the cultural ramifications of immigration and diaspora. Moreover, by juxtaposing these stories with the legend of the famous Chinese warrior woman, Fa Mu Lan, and a story about her aunt in China who committed suicide, Kingston's memoir also negotiates the transnational linkages between the American and the Chinese context of stories, both in terms of how they are told in the memoir and how they are received by the readers. Embedded in a complex mother-daughter relationship, this prevalence of the social realities of Asian American immigrant, diasporic or transnational communities invites particular interest.

---

[31] Stoler elaborates at length on the notion of "tense and tender ties" in an essay of the same title that also appears in *Haunted by Empire* (2006).

CHAPTER TWO

Discourses of "I"dentity: Maxine Hong Kingston's Mother-Daughter Aesthetic in *The Woman Warrior*

> "which collectivity does the daughter of a dark-skinned mother listen to?" (Gloria Anzandúa, *Borderland / La Frontera*)

As the previous chapter outlines, mother-daughter relationships in Asian American literature cannot be easily classified along the traditional critical practices of psychoanalytical feminism and matrilineality. This chapter looks at the aesthetic strategies of Asian American literature with which authors depict mother-daughter relationships. This aesthetic, as it relates to my primary assertion, reflects the tensions between mothers and daughters on the level of the text's content at the same time as it reflects the interconnectedness of their personal stories on the level of the text's discursive strategies. Both elements are at times at odds with each other, but the overall impression the text makes reflects the ambivalence the daughter feels about her relationship to her mother. By analyzing the discursive representation of mother-daughter conflicts in Asian American literature, this chapter attempts to answer the question whether there is a distinct subgenre of mother-daughter writing. In essence, I offer suggestions of ways to explore mother-daughter relationships in Asian American literature, and how these relationships transgress the boundaries of conventional literary genres. Although the question of an emergent mother-daughter aesthetic is certainly relevant for a number of works in Asian American literature, I will focus here on Maxine Hong Kingston's *The Woman Warrior: Memoirs of a Girlhood Among Ghosts* (1976). Kingston's memoir helps me illustrate my point that an analysis of the discursive representation of the complex mother-daughter conflict offers cues about identity politics in Asian American literature at large.

Kingston's *The Woman Warrior* is no doubt one of the most critically reviewed Asian American texts, and perhaps one of the most controversial ones in terms of genre and narrative style. More importantly in the context of my study, it is also an important publication in Asian American literature about mother-daughter relationships. Published in the late 1970s, and thus contemporaneous with manifestos of psychoanalytical feminism on the mother-daughter dyad such as Adrienne Rich's *Of Woman Born* (1976) and Nancy Chodorow's *The Reproduction of Mothering* (1978), *The Woman Warrior* addresses the psychological complexities of the mother-daughter relationship at the same time as it addresses the socio-cultural identity of a second-generation Chinese American women. Kingston's memoir starts with the explicit statement of Maxine, the main protagonist, about her confiusion as to how to make sense of her identitiy as a young Chinese American woman. Throughout the memoir, Maxine negotiates between her Chinese and her American identity only to come to the conclusion that she cannot assume "home" in either of the two cultures.

By depicting a daughter who realizes that she and her mother do not have the same concept of their Chinese American culture and history, Kingston's *The Woman Warrior* seems to suggest that the daughter's difficulty in coming to terms with her Asian American identity is related to her conflict with her mother. In relation to Werner Sollors's definition of ethnicity as related to and dependent on context (Lentricchia and McLaughlin 288), Maxine considers herself *less ethnic* and more American than her mother, a fact that widens the gap between the two generations. Furthermore, there is a sense of distrust and secrecy between parents and childen that further hinders the communication in Maxine's family. The parents do not trust their children, and because of this distrust they do not share with them their immigration stories out of fear that the children's careless spreading of this information might get the family deported by the U.S. immigration officials. Maxine remembers: "[Our parents] would not tell us children because we had been born among ghosts, were taught by ghosts, and were ourselves ghost-like. They called us a kind of ghost" (183).

As much as the parents consider her a "white ghost," Maxine also knows that within American culture, she does not belong to the white majority. But what she does not know at the beginning of the memoir is how to make sense of her family's cultural ancestry and Chinese heritage. Thus, Maxine's quest for identitiy is framed by her attempt to deduct what features in her Chinese American self are genuinely Chinese and "what is peculiar to childhood, to poverty, insanities, one family, your mother who marked your growing with stories" (5) or "just my imagination, just my family, just the village, the movies, just living" (205). As Sau-ling C. Wong[32] reminds us in this context, although multiculturalism is America's "unofficial official face," multicultural identities are subject to the continuous dilemma of examining their own sense of belonging. Wong's reading of the term Asian American as bearing a dichotomy between what is Asian and what is American epitomizes the difficulties Maxine's identity mapping entails. Throughout the memoir, Maxine makes clear distinctions between the "American life" (45) she is leading outside the

---

[32] Wong addresses this issue in her paper at the Third Biannual MESEA Conference in Padua, Italy, 27 June 2002.

family and her life at home, influenced by Chinese culture and customs, "[w]hen we *Chinese* girls listened to adults talk-story" (19 emphasis added). At the same time, there are moments in the memoir at which Maxine makes a clear distinction between her individual and her collective identity, between self and other, as it were. Addressing the issue of Maxine's selfhood both in terms of her Asian American cultural identitiy and her identity as a daughter, Kingston's memoir uses specific performative strategies that counter monolithic discourses of the traditional autobiography and thus resists classification along conventional genre boundaries. Through such strategies, Maxine's complex identity negotiations become tangible.

My main argument in the chapter is that Kingston's memoir urges us to consider the particular *contexts* from which the narrativization of Maxine's personal and collective history occurs. At times, the narrative discourse of the memoir makes it difficult to distinguish between the various narrators. Upon reading *The Woman Warrior* for the first time, many readers are confused by the emergence of multiple narrative voices. In various sections of the memoir, it is indeed not clear who the narrator is. This shifting between narrative voices and agents of narrative focalization challenges the reader to attribute facile classifications to Maxine's identity and experience as a Chinese American woman. Kingston's memoir mimics on a discursive level the process of identity negotiation that Maxine undertakes. And such negotiation of Maxine's Asian American identity between self and other, between daughter and mother, as *The Woman Warrior* challenges us to understand, cannot occur in a monolithic narrative discourse.

Narrative Discourse of Self and Other

In M. M. Bakhtin's "Discourse in the Novel," language is defined as "a living, socio-ideological, concrete thing, a heteroglot opinion" that "lies on the borderline between self and other" (282). Such a notion of identity between self and other is also central to W. E. B. Dubois' formulation of a "double consciousness" as the "sense of always looking at one's self through the eyes of others, of measuring one's soul by the tape of a world that looks on in amused contempt and pity" (45) and Elaine Showalter's rhetoric of a "double-voiced discourse" that "always embodies the social, literary, and cultural heritages of both the muted and the dominant" (201). In Kingston's *The Woman Warrior*, the mother-daughter conflict that the memoir describes renders the notion of self and other even more complex. Kingston adopts a discourse that voices both the personal and the collective cultural identity of its protagonist Maxine. Through the emergence of such a narrative discourse, the 'Other' of Kingston's

The Woman Warrior at times can be reconciled and at times needs to be reconceptualised with the 'self' in order for Maxine to be able to narrate her life story. Kingston complies with this need for multiple positions by representing select sections of the narrative through different narrative voices. Furthermore, Kingston's *The Woman Warrior* is episodic, fragmented, and experimental. This use of a polyvocal narrative discourse offers a mosaic of narrative voices in which Maxine's voice stands side by side with the voice of the legendary woman warrior Fa Mulan and the voice of her mother as a young physician in China. Packed into different chapters but told from a first person narrative perspective, each of these voices stands on its own but also contributes to a "bigger picture." But while the individual chapters do contribute to an intertextual dialogue as far as the plot development is concerned, the memoir remains largely ambiguous. Hence, the split narrative voice in Kingston's memoir performs a narration of the daughter's matrilineal inheritance which remains largely unlinear.

There are different ways to think about Kingston's use of such an experimental literary form. Both ethnic American studies and feminist literary theory offer important incentives for my reading of Kingston's memoir. All of these aspects address questions of genre, such as the question of whether women write differently from men, and the dialogue between Asian American literature as a specific literary tradition and established genre conventions in American literature. But of even greater concern, so I propose in this chapter, is Kingston's adoption of a discourse that reflects the multiple positions not just of being female and Asian American, but also of engaging in a constant conversation with the past through her identification with her mother. Such conversations that Maxine keeps with her past demand the kind of genre transgressions that Kingston's memoir undertakes in order to perform a counter-monolithic depiction of her life as a writer and as a daughter.

The definitions of genre vary: in *Genres in Discourse*, Tzvetan Todorov characterizes genre as a "horizon of expectation;" Frederic Jameson describes it in "Postmodern Consumer Society" as a "social contract;" and Jonathan Culler paraphrases genre in "Towards a Theory of Non-Genre Literature" as "a set of expectations, a set of instructions" (qtd. in Grice 77). Despite the various definitions of genre, Paul A. Bové attributes to genre "marked differences and established identities" within the category of prose narratives (Lentricchia and McLaughlin 50). Bové underscores the social construction of genre as an appropriated category in similar terms as Judith Butler has defined the social construction of gender in *Gender Trouble: Feminism and the Subversion of Identity* (1990). Like Bové, Jacques Derrida argues in his essay "The Law of Genre" that genre is superimposed, and that its totalitarian claims can thus only be considered partly valid. In *Acts of Literature* (1992), Derek Attridge paraphrases Derrida's argument well:

> The question of *genre* – literary genre but also gender, genus, and taxonomy more generally – brings with it the question of law, since it implies an institutionalized classification, an enforceable principle of non-contamination and non-contradiction. But genre always potentially exceeds the boundaries that bring it into being, for a member of a genre always signals its membership by an explicit or implicit mark; its relation to the generic field is, in the terminology of speech act theory, a matter of *mention* as well as *use*. (221, original emphasis)

To call genre therefore into question or to destabilize its boundaries, a concern that lies at the crux of postmodern literary theory, is to challenge the *status quo* of social relations. Such is also the attempt of Asian American literature of matrilineage in the sense that it shares genealogies with feminist literary theory and transnational feminism.

If literature can destabilize social norms, then the following question arises: whose norms are they and who set them to begin with? Sandra Gilbert and Susan Gubar remind us in *The Madwoman in the Attic: The Woman Writer and the Nineteenth Century Literary Imagination* (1979), "[m]ost Western literary genres are, after all, essentially male – devised by male authors to tell male stories about the world" (67). In her book *On Lies, Secrets, and Silence: Selected Prose, 1966-78* (1979), Adrienne Rich describes the beginning emergence of a feminist literary location in opposition to the male-dominated genres. In "When We Dead Awaken: Writing as Revision," Rich points out the need for a discharge of conventions of the literary genre: "A radical critique of literature, feminist in its impulse, would take the work first of all as a clue to how we live, how we have been living, how we have been led to imagine ourselves, how our language has trapped as well as liberated us; and how we can begin to see – and therefore live – afresh" (1979, 18).

In the context of transnational and postcolonial theories, the norms are set by Westerncentricism. Similar to the works of Gilbert and Gubar and Adrienne Rich, Chandra Talpade Mohanty's introduction in *Third World Women and the Politics of Feminism* (1991) observes that many, and by no means all, third world women writers, seek to make visible their distinct location in opposition to western hegemony and white supremacy. Mohanty argues that such visibility arises from and is articulated through emphasis on:

> (1) the idea of the simultaneity of oppressions as fundamental to the experience of social and political margin-

ality and the grounding of feminist politics in the histories of racism and imperialism;

(2) the crucial role of a hegemonic state in circumscribing their /our daily lives and survival struggles;

(3) the significance of memory and writing in the creation of oppositional agency; and

(4) the differences, conflicts, and contradictions internal to third world women's organization and communities. (1991, 10)

While I am hesitant to include Asian American writers under the rubric of third world women, as much as I am hesitant about the monolithic term third world women altogether, Mohanty's identification of four distinct topics does pertain to Kingston's genre manipulations and the ideological and aesthetic performances of her memoir's experimental narrative discourse.

Many critics theorize Kingston's genre transgressions by emphasizing her position as a feminist and as an Asian American author. Because of their representation of the intersection between ethnicity and gender, urges Sidonie Smith in *A Poetics of Women's Autobiography: Marginality and the Fictions of Self-Representation* (1987), female ethnic American writers carry "the potential for works of the marginalized to challenge the ideology of individualism and with it the ideology of gender" (150). Other critics have offered readings of Kingston's memoir by privileging either her contributions to feminist or to ethnic American literary canons. For instance, Estelle C. Jelinek observes in *Women's Autobiography: Essays in Criticism* (1980) that autobiographies by female authors are more a-chronical, episodic and fragmentary than men's (xx). Critics, such as Jelinek and Smith, have emphasized that in the writings of ethnic American women, such emancipatory strategies are joined by the additional need to tackle hegemonic society structures in order to articulate the aspect of "race" and culture through the discourse of writing. That the "ethnic" makes a difference, as Sato Kumiko claims in relation to Kingston's use of a highly innovative narrative mode in her experimental memoir, is certainly a well accepted, but nonetheless controversial, reading of ethnic American writing. Elaborating on Michel Foucault's question: "What difference does it make who is speaking?" (qtd. in Sato 82), Sato specifies that the author's identity is inevitably mirrored in his or her choice of genre. More specifically, Sato suggests that the identification of the author is also implied in the socio-cultural context from which the text is narrated. Sato concludes that it is the "ethnic" in contemporary writing that re-institutionalizes the author's function, a function that post-structuralist theory regards as collapsed, either "by nullifying the author," as does (Roland Barthes), or "by ideologizing it," as does Michel Foucault

(Sato 88). In the same light, the disruption of discourse beyond gender/genre limitations, argues Elizabeth Ordóñez, mirrors the minority woman's emancipation from white patriarchal laws (also of discourse) in that she is "rereading the past, reshaping the future" (19).

Both, the notion that women use genre differently than men and that ethnic American writers use genre differently from white authors lead to a conclusions that primarily emphasize differeces between the "female" and the "ethnic" by characterizing it as located in opposition to the male and mainstream. It is not so much a question of authenticity that is being addressed by such need for location, I would like to emphasize, but a question of the text's impression on the reader, an impression which arises out of the claimed authorship of a certain ethnic minority. As far as genre theory is concerned, this essentialist appropriation of gender and ethnicity is a rather shorthanded answer to the question of Kingston's unconventional use of genre in *The Woman Warrior* because it does not examine the many issues Kingston's transgression of genre normativity raises about the generic system itself. In a different project, I have argued that Kingston uses "crossover-genres" which reinforce certain genre conventions, but do so by re-appropriating them in such a fashion that exposes the insufficient scope of conventional definitions of genre (Schultermandl 2007). For the purpose of my present project, my discussion of Kingston's *The Woman Warrior* seeks to illustrate the transgressions of genre and discourse that are first and foremost emblematic of the mother-daughter conflict she depicts. This emphasis on Kingston's discursive representation of a transnational matrilineage, I would like to contend, is an example of the complexity and innovation of Asian American literary productions, but can not be considered as a synechdoche for Asian American literature altogether. Nevertheless, since the subsequent generation of Asian American female authors frame their depictions of mother-daughter conflicts in similar fashion to Kingston's, this chapter reads *The Woman Warrior* as a "mother" text from which a new form of narrative discourse of mother-daughter conflicts departs.

Towards a Mother-Daughter Discourse

Asian American authors who reinvent their personal histories of selfhood through writing about their relationships with their mothers also assert a form of power, both by writing about their experiences as Asian American women and as daughters. By revisiting and discursively constructing their own childhoods through autobiographies, memoirs, and other forms of life writing, Asian American authors perform a variety of narrative strategies that counter monolithic images of Asian American experiences. In *Begin Here: Reading Asian*

North American Autobiographies of Childhood (2007), a comprehensive analysis of Asian American life writing, Rocío G. Davis contends that "Asian North American memoirs of childhood are challenging the construction and performative potential of the national experience, particularly in the experiential categories of epistemology and phenomenology" (1). Like Davis, Lynn Bloom recognizes the potential in feminist memoirs for the daughter to assert power, not just against racism, as Wendy Ho's study (1999) suggests, but also against her own mother. Accounts of past or existing mother-daughter conflicts tend to recreate images of the mother whom the daughters, engaged in constant ambivalence between loving identification and rebellious independence, perceives as oppressive and over-present. The daughter narrator, "in recreating and interpreting her childhood and maturing self, assumes a number of the functions that her own mother fulfilled in the actual family history." This "mothering" of her own plot, continues Bloom, "is certainly a reversal of the [mother's] *power and dominance* that prevailed during the [years of the daughter's adolescence]" (Davidson and Broner 292, emphasis added). In constrast to Bloom, Judith Butler considers such acts of self-creation in terms of their subversive potential against hegemonic discourses that rely on binary oppositions. In *Gender Trouble: Feminism and the Subversion of Identity* (1990), Butler delineates the signifying practices of identity mappings in the following way: "As part of the epistemological inheritance of contemporary political discourses of identity, this binary opposition is a strategic move within a given set of signifying practices, one that establishes the 'I' in and through this opposition and which reifies that oppression as a necessity, concealing the discursive apparatus by which the binary itself is constituted" (184).

This narrative discourse between self and other relies on specific narrative strategies that allow for a narrative perspective that can emcompass both the daughter's and the mother's stories. Such a discourse can either fuse the two narrative instances, thereby bridging the gap between a daughter and her mother, or it can widen the ideological gap by pitting the mother's narrative against the daughter's. In her groundbreaking book, *The Mother/Daughter Plot: Narrative, Psychoanalysis, Feminism* (1989), Marianne Hirsch defines a narrative discourse that combines the daughter's and the mother's perspective. This "mother/daughter plot," so Hirsch contends, is a literary perfomance which gestures toward a sense of solidarity on the narrative level between mother and daughter:

> The story of female development, both in fiction and theory, needs to be written in the voice of mothers as well as in that of daughters. It needs to cease mystifying maternal stories, to cease making them the objects of a 'sustained quest.' Only in

> combining both voices, in finding a double voice that would yield a multiple female consciousness, can we begin to envision ways to 'live afresh.' Only thus can feminists begin to imagine a social and ideological revolution that feminism has only begun to effect. (1989, 161)

While Hirsch's defintion of a mother/daughter plot mostly deals with the representation of female identitiy on the level of narrative discourse, Nan Bauer Maglin asserts that in the literature of matrilineage, women writers need to address the ambivalence about their relationships with their mothers and that this ambivalence shapes their works on a thematic and, to a certain degree, also on a narrative level. Maglin's identifies five interconnected themes in the literature of matrilineage:

> (1) the recognition by the daughter that her voice is not entirely her own;
> (2) the importance of trying to really see one's mother in spite of or beyond that blindness and skewed vision that growing up together causes;
> (3) the amazement and humility about the strength of our mothers;
> (4) the need to recite one's matrilineage, to find a ritual to both get back there and preserve it;
> (5) and still, the anger and despair about the pain and silence borne and handed on from mother to daughter" (Davidson and Broner 258).

Hirsch's and Maglin's projects are not so dissimilar, even though their attempts to contextualize the literary representations of mother-daughter conflicts connote different feminist subject positions, one foregrounding unity and the other one difference.

While both projects are equally innovative in their recognition of the mother-daughter conflict as formative element of a text's narrative strategy, they both adopt discourses of identity that are based on binary opposition. Jessica Benjamin's intersubjective theory offers a different approach to identity formation between mother and child, and, as Yi-Lin Yu's recent study about maternal subjectivity in Amy Tan's *The Joy Luck Club* argues, also about the narrativization of the mother-daughter conflict. According to Benjamin's formulation in *Bonds of Love: Psychoanalysis, Feminism and the Problem of Domination* (1988)

> [t]he intersubjective view maintains that the individual grows in and through the relationship to other subjects. Most important, this perspective observes that the other whom the

> self meets is also a self, a subject in his or her own right, It assumes that we are able and need to recognize that other subject as different and yet alike, as an other who is capable of sharing a similar mental experience. Thus the idea of intersubjectivity reorients the conception of the psychic world from a subject's relation to its object toward a subject meeting another subject" (19-29).

Unlike the subject-object theory of the Freudian psychoanalytical tradition, Benjamin's intersubjective theory offers a critical framework through which mother and daughter can both be their own subjects. Benjamin thus proposes that identity does not need to rely on binary oppositons. In light of the daughter's identity negotiation between self and other, this absence of a binarity enables a woman to imagine herself in a fashion that does not demand a hierarchical division between her self and her (m)other but that "breaks down the oppositions between powerful and helpless, active and passive" (48) one that "counteracts the tendency to objectify and deny recognition to those weaker or different – to the other" (48).

In relation to the mother's selfhood and the narrative representation of her selfhood, Yi-Lin Yu's recent study offers an interesting appropriation of Benjamin's intersubjective theory. Yu analyzes the narrative construction of maternal subjectivity in Tan's novel and argues that Tan's *The Joy Luck Club* exhibits a narrative strategy that allows the mothers "to reconstruct and make significant and coherent the histories and life stories that they might have lost or forgotten after their emigration to their new adopted country, America" (n.p.). Through a pattern of interlocking narratives, some told by the mothers and some by the daughters, proposes Yu, Tan's novel demonstrates that "storytelling is built upon mutuality in which the acts of telling and listening are conducted simultaneously: one cannot work without the other" (n.p.). While Tan's novel successfully establishes through such a narrative technique a dialogue between mothers and daughters, I would like to argue here that Kingston's memoir offers a more complex rendition of this mutuality by fusing the mother's and the daughter's narrative voices into a narrative discourse that operates with a first-person perspective that can be mother and daughter at the same time. Through such a literary representation of the mother-daughter conflict, Kingston's memoir aestheticizes this intersubjective identity model by discursively blurring the ego-boundaries between what can in part be divided into the mother narrator and the daughter narrator.

Kingston's *The Woman Warrior* exhibits a narrative strategy which counters binary oppositions between mother and daughter while still emphasizing the daughter's ambivalence about her selfhood. On the level of narrative discourse,

Kingston achieves this by using multiple first person narrative perspectives, sometimes without making it clear for the reader who the narrator of the individual chapters is. At times, it is not clear whether Maxine, the main protagonist of Kingston's memoir, adopts different narrative perspectives or whether there are different narrators. Some critics suggest that the narrative discourse of Kingston's memoir can be divided into Kingston's voice and Maxine's voice. Patricia P. Chu, for instance, points out the "narrator's double perspective": a complex discourse in which Kingston "'speaks' as an adult recalling, and to some extent reliving, her experiences and perspectives as a girl growing up in Stockton, California, in the 1940s and 1950s" (86-87). Similarly, Sidonie Smith observes in her essay "Filiality and Woman's Autobiographical Storytelling" a division of Kingston's discourse into "two sets of stories: those of the dominant culture and those of an ethnic subculture with its own traditions, its unique stories" (Wong 2001, 58). Such are also Rosetta P. Haynes' observations that Maxine's narrative voice can be divided into an American and a Chinese "I" (137). Lee Quinby has attempted to resolve the maze of such multiplicity of Kingston's narrative "I" in his formulation of an "ideographic self" with which Kingston places herself in–between different cultures. Addressing *The Woman Warrior*'s often contested categorization as autobiography, Quinby explains that by using an autobiographical genre, Kingston attempts to defy and challenge the existence of a traditional "I" with assets to totalitarian authority. Instead, Kingston's use of an "ideographic self" that negotiates between the American "I" and the Chinese "I" "valorizes individual freedom while at the same time defining selfhood as an ensemble subjectivity [sic]" (Smith and Watson 306). Quinby's suggestion of an ideographic self, as Rosetta R. Haynes specifies, is closely connected to the "Western totalized and disconnected 'I' of autobiography [and] more accurately describes the Western male 'I' of traditional autobiography" since [w]omen were not traditionally defined as independent or disconnected (Hoeveler and Boles 137).

Not only do all of the above considerations of the narrative discourse which Kingston employs in her memoir operate with an understanding of identity as based on binary oppositions between self and other, these considerations hardly address the cultural and psychoanalytical aspects that characterize the mother-daughter conflict, one whose very nature demands a closer look into the struggle between independence and identification. Taking my cue from Benjamin's intersubjectivity theory, I argue that Kingston's discourse cannot be divided into an American and a Chinese voice, as seems to be the consensus among the scholars I cite above, nor can it in fact be divided at all. Instead, I propose that Maxine re-invents herself through a narrative voice that can be both self and other, and which enables a narrative performance of identity that expresses ambivalence through a foregrounding of context rather than essential difference.

A different way of reading her memoir is to assume that Maxine has both a personal voice with which she rebels against the mother and the mother-culture and a collective voice with which she reconstructs her matrilineal heritage. In the context of my project on the representation of mother-daughter conflicts, the idea that Maxine can narrate both her self and her collective history is very appealing and invites a closer look at the strategies with which Kingston constructs the narrative discourse that allows for such ambivalence. The emergence of either of Maxine's discourses is context-specific and is a direct response to socially imposed categories that objectify her. In her conversations with her mother, for instance, Maxine maintains her personal voice, a voice that underscores her distinction from the cultural heritage her mother embodies. With this voice, Maxine explores her affinities with the dominant American culture, for instance, when she renders herself "American feminine" (11) and aspires to becoming "a lumberjack in Oregon" (47) because she wants to liberate herself from the image of womanhood her mother represents. All these attempts originate in Maxine's maintenance of an "American life" (45), one that is separate from the life she is leading at home, the place where "we Chinese girls listened to the adults talk-story" (19).

Such a reading practice also invites a more thorough investigation of the contexts in which the different narrative voices emerge. In the following section, I will approach a reading of Kingston's narrative strategy, analyzing, in particular, the various tendencies within Maxine's "I"dentity. Kingston emphasizes the context from which her narratives emerge in order to distinguish between the multiple cultural environments she is exposed to. In the chapter "Shaman," for instance, Maxine realizes that her understanding of her Chinese cultural ancestry can only occur through the frame of the U.S. circumstances of her present life. Telling the story of her mother's life in China, Maxine starts with the imminent here and now, that is, the U.S. setting she lives in, and weaves the narratives of her collective past into her personal live story. Alternately, she travels back and forth in her accounts and bridges the present with the past, the American with the Chinese, through numerous comparisons of how Chinese customs translate into a U.S. context. Yet, her conflict with her mother complicates this identity mapping. For instance, Maxine directs her frustration with misogynist Chinese proverbs like "Girls are maggots in the rice" and "It is more profitable to raise geese than daughters" (43) solely at her mother Brave Orchid, thus distancing herself from her mother. By constantly accusing her mother of not treating her in the same openly loving way as American mothers do, Maxine further alienates her mother. Ideologically, this sense of alienation keeps mother and daughter apart, thus rendering them even more powerless in the face of patriarchy. This aspect gains further importance considering the fact that in *China Men* (1980), Kingston's fictional biography of her father, Maxine much more readily allies with her father against racist American policies and, with considerably more empathy than for her mother's struggle against racism and sexism, accepts her father's achievements in life. Because of its intertextual relationship to *China Men*, Kingston's memoir is a powerful depiction of the daughter's favoring of the dominant culture in ways that duplicate the dynamics of post-Oedipal assimilation to and acceptance of the father as means of separation from the mother.

Such attempt at separation from the mother becomes evident in sections and chapters of the memoir in which Maxine clearly distinguishes her voice from her mother's voice. In the first chapter, "No Name Woman," Maxine emphasizes this difference in her re-appropriation of a story her mother told her about her aunt who committed suicide. After the story Maxine's mother tells about the aunt in China who was ostracized by her village and punished by her "family's deliberately forgetting her" (16) for the shame she brought upon them in their eyes, Maxine offers four alternative readings that all deal with the possible circumstances that led to her aunt's pregnancy out of wedlock. While the mother's narrative does not offer any further details other than explaining: "She could not have been pregnant, you see, because her husband was gone for years" (3), Maxine's versions of the story are more sympathetic toward the aunt. In one version, she imagines her aunt being the victim of sexual assault, the man who raped her "not much different from her husband. They both gave orders: she followed" (7). In another version, Maxine envisions her as the lone romantic, who, deserted by her husband who left for the "Gold Mountain," took a lover and "gave up everything for sex" (6). In the third version, Maxine imagines her as a "wild woman" who "kept rollicking company" (8) and used her lovers to fill her sexual appetite. In the forth finally, Maxine considers her outside the traditional narratives of romantic love and imagines her as independent girl who "combed individuality into her bob" (8) and considered sex as a means of social rebellion.

The fact that Maxine relates a story her mother used to tell her and then deconstructs that story, speculating about the alternative readings of her aunt's suicide, takes into consideration the possibly strategic omissions her mother made to the 'real' story. Knowing that her mother's version of the story is supposed to serve as a cautionary tale to warn her about the dangers of premarital sex, Maxine seeks to uncover the facts behind the mother's story. She soon realizes, however, that storytelling inevitably entails performing a literary gesture to fulfill a specific purpose. This inherent purpose of storytelling becomes clear to Maxine when she asserts that the story only fulfills its function if she can relate it to her own life. Maxine says about her aunt: "Unless her life branches into mine, she gives me no ancestral help" (8). And the same premise that applies to the function of the story about "No Name Woman" also holds for Maxine's authorial choices as a narrator of her personal and her collective identity.

Her most apparent choice in the context of her relationship with her mother is to recall incidents of mutual misunderstanding between her and Brave Orchid. Maxine consciously breaks away from the Chinese heritage her mother embodies; in matrophobic rejection of her mother's "slave" identity – as evoked by Kingston's interpretation of the Chinese word for the first person singular female pronoun – Maxine deliberately burns food, neglects the household, and decides to become "a lumberjack in Oregon" rather than take her mother's place at the family laundry (47). Maxine also subscribes to white American ideals of femininity. Conversely to her mother's loud voice of imperfect immigrant English and her pigeon-toed legs, she walks and talks "American feminine" (11), in fear of otherwise attracting "no dates" (47). Due to such disassociation from her mother, Maxine encounters difficulties in placing herself within the line of matrilineage that her mother represents. She considers Brave Orchid to be "mean" (51), and in rebellion against her mother's maternal authority, constantly refuses to accept her advice: "my sweater lost somewhere (probably not worn because my mother said to wear a sweater)" (181). It becomes clear throughout the memoir that Maxine's mischaracterizations of her mother's peculiarities do not refer to single incidents but are largely based on her overall negative attitude toward Brave Orchid. When the latter, bringing her children to their family laundry, places the baby's crib in the shop window, for instance, Maxine believes her mother to be boastful of her new-born, showing it off to the people of Chinatown. However, as a conversation with her mother clarifies years after this incident, Brave Orchid (a successful physician in China) always put the cradle as far away from the laundry fumes as possible (104-5). As most forcefully depicted in the dialogic exchanges with her mother, the fact that she misinterprets her mother's intentions and discharges herself of her mother's markers of ethnicity are at the core of the mother-daughter conflict between Maxine and Brave Orchid.

But these incidents between Maxine and her mother are clearly characterized as childhood memories and are thus subject to misremembering or misrepresentation. Maxine contends: "maybe [...] what I once had was not Chinese-sight at all but child-sight that would have disappeared eventually without such struggle" (205). Indeed, the mother's narrative often counters the narrative realities that Maxine constructs in her stories. Through such moments in the text, the mother's concerns for her daughter and for the continuity of Chinese customs in the family become tangible. For instance, the fact that Maxine does not know her mother's age makes her seem like one of the "White Ghosts [who] can't tell Chinese age" (104), thus evidencing Brave Orchid's concern that her own daughter does not really know her. For Brave Orchid, her American children seem "like the ghosts" and "have no memories" (167). In anticipation of Maxine's inability to understand the stories she tells about her life in China, Brave Orchid transfers facts of her Chinese past into the American context of the present: "In China, the bridges are nothing like the ones in Brooklyn and San Francisco" (87). Brave Orchid's acknowledgment of the cultural differences between her and her daughter becomes explicit in her need to reframe her stories about China through an American context. While this practice of translating for her daughter her Chinese heritage does not withstand the issue of manipulative representation, such as is the case with the narrative on Maxine's aunt, what it does reiterate is the discursive performance of storytelling that runs within Maxine's family.

While Brave Orchid's comments exhibit her awareness of the need to recontextualize her Chinese stories within American culture, Maxine has yet to learn the code her mother uses to articulate memory and culture. Maxine takes personal offense when her mother, because the Chinese "like to say the opposite," calls her ugly, noisy, and lazy (203). Only when she moves out does she start to adopt a different perspective. Whether this is a more mature perspective or just a different one is not so much the concern of my argument here. What is important, however, is that Kingston stresses a shift in context or space, both physical and discursive. In other words, Maxine has to leave their mother-daughter relationship in order to distance herself from the ramifications of her psychological disputes with her mother which largely influences her perception of the Chinese heritage she is connected to. When her mother expels her from home, Maxine is inevitably forced to re-negotiate her cultural identity, pragmatical reasoning being her "new way of seeing" (204). Revisiting her ethnic and gender socialization from a less emotional and more analytical perspective, Maxine sorts out real childhood experiences from those childhood traumata she possibly only imagined and acknowledges that she might have misremembered certain incidents. But before she can do so, she needs to express her anger and frustration. Eventually, maybe "because [she is] the one with the tongue cut loose" (197), Maxine tells her mother what she calls the "true things" about herself, basically all the reproaches and hostilities that she cultivated over the years. Thus, her cut-loose tongue, initially intended by her mother to free Maxine from Chinese patriarchal restrictions to devout and passive femininity, becomes the weapon the culturally and personally alienated adolescent daughter directs against her own mother. Therefore, Maxine blames Brave Orchid for having cut her tongue in order to make her "talk weird" and to make her "flunk kindergarten" (201). As absurd as Maxine's accusations may sound, what she really implies is that her mother's inability to speak English flawlessly gave Maxine "a zero IQ" (201). The underlying assumption in Maxine's reproaches is that her mother, who speaks a form of immigrant English, is the reason for her lack of success in American society.

While there is a great deal of confrontation and anger in what Maxine says to and thinks about her mother, in the memoir such points of conflict are juxtaposed with sections in which Maxine celebrates the strong tradition of storytelling that has been at the center of her family, a tradition that her mother taught her. The fact that her mother taught her the art of storytelling is pivotal in that it establishes a shared tradition between Maxine and Brave Orchid. In relation to Maxine's earlier complaints that her mother didn't teach her anything useful, this appropriation of the art of storytelling also shows her from a more sympathetic side towards her mother. On the level of narrative discourse, the sections in which Maxine narrates her connectedness to her symbolic *mother* figures use a first-person narrative perspective which relates her to her collective mother-culture. With this inclusive discourse, Maxine tells several stories of strong Chinese women: the story of Fa Mu Lan, the legendary warrior woman, the story of her mother's successful life in China, and the story of her aunt's suicide by drowing herself in the family's well, an act of defiance and rebellion against the silence the family imposes on her once she gets pregnant out of wedlock. In contrast to the distance her personal stories about her mother convey, these stories show compassion with and pride of her symbolic mother figures. In these sections she speaks with gratitude and compassion of the strength the women have brought forth to surmount the legacy of misogynist Confucian Chinese culture and customs. Such rhetorics also prevail in Maxine's acknowledgement of her similarity to Fa Mu Lan, the legendary woman warrior Kingston evokes in the title of her memoir:

> The swordswoman and I are not dissimilar. […] What we have in common are the words at our back. The idioms for *revenge* are 'report a crime' and 'report to five families.' The reporting is the vengeance – not the beheading, not the gutting, but the words. And I have so many words – 'chink' words and 'gook' words too – that they do not fit on my skin. (53 original emphasis)

In this context, matrilineage does indeed serve as a source of inspiration for Maxine. Most specifically out of her need to affirm her Chinese American identity in the face of the double marginalization of ethnic minorities in the

U.S., Maxine embraces the discourse of her cultural heritage. In this context, she draws on the *chink* and *gook* words she rejects when in direct confrontation with her mother. But fighting for emancipation of ethnic minorities in the U.S., Maxine takes up the "sword" of her Chinese ancestors and seeks revenge. For instance, when working at an art supply department and at a land developer's association, Maxine refuses to order what her boss calls "more of that nigger yellow" and to type invitations to a banquet hosted at a restaurant that "is being picketed by the CORE and the NAACP" (48). There, the sword of the warrior woman of her mother's talk-story inspires Maxine's struggle for ethnic emancipation, both for her own and for other ethnic groups in the U.S. It is interesting to note that with the female persons / personae who live in China, including Fa Mu Lan, but also her own mother, she identifies much more readily than with the Chinese American women in her familiy in the U.S. Until Maxine resolves the intricate dynamics of the mother-daughter conflict that dominated her growing-up and reconciles with Brave Orchid, her voice of revenge and retaliation against the sexism and racism she witnesses and experiences remains "a bad, small person's voice that makes no impact" (48) and is largely "unreliable" (49).

Only at the end of Kingston's memoir, once Maxine has resolved her conflict with her mother, can also her ambivalence about her identification with her mother be resolved. Towards the end of the novel, Maxine tells a story that she and her mother both imagined. At that point, her memoir displays a narrative discourse which equally incorporates the perspectives of Maxine and of her mother: "Here is a story my mother told me, not when I was young, but recently, when I told her I also talk story. The beginning is hers, the ending is mine" (206). This story is carried by the discourse of the daughter who accepts traditional Chinese storytelling into her own discourse, in fact even makes it her discourse. This discourse constitutes a success in the transference of the daughter's cultural collective past, especially in the diasporic context of immigrant families. The fact that this final story "translated well" (209) is emblematic of a general understanding that mother and daughter can both *own* the narrative discourse of Kingston's memoir. Such a literary performance also implies that the psychological chasm between mother and daughter can be resolved.

Minority/Mainstream Discourses and the Politics of Location

This emphasis on context and interconnectedness liberates Asian American literature from essentialist notions of culture and ethnicity. Kingston's use of a narrative discourse whose representation of both the filial and the maternal voice by emphasizing the interconnectedness between individual and collective identitiy is an important achievement in light of ongoing discussions in ethnic American literary studies about the distinction between mainstream and minority discourses in American literature. This division between mainstream and non-mainstream literatures enacts a dividing line between what American society recognizes as American and what it deems as "other." As Derek Parker Royal rightly observes, "[t]he question of what it means to be an American goes hand in hand with the question of how to define American literature" (147). In a similar light, Paul Lauter suggests "the Great River theory of American Letters," which labels texts by so-called minority authors as "minor rills and branches" (6). Lauter's clever metaphor implies that the very suggestion of a mainstream/minority literature can be seen as an act of reenforcement of existing power divisions in American society. This more or less subliminal implementation of power struggles is another form of domination, and to explore Kingston's narrative aesthetizication of the mother-daughter conflict in this context offers another interesting reading practive of the genre subversions which *The Woman Warrior* performs.

Since the division between mainstream and minority literatures also echoes the social pratice in the U.S. of distinguishing between mainstream and minority authors, the use of the monolith "minority" also raises issues about the ways in which Asian American authors' literary performances are classified both on the American literary market and in society at large. The question that I am asking her is not so much whether Kingston is a minority author. I am much more interested in the ways in which Kingston's use of a mother-daughter aesthetic which refutes binary oppositions resists reading practices which seek to categorize Asian American literature in essentialist and monolithic terms. Because Kingston's memoir foregrounds the question of authorial agency in relation to the mother-daughter conflict, questions about the relationship between author and text cannot be entirely neglected. These questions are especially important in the context of discussions about the role of the author as agent of authenticity for the context of her work. While I do not mean to argue that looking at Kingston's memoir offers new insights in relation to the question of her authorial agency, I would like to extend the critical conversations that emerged about Kingston's agency as an author to my discussion of Maxine's comments on authorial agency. In this light, the mother-daughter context in which I read Kingston's memoir is worth exploring, starting with Maxine's ultimate understanding that identity and discourse cannot be contained through binary oppositions.

This need to tackle binarity is a central issue in feminist literature. In her essay "Choosing the Margin as Space of Radical Openness," published in her

1989 collection of essays *Yearning: Race, Gender, and Cultural Politics* and somewhat a more direct response to Rich's formulation of a politics of location, hooks identifies women of color writing as a space "where we begin the process of revision" (1989, 145) from multiple points of view:

> I have been working to change the way I speak and write, to incorporate the manner of telling a sense of place, of not just who I am in the present but where I am coming from, the multiple voices within me. [...] When I say then that these words emerge from suffering, I refer to that personal struggle to name that location from which I come to voice – that space of theorizing. (146)

Important for feminist postmodernist aesthetics, hooks's "placing" of such struggle of naming within the medium of language challenges the idea that identity can only be constructed in essentialist terms. The contrary becomes evident from hooks' questions: "Dare I speak to oppressed and oppressor in the same voice? Dare I speak to you in a language that will move *beyond the boundaries of domination* – a language that will not bind you, fence you in, or hold you?" (146, emphasis added).

hooks contributes to the launching of a critical discourse in feminist theory which refuses to think in terms of a center/margin dichotomy. In her essay "(De)Centering the Margins?: Identity Politics and Tactical (Re)Naming," AnaLouise Keating critiques U.S. feminist theory and its reproduction of the center/margin oppositionality in women writers' alleged exclusive location within the margin. In her essay "Woman Skin Deep: Feminism and the Postcolonial Condition," Suleri, asserts that "until the participants in marginal discourses learn how best to critique the intellectual errors that inevitably accompany the provisional discursivity of the margin, the monolithic and untheorized identity of the center will always be on them" (757-58). Suleri argues that feminists of color who operate with an unconditioned acceptance of the division into discourses that emerge from the center and discourses that emerge from the margin reinforce the very marginalization they experience in the first place. By adopting a politics of location from within the margins, argues Suleri, women writers of color have largely contributed to the critical practice of reading women of color feminist texts through frames of stereotypy that reduce possible critical receptions to mere "celebrations of oppression, elevating the racially female voice into a metaphor for 'the good'" (759). Like Suleri, AnaLouise Keating cautions of such practices which, despite the fact that the margin can also be considered a secure place from which women writers of color can counter-write double marginality, essentialize and thus "other" women writers of color on the discursive level.

That there are strategies for woman writers to achieve visibility without reverting to what Spivak terms "strategic essentialism," illustrates AnaLouise Keating's study *Reading Women Writing Women* (1996). Keating cites as one of the most influential and widely recognized formulations of a non-essentialist intervention Gloria Anzaldúa's concept of the *borderland.* In her experimental autobiography *Borderlands/La Frontera: The New Mestiza* (1987), Anzaldúa targets the notion of a universal margin and dismantles it as inappropriate, because unspecific, location of the feminist theory and practice of women of color. Already years before the publication of *Borderlands/La Frontera*, Anzaldúa describes the act of writing as a necessity for the women to establish visibility in a white, male dominated world. In her essay "Speaking in Tongues: A Letter To Third World Women Writers," which appeared in *This Bridge Called My Back: Writings By Radical Women of Color*, the 1981 anthology co-edited with Cherríe Moraga, Anzaldúa facilitates an understanding of the underlying dimensions the process of *writing one's self* reflects in women of color literatures:

> The act of writing is the act of making soul, alchemy. It is the quest for the self, for the center of the self, which we women of color have come to think of as 'other' – the dark, the feminine. Didn't we start writing to reconcile this other within us? We knew we were different, set apart, exiled from what is considered 'normal,' white-right. And as we internalized this exile, we came to see the alien within us and too often, as a result, we split apart from ourselves and each other. Forever after we have been in search of that self, that 'other' and each other. And we return, in widening spirals and never to the same childhood place where it happened, first in our families, with our mothers, with our fathers. The writing is a tool for piercing that mystery but it also shields us, gives a margin of distance, helps us survive. And those that don't survive? The waste of ourselves: so much meat thrown at the feet of madness or fate or the state. (Moraga and Anzaldúa 169)

It is such a discourse that equally represents self and other which characterizes the mother-daughter aesthetic of Kingston's memoir.

In their collection of essays, *De/Colonizing the Subject: The Politics of Gender in Women's Autobiography* (1992), Sidonie Smith and Julia Watson argue that "autobiographical practices can be productive in that process as the subject, articulating problems of identity and identification, struggles against coercive calls to a 'universal humanity'" (xix). As such, Smith and Watson position their definition of a decolonization of the subject in autobiographical practices in opposition to the questions that Foucault, Lacan and Spivak raise about the possibility of a decolonization of the subject in the face of the multiple power structures in which the subject is imbedded: Foucault about social power structures; Lacan about patriarchal power structures; and Spivak about postcolonial power structures. In this sense, Smith and Watson's take on decolonization of the subject is a more optimistic one, precisely because it takes into consideration the "perspectival adjustments" necessary for an analysis of life writing beyond the Eurocentric literary tradition. Similarly, Caren Kaplan's essay in the collection devotes its attention to the question of generic boundaries of autobiographies in pursuit of an answer to the question "whether or not autobiography is recoverable as a feminist writing strategy in the context of transnational affiliations" (116). Kaplan proposes a "discourse of situation" (117) which offers a possibility of decolonizing the subject.

By emphasizing the multiple contexts that play out in the narrative representation of the mother-daughter conflict, Kingston's memoir successfully recovers the collective within the personal identity negotiation of Maxine's narrative discourse not in a syncretic way but in a manner that suggests that although the two are at odds with each other, there can still be a viable discourse of selfhood that blurrs the ego-boundaries of the two women. This discourse of "I"dentity privileges the individual while reconciling it with the collective throught the contextual and "perspectival adjustments" that are needed to decolonize the narrative self. Such an understanding is important in the context of this project in that it limns the potential of inviting through the analysis of the mother-daughter conflict an understanding of the possibilities of non-essentialist identity politics within Asian American literature at large. Because Maxine, as the narrative strategy of *The Woman Warrior* demonstrates, needs to find her sense of authorial agency through her negotiations of the multiple contexts from which the narrativization of her self emerges, Kingston's memoir resists essentialist classification along a binary opposition that seeks the distinguish clearly between her Chinese and the American identities. While Maxine tries to separate herself from her mother by underscoring the difference she perceives between her Chinese life and her American life, the narrativization of her conflict with her mother bridges on the discursive level this distinction between self and other that Maxine seeks to make. Hence, even in those passages of the novel where Maxine foregrounds the insurmountable differences between her mother and herself, the memoir yokes together the two women's lives and discourses by presenting them as literary performances that contribute to the construction of a narrative of selfhood that spans several generations of women, that conjoins historical with personal renditions of the past, and that illustrates how the narrative recovery of the past is an essential part of Maxine's present sense of self. It is through this narrative performance that Kingston's memoir proposes a strategy of overcoming a severe mother-daughter conflict and thus, by extension, evokes a discursive strategy for a transnational feminist solidarity which unites Maxine with her matrilineage. In other words, what is transnational about Kingston's depiction of the mother-daughter conflict is not just the recovery of Chinese culture from a diasporic location, but the discursive situation from which Maxine launches her life telling. This position lays bare the underlying structures of power and privilege both in the context of Chinese American and Chinese communities. The fact that there is a link between the different generations of women in Maxine's family, to the same extent as there is a link between the historical and the mythical accounts of her family heritage, suggests another form of Kingston's ability to transgress boundaries. All of these strategies to transgress linear representations of history and identity are amplified in the context of mother-daughter conflict that Kingston's memoir depicts.

CHAPTER THREE

The Politics of Transnational Memory in Amy Tan's *The Joy Luck Club*

> "I can never things I didn't understand in the first place" Jing-mei Woo in "The Joy Luck Club"

With the publication of her debut novel *The Joy Luck Club* in 1989, Amy Tan launched a wave of intensive academic and popular interest in Asian American mother-daughter literature and brought Asian American women writers to a large readership in ways that no other writer has since been able to achieve. Much more accessible than Kingston's *The Woman Warrior*, Tan's novel opened up a market for Asian American fiction on mother-daughter relationships, so much so, that the often-quoted "Amy-Tan Phenomenon" continues to be the ground of all comparison in mother-daughter literature in North America and, most recently, also in Asia.[33] Critics, and probably authors as well, have been trying to crack to code of Amy Tan's immensely successful first novel. In her essay "Sugar Sisterhood: Situating the Amy Tan Phenomenon," Sau-ling C. Wong takes into consideration the literary and social circumstances that might have contributed to Tan's crossover success. Its subject matter, argues Wong, is one of the most important factors for the novel's success with a mostly white female reading audience which "appears to have a keen appetite for mother-daughter stories by and about women of color" (1995, 177). Given the large amount of mother-daughter writing by and about Asian American women, subject matter cannot be assumed to have had the greatest impact on the emergence of the Amy Tan Phenomenon. On the contrary, as Wong argues, the novel caters well to the expectations of its reading audience by offering "a convergence of ethnic group-specific literary tradition and ideological needs by the white-dominated readership – including the feminist readership – for the Other's presence as both mirror and differentiator" (177).

The fact that Tan's success was carried by a predominantly white, predominantly female audience places the novel at the heart of ongoing controversies about the cross-cultural reception of multi-ethnic American literatures. The question of why these readers were so taken by the complex relationships

[33] See, for instance, Tamara S. Wagner's "'After another round of tissues': 'Bad Time' Fiction and the Amy Tan-Syndrome in Recent Singaporean Novels" (2003).

between the first-generation Chinese immigrant mothers and their American-born daughters is worth exploring. In the context of globalization in general and China's growing economic power in particular, Tan's depiction of China and of Chinese American women offers many incentives for a discussion of how American readers have been viewing China in the past few decades. Yuan Shu's recent deconstruction of the unmistakably "Asian values" in Tan's novel, and his observation of a common conflation of Asian and Asian American cultural identities on the part of a non-Asian American college student audience, makes apparent the persistent and preconceived notions about the exoticism of Asian American literature's depiction of the "Other." Shu's main observation is that reading audiences of *The Joy Luck Club* bring to the text existing notions about Asian and Asian American culture. These assumptions about the nature of Asian American identities often echo prevalent stereotypes and are pivotal to Fatimah Tobing Rony's assertion that "the exotic is always already known" (6). The occurrence of such preconceived reading practices of Asian American texts stresses the importance of investigating Tan's politics of representation of Chinese and Chinese American culture through the complex and conflictive mother-daughter relationships, the subject of Tan's novel.

In this chapter I look at Tan's discursive construction of the cultural memory with which the mothers and daughters approach their matrilineage. I am most interested in the daughters' appropriations of their Chinese heritage through the use of memory as cultural vehicle. In *The Joy Luck Club*, memory is a cultural narrative which serves the function of narrating the mothers' appropriations of their lives in China and their immigrant experiences in the U.S.; memory also has the function of delineating the daughters' experiences of growing up as daughters of immigrant mothers and dealing with their mothers' memories of a country and culture with which they themselves are not familiar. My main focus of attention is on the daughters' relationship to her mother and thereby to their cultural heritage. My analysis of the daughter protagonists' difficult relationships with their mothers and, by extension, with their Chinese heritage, follows Sau-ling C. Wong's suggestion that the "Americanized daughter, who needs to be enlightened on things Chinese, serves as a convenient, unobstrusive stand-in for the mainstream reading public" (1995, 197). Therefore, the aspect of the daughters' relationships to their Chinese heritage that I am most concerned with is their difficulty in establishing a sense of feminist solidarity with their mothers and their collective, matrilineage ancestry. This difficulty, as I argue in a later section of this chapter, becomes apparent from one protagonist's actual experience of China: when Jing-mei travels to China in order to meet her twin half-sisters, the image she created of China based on her mother's storytelling and her personal experience of China as an

American tourist collide. I propose the term *belated memory* for this confrontation between memory and experience, a confrontation through which her memory of her mother's homeland is being validated through her personal experience. For this purpose, I focus for my present project on the first and the last chapters of the novel, two of the four that Jing-mei narrates; the fact that in the first chapter, Jing-mei narrates her mother's memories of China and in the last chapter narrates her personal experience of and in China lends itself well for an investigation of the narrative representation of memory and exemplifies the belated nature of the daughter's memory. I begin by placing Tan's novel in the context of memory studies in ethnic American literatures before I emphasize the transnational aspects that characterize the difficulty Chinese American daughters have in remembering their cultural legacies.

Cultural Memory in Multi-Ethnic American Literature

The use of memory as literary performance of ethnic consciousness in U.S. culture has been discussed in literary scholarship with considerable attention to the specific functions memory has in establishing alternative histories of American culture. First and foremost, two collections of essays, *Memory, Narrative, and Identity: New Essays in Ethnic American Literatures* (1994) and *Memory and Cultural Politics: New Approaches to Ethnic American Literatures* (1996), edited by Amritjit Singh, Joseph T. Skerrett Jr. and Robert E. Hogan, recognize cultural memory as ubiquitous trope in ethnic American literatures. The two collections point out the political implications that memory has, especially in the context of American culture studies: "What we study are the traces of memory in language and narrative and the ways individual writers challenge it: opposing to memory its dark shadow, forgetting; reconsidering its relation to history and oral tradition; erasing and revisiting it; preserving or recovering it" (Singh et al. 1994, 17). G. Thomas Couser rightfully observes that for ethnic minorities, who have been excluded from mainstream history, "the only history *is* memory" (Singh et al. 1996, 107, original emphasis). The diasporic experience of first-generation immigrants and their American-born children often determines memory as the only viable means of staying in touch and symbolically *returning* to their cultural origins. What Richard Rodriguez claims for the cultural transmittance among the Mexican immigrant population echoes the function of diaspora memoric in general: "Like the wandering Jew, Mexicans had no true home but the tabernacle of memory" (Mendoza and Shakar 197).

This exploration of cultural memory is especially important for women writers who write the complexities of gender and ethnicity into American history. bell hooks, for instance, asserts: "Remembering makes us subjects in history. It is dangerous to forget" (Mariani 54). In her book *Yearning: Race, Gender, and Cultural Politics* (1990), hooks affirms that "[t]here is an effort to remember that is expressive of the need to create spaces where one is able to redeem and reclaim the past, legacies of pain, suffering and triumph in ways that transform present reality" (1990, 147). The politics of memory in ethnic women's writing is, in the words of hooks, "a struggle of memory against forgetting" (ibid.). In her essay "Narrating Memory," Terry DeHay observes that "[t]he minority woman must look to her history, both to preserve it and to find out who she is. She needs to have a clear vision of her past, in order to re-vision the present. This is the process of re-membering" (Singh et al. 1994, 31).

In the literature of matrilineage, memory is the main device through which the American-born daughters connect with the lives of their foremothers. Through memory narratives, women writers of color have been honoring and preserving the culture of their foremothers, a culture that has been excluded for generations from history in general and mainstream literature in particular. This re-claiming of their own and their community's histories, their collective memories, and the minority cultures preserved by their mothers, allows women writers to assert their identities in a society that doubly marginalizes them. Through stories of multi-layered memories, many Asian American women writers portray the interconnectedness of the daughters' lives with their ancestors' as carriers of their cultural legacies. In her cultural narrative "Grandma's Story," Vietnamese American writer, filmmaker, and composer Trinh T. Minh-ha, for instance, describes a daughter's collective memory as a source of cultural richness. In particular, Trinh acknowledges that in this act of remembrance itself, lies the possibility to establish feminist solidarity and female alliance:

> The world's earliest archives or libraries were the memories of women. Patiently transmitted from mouth to ear, from body to body, hand to hand. In the process of storytelling, speaking and listening refer to realities that do not involve just the imagination. The speech is seen, heard, and smelled, tasted, and touched. It destroys, brings to life, nurtures. Every woman partakes in the chain of guardianship and of transmission. (1989, 121)

Traditionally, the literature of matrilineage recognizes the cultural collective as continuum whose continuity depends on the individual woman and her interaction with her culture. As Trinh's quote suggests, the interconnectedness between the individual members helps preserve a history and tradition that are separate from that of the dominant culture. Hence, the claiming of literary and biological foremothers is a highly political act of commemoration of those who are forgotten in Western mainstream history. However, the question that is most interesting in this context is *what* the American-born generation (including American-born daughter Amy Tan and the protagonists in her novels) is remembering, and, by logical extension, what it is more or less in line with Kingston's concept of "deliberately forgetting" (1976, 16).

Belated Cultural Memory

Amy Tan's *The Joy Luck Club* emphasizes the politics of representing cultural memory by narrativizing memory. Composed of four sets of four first person narratives told by four immigrant Chinese American mothers (Suyuan Woo whose stories are narrated by her daughter Jing-mei, Lindo Jong, An-mei Hsu, and Ying-ying St. Clair) and their American-born daughters (Jing-mei Woo, Waverly Jong, Rose Hsu Jordan, and Lena St. Clair), Tan's highly acclaimed first novel forcefully combines the cultural narrative with the conflicts innate to the mother-daughter relationship. In her portrayal of mothers and daughters who are emotionally alienated from each other because of cultural differences, Tan challenges the idea that the daughter is the embodiment of her mother's personal memory. Although often claimed as an example of matrilineal mother-daughter texts,[34] *The Joy Luck Club* epitomizes the American–born daughter's difficulty re-membering her collective heritage. This difficulty complicates the daughter's interaction with her mother, and, as evident from Jing-mei's case, also with her mother's memory.

Memory plays a central role in the novel, both thematically as well as structurally, so much so that critics have referred to the novel as "a collection of intricate and haunting memories" (Shen 234). For instance, already in the dedication of the novel does Tan evoke memory as the overriding theme. Tan writes: "To my mother and the memory of her mother" and then below "You asked me once what I would remember. This, and much more." The two inscriptions represent memory as a vehicle of matrilineage and at the same time open up the dialogue about the potential of memory as a parameter of cultural identity. Furthermore, the chapters of the novel that Jing-mei narrates also present three kinds of narratives: her memories of her mother, incidents that occurred when Jing-mei was a young girl, a young adult, and an adult woman in her early thirties, and her mother's memories, framed by her own narratives

[34] Marina Heung engages Tan's novel as example of an intact mother/daughter plot after. See also, Suzanna Danuta Walters' argument in *Lives Together / Worlds Apart* (180-84).

of her present life after her mother's death. Moreover, memory also configures the narrative structure of the novel. The absence of a chronological plot development foregrounds the episodic and flash-back like emergence of different memories of specific life situations. For instance, the first set of narratives, all headed under the title "Feathers from a Thousand *Li* Away," depicts the mother's lives as young girls in China; the second set, "The Twenty-Six Malignant Gates," depicts their lives as immigrant mothers of American-born daughters and their relationships with their daughters as young girls; the third set, "American Translation," narrates the relationship between the mothers as old women and their adult daughters; and the forth set, "Queen Mother of the Western Skies," depicts the mothers' lives in China as adult women and their immigrant experiences in the U.S. The narrative voices of these four sections are alternating: the mothers narrate the first and the last set of narratives and the daughters the middle ones. This general pattern is disrupted by the fact that Jing-mei tells a narrative in all of the four sections, including the first chapter of the first sect, and then the closing chapters of each of the other three sets of narratives. While the mothers and daughters interweave their present lives with memories of the past, Jing-mei's stories additionally contain episodes that depict her mother's memories. Therefore, in Jing-mei's role as a daughter and in her narrative agency lie the most complex aspects of memory in Tan's novel.

Through this interconnectedness of the mothers' and the daughters' stories, Tan's novel depicts the past as being interconnected with the present. In line with Ben Xu's assertion that "If the past casts a shadow on the present through memory, the present also re-imposes on the past by means of memory" (7), the thematic complexity of memory becomes evident in the novel in the fact that the daughter protagonist Jing-mei Woo has difficulty retaining and retelling the story that her mother used to tell her. The story in question is a story of loss as well as of survival: it is the story of her mother's flight from the invasion of the Japanese troops in China during World War II, a flight during which she is forced to abandon her young twin daughters along the roadside at the outskirts of Kweilin; but it is also the story of the Joy Luck Club's weekly meetings her mother hosts in China to celebrate with her neighbors the fact that they survived the hardships in their war-torn communities. While with the founding of the Joy Luck Club with the Chinese immigrants in San Francisco and their weekly meetings, Suyuan Woo adds a new chapter of survival to her life story, she is unable to reconnect with the daughters she had to give up in China, and thus her story of loss remains one of loss. It is this story of loss that her daughter Jing-mei symbolically inherits, and along with it the mission to complete her mother's quest to reunite with her half-sisters in China.

However, it becomes clear in the opening chapter of the novel that Jing-mei finds herself to be ill-equipped to fulfill this task. Never having taken her mother's stories seriously and never having anticipated the cultural importance her mother's stories hold ("I never thought my mother's Kweilin Story was anything but a Chinese fairy tale" [25]), Jing-mei cannot rely on her memory in order to fulfill her role as her mother's successor, symbolically as the fourth player at the Sunday night mah jong game her mother used to host, and figuratively as the person who should recover her mother's lost daughters. The reasons for Jing-mei's inability to tell the story of her cultural memory are testimony to her degree of alienation from Chinese culture and are the result of her life-long conflict with her mother. This, we learn throughout the novel, now comes to be a detrimental loss to Jing-mei, who, after her mother's death, finds herself unable to keep the memory of her mother alive and recognizes this as a missing link in her own identity quest.

Jing-mei Woo's difficulties assuming the responsibility of perpetuating the matrilineal heritage forcefully illustrate the complexity of memory. Since her mother's recent death, Jing-mei is confronted with the challenge of taking over her mother's place, figuratively as well as literally, at the monthly mah-jong game. There, her ineptitude to replace her mother becomes the epitome of a generation of culturally alienated daughters who are unable to handle their ancestral memories. Such inability leaves the Joy Luck mothers with the feeling of being emotionally and culturally duped: "Imagine, a daughter not knowing her own mother!" (40). The Joy Luck mothers are appalled by the fact that Jing-mei knows so little about her mother's hardships in China, her mother's children before she immigrated to the U.S., and her mother's dedication to the Chinese American community. They are terrified by the idea that Jing-mei's ignorance about her mother's live pushes the memory of Suyuan more and more into the past and into the forgotten. This fear of being forgotten, as becomes evident from the Joy Luck mothers' reactions, is prominent among the first-generation immigrant women of the Joy Luck Club: Jing-mei realizes:

> And then it occurs to me. They are frightened. In me, they see their own daughters, just as ignorant, just as unmindful of all the truths and hopes they have brought to America. They see daughters who grow impatient when their mothers talk in Chinese, who think they are stupid when they explain things in fractured English. They see that joy and luck do not mean the same to their daughters, that to these American–born minds 'joy luck' is not a word, it does not exist. They see daughters who will bear

> grandchildren born without any connecting hope
> passed from generation to generation. (40-41)

This passage epitomizes the immigrant mothers' desire for prolongation and recovery of their cultural heritage and their personal achievements after immigrating to the United States.[35]

Therefore, memory in *The Joy Luck Club* unfolds as an important vehicle for the second-generation immigrant daughter to explore her cultural heritage of her family's country of origin. Reiterating Marianne Hirsch's notion of "postmemory" (1997), Agnieszka Bedingfield argues that ethnic memory between different generations of members of immigrant families relies on three main components: transference, translation, and transcription. These three constituents of the diasporic memory, in Bedingfield's terminology, define the cultural memory of the diasporic condition as "trans-memory," characterizing first-hand memories that the second-generation immigrant authors handle through the process of transference, translation, and transcription. Such reliance on indirect memory refers to the concept which Marianne Hirsch describes as "the experience of those who grew up dominated by narratives that preceded their birth, whose own belated stories are evacuated by the stories of the previous generation shaped by traumatic events that can be neither understood nor recreated" (1997, 22). Bedingfield's appropriation of Hirsch's concept of postmemory as "second-generation memories of cultural or collective traumatic events and experiences" (ibid.) denotes aptly the Joy Luck daughters' complex task of dealing with their own experience.

I would like to expand Bedingfield's definition of trans-memory by addressing the transnational representation which becomes evident in the daughter's narrative agency. Any form of cultural appropriation from the perspective of diaspora and exile is often determined by a person's attempt to achieve a sense of self that recuperates partially the cultural origin into the diasporic location. Stuart Hall's definition of identity as production is helpful in this context (222). Hall argues that cultural identity "is not some universal and transcendental spirit inside us on which history has made no fundamental mark. It is not once-and-for-all. It is not a fixed origin to which we can make some

---

[35] Numerous critics have focused on the mothers' need for a preservation of their collective memory. See, for instance, Chandra Tyler Mountain, "'The Struggle of Memory Against Forgetting': Cultural Survival in Amy Tan's *The Joy Luck Club*," *Paintbrush* 22 (Autumn 1995): 39-50; Michael Delucchi, "Self and Identity Among Aging Immigrants in *The Joy Luck Club*," *Journal of Aging and Identity* 3.2 (1998): 59-66; and Claudia Kovach Smorada, "Side-Stepping Death: Ethnic Identity, Contradiction, and the Mother(land) in Amy Tan's Novels," *Fu-Jen Studies: Literature and Linguistics* 24 (1991): 31-45.

final and absolute Return [sic]. [...] The past continues to speak to us. But it no longer addresses us as simple, factual 'past,' since our relation to it, like the child's relations to the mother, is always-already 'after the break'" (226). In the portrayal of Jing-mei's attempt to relate to Chinese culture through the memory of her mother's life, Tan's novel provides an interesting case study for Hall's concept of a diasporic production of identity. If we take for granted Hall's assertion that the past continues to speak to Jing-mei, then we need to explore the different ways this interaction between present and past affects her ability to understand the origin of her Chinese ancestry. Transnational feminism lends viable tools for this discussion of memory and identity. Most forcefully, emphasizing the representation of the "Other" culture within Jing-mei's narratives in the tradition of transnational feminist theory, brings into sharper focus the ideological underpinnings that reverberate in Tan's depiction of a mother-daughter relationship that integrates memory as a component of their personal interaction and of their collective responsibility.

Tan's treatment of an unreliable memory, rooted in and overshadowed by a fierce mother-daughter conflict, raises issues about the preservation of cultural memory of the diasporic 'home' land. Both first- and second-generation immigrant women, as the examples of Jing-mei Woo and Lindo Jong suggest, ultimately have to return to China in order to be able to define their ethnic consciousness without relying on imposed stereotypes they have about Chinese culture and about American culture. Through this return to the origins of their cultural heritage, Tan implies a certain belatedness of memory as part of the diasporic experience of Asian Americans. What is most interesting about this intervention of a belated memory is that the second-generation American daughters experience a certain kind of displacement and alienation not only in relation to their mothers' pasts, but also in relation to the influence their mothers' lives in China continue to have on their lives in the U.S. In this context, memory becomes a contestant of cross-cultural communication as well as a vehicle of transnationality. The term belatedness, in this specific context, echoes the meaning of the term in Spivak's usage, namely as reference to the "time lag between sign and referent in colonialist cultural indoctrination" (Joseph 2002, 73), but does so in its reversed form. While Spivak's use of the term belatedness emphasizes the experience of subaltern subjects with American indoctrination (1999, 141-42), my use of the term belatedness implies the confrontation between memory of and lived experience in the 'homeland' from the second-generation immigrant daughter's transnational perspective.

Mothers and daughters in *The Joy Luck Club* experience this aspect of transnationality through memory quite differently, and the representations of their memories in Tan's novel invite an intertextual reading that structures thematically the individual chapters according to a specific subject. For instance, the vignette which precedes the first chapter of the novel initiates the reader into the issue of loss and recovery and the role that memory plays in this context.[36] The theme of loss and recovery then appears throughout the stories told by Jing-mei, both in relation to her mother's life and to her own. The swan that the old woman in the vignette loses and the single swan feather that she is able to keep upon immigrating to the U.S. signifies her transition from actual lived experience in a specific culture to the symbolic recovery of that experience through memory. The depreciation from "a swan too beautiful to eat" to "only one swan feather" (17), together with the implied trauma of her immigrant experience ("And then she had to fill out so any forms she forgot why she had come and what she had left behind") characterizes this transition from lived to related experience though memory and emphasizes the implied shifts and alterations. While it is the old woman, possibly an iconic figure for the entire generation of the Joy Luck mothers, who experiences this transformation from lived experience to remembered experience in the vignette, in the first and the last chapter of the novel it is "her" daughter who is supposed to come to terms with this shift. And as already announced in the vignette, the difficulty of getting the daughter to understand the significance of the swan feather, hence of the mother's memory, and to give the mother the power to tell her daughter "in perfect American English" (17) about the significance of the swan feather, constitutes a major problem in the transmittance of the mother's memory. The novel's narrative structure shifts in the sense that Jing-mei's narrative voice from narrating her memories to narrating her mother's memories. This shift amplifies the geographic binary opposition between China and the U.S., and the temporal binary opposition between the distant past and the recent past or even the present. The first and the last chapter of the novel elaborate on this theme of loss and recovery. For instance, Jing-mei's inability to recover her mother's stories through memory is rooted in her lack of understanding of the circumstances depicted in her mother's stories. In other words, Jing-mei's inability to do justice to her mother's life story stems from the fact that her mother always remains a cultural "Other" to her. Thus, the shift in the narrative situation form a homodiegetic to a heterodiegetic narrator mirrors the shift on the level of physical location.

---

[36] For instance, Wendy Ho even uses the subject matter of the first vignette, the "swan-feather mothers and coca-coal daughters" as entry point into her discussion of Tan's novel (1996, 327-45).

In the context of Jing-mei's act of remembering her mother's stories, this trans-memory is not only set in a different narrative diegesis but also in a different geographical, geopolitical and cultural space which contributes to the discursive "othering" of the mother's memories. If memory is a symbolic recovery of the past into the present, the diachronicity of memory also employs temporal difference as a marker on an "Other" time. The novel operates with two different mechanisms of enforcing this othering of the mother's memories: one is through Jing-mei's difficulty remembering her mother's life stories precisely because they are so foreign to her, and the other one is through her trip to China, during which her trans-memories are being renegotiated. The discursive juxtaposition of her trans-memory with her experience renders her relationship to her collective past a belated memory. Because she cannot rely on her memory of her mother's stories, despite the fact the she is supposed to be the missing link between her mother and her mother's past life in China, Jing-mei travels to China to meet with her half sisters. This meeting can be seen as her personal encounter with the subjects of her mother's stories, and thus, by extension, with the embodiment of her mother's memories of China. Therefore, to meet the subjects of the story, a story that she mistook until recently for a "Chinese fairy tale" (25), echoes the reversal of the shift from experience to memory that the old woman in the vignette confronts. These two circumstances, Jing-mei's encounter with the subjects of her mother's past life through storytelling and through first-hand experience, as I illustrate throughout the remaining part of this chapter, determine the complexity of memory in the transnational context of the relationship between mothers and daughters in *The Joy Luck Club*. Thus, on behalf of a generation of Americanized daughters, Jing-mei asserts: "I can never remember things I didn't understand in the first place" (19). This statement contains the dilemma of the entire generation of Joy Luck daughters, who realize that in order to be able to embrace their cultural heritage they need to be able to understand their mothers' life stories even if they are set in a time and place that is foreign to them.

Recovering the Past through Memory

The first way in which Jing-mei learns about her Chinese heritage is through her mother's storytelling. Despite the fact that Jing-mei assumes the narrative agency of her mother's life after Suyuan Woo's death, and thus seems to be able to lend her own narrative agency to the accounting for her collective, matrilineal voice, she also appears to be aware of her position of an outsider when doing so. This insider/outsider duality of her cultural agency can appear confusing and misleading on the level of narrative structure, since it is never quite clear whether she is indeed a reliable narrator of her mother's life or whether she fills the gaps in her cultural understanding with acquired and internalized stereotypes about Chinese culture. This is important in the following analysis of Jing-mei's explicitly distanced depiction of her mother and of Chinese American culture. Jing-mei's narratives follow a clear pattern: the first person narrative perspective shifts from Jing-mei to Suyuan, from mother to daughter. This shift in the narrative perspective raises the question as to how reliable a narrator of her mother's stories she can be. The question arises because at different instances in the novel, Tan depicts Jing-mei as unable to understand and relate to the cultural customs her mother continually practices within the Chinese American community, such as her mistaking of the monthly gatherings of secret meetings of an illegal group (28). Because these implied mis-interpretations precede the supposedly true story about Suyuan Woo's life in China, her role as a reliable narrator is questionable. For instance, immediately before Jing-mei re-narrates the event of her mother's having to leave behind her twin daughters when fleeing from the Japanese troops, she calls attention to the fact that she is confused about the stories of her mother's life and never knows what is true and what is just "a Chinese fairy tale" (25). This is different from Kingston's use of a mother-daughter aesthetic in *The Woman Warrior* because the reader always knows who is speaking in which chapter of *The Joy Luck Club*. In fact, the individual chapters of the novel bear the names of their narrators. Hence, with the exception of the chapters in which Jing-mei tells her mother's stories, their narratives are always characterized by an auto-diegenic narrative situation, one in which the main protagonist is also the narrator. And even in the chapters where Jing-mei tells her mother's stories, the narrative situation is made explicit through the framing of Suyuan's narrative by her daughter's introduction, in which she gives the context of her own storytelling as well as of the context in which her mother used to tell her these stories.

Exceeding the narratives of the "generational conflict" (Lowe 1991, 26), the individual stories of *The Joy Luck Club* capture the complexity of cultural memory in a transnational context. The retention of cultural memory and the related ethnic and gender consciousness is different for the two generations of Chinese American women in the novel. The mothers ("aunties") of the Joy Luck Club feel an immediate sense of loss of their Chinese homeland and experience this special transition and cultural transference most directly. Told from their post-immigration perspectives, the mothers' narratives in Tan's novel convey the sense of ambiguity toward the Chinese homeland. On the one hand, the narratives depict candidly the hardships and struggles young women deal with in misogynist, patriarchal Chinese culture and within the Confucian family traditions. On the other hand the narratives describe how the mothers made use of their sharp insight of and familiarity with the dynamics of traditional Chinese culture in order to subvert the impositions and restrictions on their own lives and to free themselves from oppression. Lindo Wong's story "Red Candle" is good example of the double message the mothers' narratives send. Instead of succumbing to the misogynist rules that determined her acceptance of an arranged marriage, Lindo makes use of the Confucian family model[37] and gets out of the marriage by claiming that the family's ancestors appeared to her in a dream and announced to her that one of the family's servant girls is their son's "true spiritual wife" (65). And by convincing the inlaws that the ancestors had discovered that the girl was "of imperial blood" (65) and had impregnated her with the longed-for male family heir, Lindo not only saves her own life but also the life of the servant, whose secret pregnancy with the delivery man's child she turns from a potential disgrace to a prophecy (65).

In addition to this ambiguous relationship to traditional Chinese culture, the mothers have very contradictory opinions about life in the U.S. On the one hand, the mothers find very compelling the exceptionalist notion that "[y]ou could become anything you wanted to be in America" (132) while on the other hand, they criticize American culture for its lack of values. The very same is true for the way they raise their daughters. Thomas J. Ferraro argues in *Ethnic Passages: Literary Immigrants in Twentieth Century America* (1993) that despite that fact that the search for a better life is often the family's main motivation to immigrate to the U.S. in the first place, immigrant parents also want their children to honor their home-culture. While they do wish their daughters to become prodigy children and to take advantage of the seemingly endless possibilities American culture has to offer, the Joy Luck aunties also criticize their daughters for being too American and not Chinese enough. In many instances, the mothers become aware of the fact that it is difficult to have the best of both worlds: Lindo Jong articulates this wish: "I wanted my children to have the best combination: American circumstances and Chinese character. How could I know these two things don't mix? (254).

[37] In *Between Worlds*, Amy Ling lists the Three Obediences and Four Virtues Confucius attributed to Chinese Women: "The Three Obediences enjoined a woman to obey her father before marriage, her husband after marriage, and her eldest son after her husband's death. The Four Virtues decreed that she be chaste; her conversation courteous and not gossipy; her deportment graceful but not extravagant; her leisure spent in perfecting needlework and tapestry for beautifying the home" (3).

The function of the mothers' narratives seems to be to define the ongoing identity negotiation between their origins in China and their new beginnings in the U.S. The arrangement of the individual narratives, two sets of four stories that symbolically embrace the daughter narratives, define the mothers' stories as a backdrop of the daughters' identity negotiations and as a frame in which the daughters' searches for selfhood take place. I would even suggest that the mothers' lives, because they are communicated through the stories they tell, constitute the reason for the daughters' identity negotiations. By having to learn how to confront and best interpret their mothers' stories, the daughters experience the ways in which memory influences their ongoing identity negotiations. In addition, the mothers' narratives express strong criticism of the one-dimensional representation of Chinese Americans in American popular culture. They are particularly appalled when their own daughters use them to single out the flaws of their cultural heritage. When Waverly Jong inquires details about the alleged cruelty of Chinese customs, her mother Lindo replies: "Chinese people have many things. [...] Chinese people do business, do medicine, do painting. Not lazy like American people. We do torture. Best torture" (91). By using playfully and subversively stereotypical images of Chinese culture, Lindo applies what Sau-ling Wong has described as "counter-Orientalist" agency in order to decolonize concepts of Chineseness in the U.S. (Palumbo-Liu 190-91). For instance, Lindo asserts that supposedly traditional Chinese proverbs in fortune cookies are invented "nonsense" attempts at correcting misconceptions about Chinese culture in the U.S. (Kim 1982, 23-32). Thus, when the daughters define their mothers by means of orientalist stereotypes of Chinese culture, as Jing-mei Woo does by claiming that Chinese mothers communicate their love "not through hugs and kisses but with stern offerings of steamed dumplings, duck's gizzard, and crab" (202), the readers need to be aware of the problems that such orientalist depictions entail and need to challenge the daughters' biased representations of their immigrant Chinese American women.

The question that remains, however, is the question to what extent Tan solicits or averts such responses? For instance, the fact that the mothers' stories are set, to a large degree, in the past and the daughter's in the present also amplifies the cultural chasm between mothers and daughters. One can argue that this dichotomization on the level of the narratives' temporalities epitomize the complex dynamics of the mother-daughter relationships of the novel. Moreover, as unreliable as the depictions of Chinese culture may be on account of Jing-mei's narrative ambivalence, the intervention of the joy luck mothers' stories does provide details about Chinese culture and customs that Jing-mei might not be able to present. Tan's use of details and other references to Chinese culture, however, has often been target of criticism. In "Sugar Sisterhood," Wong points out numerous misuses and mistranslations of Chinese words and the faulty characterization of typically Chinese customs (Palumbo-Liu 1995, 180-85). In her essay "Autobiography as Guided Chinatown Tour?: Maxine Hong Kingston's *The Woman Warrior* and the Chinese-American Autobiographical Controversy," Wong calls attention to Kingston's quasi-authentic depiction of the Stockton Chinatown. By the same token, Tan's depictions of Chinese traditions, especially when articulated through the perspectives of the "aunties," also run the risk of exoticizing Chinese American culture. Wong speaks of an "Othering accomplished by temporal distancing" (Palumbo-Liu 1995, 186), one that enforces the binary opposition between the U.S. (present) and China (distant past). This temporal difference between the individual sets of stories, Wong concludes, discursively pits mothers and daughters, as well as the cultures they "represent," against each other in ways that replicate the dynamics of the mother-daughter conflict itself.

Experience and Ideology in the Motherland

The second, and more immediate, way for Jing-mei to experience the culture of her mother's homeland is during her trip to China. Her trip to China is an important moment in the novel, both in terms of content and in terms of narrative structure. For instance, during this trip, the binary opposition between the U.S. of the present and the China of the past is being reconfigured, and, as I will point out below, reinforced. While many critics have discussed the narrative strategies of the beginning of Tan's novel, I see in the closing chapter a crucial aspect that helps us understand *The Joy Luck Club* in terms of its discursive construction of the mother-daughter relationship in Asian American literature and that helps locate Tan's novel within Asian American critique at large. Catherine Romagnolo argues that the narrative beginnings in *The Joy Luck Club* are of "ideological significance" because of their resistance to discourses of "authentic origins" in the question of the protagonists' identities (90). Romagnolo proposes that reading critically these ideological dimensions of the narrative beginnings brings into focus "a critique of the very concept of origins – especially in its relation to 'American,' 'Chinese,' and 'Chinese American' identity" precisely because such a critique "illuminates the discursive constructedness of authenticity, origins, and identity, thereby problematizing reductive cultural representations of female, American, and Asian American subjectivity" (90). While critics like Romagnolo pay close attention to the expository quality of the first few pages of Tan's novel, I would like to argue that the same "ideological significance" that holds for the narrative beginnings also applies to the narrative ending of the novel. Because Tan's narrative style in *The Joy Luck Club* is circular, and because the individual chapters dialogue with one another on an intertextual level (Souris), the closing chapter reiterates Tan's strategies of narrativization of Chinese American cultural memory. In this last chapter, Tan's treatment of authenticity and origin is, contrary to Romagnolo's observation about the narrative beginning, not so subversive but operates with a highly essentialist approach. This completion of the narrative plot and of the thematic diversity of the novel's various accounts of Chinese American culture climaxes with Jing-mei's trip to China.

Jing-mei's trip to China constitutes the climax of her identity quest and ideological appropriation of China. During this trip, her very first trip to China, she is supposed to meet the twin daughters from her mother's first marriage. It has been Suyuan's wish throughout her life to find the abandoned babies and bring them into the family, just as much as it has been her wish that Jing-mei would understand and cultivate her Chinese heritage. Both events occur during this trip, which lends the novel a rather unforeseeable happy ending: Jing-mei not only finds her mother's "daughters in China" (39), she also finds her Chinese identity. Interestingly, Tan does not challenge this sudden metamorphosis from an American to a Chinese woman. Quite on the contrary, the novel reiterates the same essentialist argumentation that ethnicity and culture are biological predispositions, an argumentation it offers in the first chapter. Whereas at the beginning of the novel, the joy luck aunties try to convince Jing-mei that "[her] mother is in [her] bones" (40), at the end of the novel Jing-mei concurs with her mother's argument that her Chineseness "is in [her] blood, waiting to be let go" (267) and experiences this transformation as soon as she enters China: "I feel the skin on my forehead tingling, my blood rushing through a new course, my bones aching with a familiar old pain. And I think, my mother was right. I am becoming Chinese" (267). Commenting on how her make-up melts away in the hot, humid climate, Jing-mei describes this dissolving of her American identity and the surfacing of her genetic "racial" traits– hence the reference to how more naturally Chinese her eyes and hair look (272), two of the most pronounced facial features that distinguish Asians from Caucasians. Underlying this metamorphosis seems to be a variation of the Melting Pot hypothesis which locates the manifestations of a person's ethnicity as immediate response to his/her physical immersion into a foreign country. By the same token, Tan seems to imply that culture and ethnicity are pre-encoded, rather than "learned," features of a person's identity. Jing-mei's automatic transformation from American to Chinese stands in strong opposition to the previous parts of the novel, where she is unable to understand Chinese culture. For instance, while she repeatedly points out how limited her passive knowledge of Mandarin is, she now asks her father, who accompanies her on this trip, to tell her about her mother "in Chinese" (281).

Tan's depiction of Jing-mei's transformation appears to be a *deus-ex-machina* solution to the complicated process of ethnic identification which many second-generation immigrants face, but one that seems nevertheless tailored after a specific discourse of ethnic American identity: one that defines Chinese American identity as being Chinese *and* being American. The implication that Jing-mei turns Chinese just because she went to China is as troublesome as the related notion that only by going to China will she ever come to terms with her Chinese American identity. This emphasis of a possible "return" to China also alludes to the reading of the term Chinese American as Chinese people who live in America without taking the dynamics of diaspora and transnationalism into consideration. This is especially interesting because in contrast to Jing-mei's mysterious metamorphosis, Lindo Jong describes her return to China in quite opposite terms. Visiting China after almost forty years, Lindo realizes that she was no longer "one hundred percent Chinese" and that no matter how hard she tried, people immediately recognized her as a foreigner and "charged [her] high foreign prices" (266). Lindo Jong's emphasis on her loss of authenticity articulates well immigrants' acculturation to the U.S. and the resulting cultural distance from their homeland.

I would like to return once more to Jing-mei's feeling that she is "becoming Chinese." It is important to note that she utters this statement at the very beginning of the novel's last chapter, and that by so doing, she sets the tone for her identity negotiations in China. For instance, we get the sense, as the final chapter unravels, that Jing-mei is being transformed from a cultural outsider to a cultural insider. For instance, Jing-mei is clearly being characterized as an outsider to the reunion between her father and his relatives. A mere bystander who is, at times, unable to follow their conversations, she observes the meeting of her Chinese American father with his Chinese relatives but never really participates in it. Similarly, Jing-mei's bafflement "This is communist China?" (276), when she sees for the first time their hotel, "a grander version of the Hyatt Regency" (276), echoes her expectations of the much less modern, or should I say less westernized, China. Tan goes to great lengths presenting the details of the "magnificent" hotel, thereby giving expression to Jing-mei's surprise at the possibility of such luxury in China and at the comparatively inexpensive rate at which such luxury can be obtained. A particularly striking moment in the last chapter is when she takes inventory of the American products in her room, naming each and every one of the many items in the mini-bar, only to reaffirm her initial disbelieve, "This is communist China?" (277), at the availability of American consumer goods. As much as she questions the concept of communist China, she is unable to discern that the consumer goods provided in upper class hotels cater to the tastes and needs of tourists like herself and can hardly be taken as signs of Chinese cultural development but as tokens of cultural commodification purported via mass tourism.

On the discursive level, Jing-mei's rehearsal of American consumer products and her incredulous comment about the luxury of communist China in the last chapter also foreshadow possible means of identification between her and an American reading audience. As Sau-ling Wong points out, the fact that Jing-mei names the individual items by their brand names and that she does not use any brand names for the Chinese products she sees (Palumbo-Liu 1995, 186-87) also connotes a degree of cultural othering. The Chinese products, such as the shower gel she uses, do not have names but are characterized through their similarities and comparisons to products she knows to be Chinese, as the fact that the shampoo remindes her in "consistency and color of hoisin sauce" (278) shows. Finding her preconceived notions of Chinese culture affirmed, Jing-mei feels finally reassured in her ideas about what her experience in China should be like: "This is more like it, I think. This is China" (278). What becomes evident from this chapter is that Tan not only characterizes China as a place that remains locked in another time because it is locked in the stories of a former time, she also defines China to be backwards in relation to a contemporary setting. In Jing-mei's assessments of modern Chinese culture, memory seems to become unnecessary in the last chapter since Jing-mei now gets to experience what she has, up until then, only heard of through the memories and storytelling of the older generation.

In this light, her alleged "becoming Chinese" implies that after her transformation from American to Chinese, she is able to assume to role of a cultural insider, one who exudes authority in her assessment of Chinese culture and life style. This authority gives weight to her assertion that China remains a temporal "Other" in relation to the U.S. Now an insider, she can be trusted, and her judgment makes sense to an American reading audience who might share a similar sense of displacement when matching the imaginary notions of Chinese culture with their experiences of China through mass tourism. While memory can be contested, Jing-mei's first-hand experience cannot. In this context, Jing-mei experiences in China the same backwardness that she attributes to the China of her mother's stories. Jing-mei goes to seek proof of her preconceived notions of China. And in the fact that she did find them, she sees herself justified in her distancing from Chinese culture as well as in her conflictuous relationship with her mother. It is this experience, the one that validates in a belated context the stereotypical images of China that she has come to internalize on the basis of her mothers' stories, which the term "belated memory" implies.

In the previous section of this chapter, I have pointed out Tan's depiction of the daughters' orientalist and the mothers' counter-orientalist practices of self-identification. This observation leads me to my main focus for this project, namely the question about female solidarity. On the level of thematic representation, the mothers' experiences are largely interchangeable and contribute to the creation of a stereotypical image of Chinese women. The narratives of their lives in China are all set in the same era, capturing the mother's lives as daughters negotiating their own relationships to their mothers and as mothers negotiating their relationships to their daughters. At the same time, the sets of narratives about the mothers' lives in China also symbolically introduce the reader to the Chinese culture configured through the lives of the mothers as young Chinese women. On the discursive level of the mothers' narratives, the uniformity of settings in the past and in traditional Chinese culture characterize China as homogeneous country for which the mothers appear as "authentic" spokeswomen. The issue of authenticity in the mothers' narratives is especially interesting, since the mothers' narratives are full of generalizations about China. For instance, An-mei Hsu's account of China exemplifies this approach: "That was China. That was what people did back then. They had no choice. They could not speak up. They could not run away. That was their fate" (241).

There are also problems of representation of Chinese women in the novel that become apparent from a juxtaposition of the mothers' and the daughters' narratives. What is problematic is that by setting the mother's stories in the past and the daughter's stories in the contemporary, Tan creates distance and reinforces the difference between the two generations of women. By juxtaposing China of the past with America of the present, the novel decontextualizes the mothers' experiences from the experiences of a non-Chinese American readership not only on the level of culture but also on the level of temporality. For instance, the fact that Jing-mei's narratives about her present life are told in the present tense and her memories of her mother in the past is, although entirely plausible, is still a stylistic gesture that amplifies this difference in temporalities. This emphasis on a Chinese culture that is confined to the past makes plausible why the daughters have such a hard time identifying with their mothers. This notion of an "old China" reinforces the stereotype of immigrant Chinese women as backward and unprogressive and defines Chinese culture as old-fashioned. By choosing pre-communist China as narrative setting for the life stories of the maternal generation, the novel leaves out almost entirely comparative accounts of contemporary China. With the exception of the Hsu family, whose recent trip to China, a trip which left them nine thousand dollars in debt after they paid off the gifts and treats for the relatives they went to visit, none of the stories depict any "modern Chinese subject" (Rey Chow 1991) other than the needy and greedy relatives. On the contrary, many of the mothers comment in their stories on the backwardness of traditional Chinese culture. Lindo Jong's reference to arranged marriage makes that apparent: "That was how backward families in the country were. We were always the last to give up stupid old-fashioned customs" (51). Unlike the daughters' negative stereotypical comments on China, the mothers' overgeneralizations do not stand challenged or corrected. Given narrative authority through correcting the daughters' misrepresentations and their lived experiences, the mothers seem to be representing authentic China. Not only does this portrayal of the mothers as authentic voices fail to acknowledge the intervention of their Americanized narrative perspectives, it also echoes the commonplace critique in transnational feminism that receiving texts by ethic writers as "'windows' into the presumed alterity of other cultures" (Amireh and Majaj 2) reinforces and often over-exaggerates cultural difference. This emphasis on difference singles out the mothers as cultural aliens and, in the specific context of the mother-daughter dyad, supports the daughters' cultural and emotional disassociation from their mothers.

Recognizing the danger of such generalizations, Rey Chow offers two useful concepts for a critical evaluation of Western mass media's depiction of "the other country" (1991, 83). This is important given that, as Patricia P. Chu reminds us, *The Joy Luck Club* first appeared on the American book market the same year the massacre at Tienanmen Square made the global news (Chu 2000, 167). Although these circumstances are coincidental, Chow's critique of Western representation of China addresses well the existing political and cultural interest in East Asia and frames the release of Tan's literary debut with prevalent images on China in mainstream American culture. In her critique of American coverage of the "China crisis," for example, Chow refers to a sensationalist interest of the West that manifests itself in what she calls "China watching." Symptomatic of China watching, Chow specifies, are detailed depictions in which U.S. mass media depicts the Chinese government as controlling and ruthless and portrays the protesters without respecting their right to anonymity (1991, 83). The other concept, the "*King Kong* syndrome," which Chow defines as intricately connected to the sensationalism that is at the center of China watching (1991, 84), echoes Gayatri Chakravorty Spivak's contention that the "third world" is often depicted as the site of "raw" materials that invoke "monstrosity" which appears in contrast to the First World both as entertainment and as evidence for the persisting Western notion of cultural elevation (1987, 90). These two syndromes of orientalist gazing at China/the third world are ubiquitous in representations conveyed through American mass media. Chow asserts: "Locked behind the bars of our television screens, we become repelled by what is happening 'over there,' in a way that confirms the customary view, in the U.S. at least, that ideology exists only in the 'other' (anti-U.S.) country" (1991, 84). In a different essay, Chow defines the "fascination with the native, the oppressed, the savage, and all such figures" as "a desire to hold onto an unchanging certainty [...] a desire for being 'non-duped,' which is a not-too-innocent desire to seize control" (1996, 141). The fascination with violent and/or sensational spectacles 'over there' therefore assures the West that, guarded by democracy and political and social freedom, 'over here' everybody is safe and everything is in order.

Hence, Tan's depiction of a China of the remote past, argues Patricia Chu, fails to acknowledge the "vision of early-twentieth-century China as a country in which modern and traditional elements coexist, a country that, like the United States, is constantly changing" (156). This creates the impression that, in contrast to the modern US, Chinese culture is frozen in the past and explains why the daughters are so resentful in their identification with their matrilineal heritage. Given that they were brought up by their mothers to embrace the possibilities the American Promised Land symbolizes and given that they have internalized the freedom of post-women's rights movement U.S., how could the daughters relate to misogynist ideas of womanhood in the China of the early twentieth century? What is striking in the context of this discursive distance is that Tan's novel does not expose the bias with which the daughters view their mothers' Chinese pasts. As becomes evident from the yuppie lifestyles of career woman Waverly Jong or the comfortable financial situation of suburban housewife Rose Hsu Jordan, the daughter's upper-middle class status hardly reflects the hardships and struggles which their mothers experienced upon arriving in the U.S. or their previous economic and social dependency on the patriarchal family system in China.

It is in this context that I argue that Jing-mei's trip to China serves the function in the novel of recovering her mother's past instead of discovering a modern image of Chinese femininity. Although she does meet modern Chinese women, such as her twin half-sisters, there is no suggestion in the novel that these women imply to Jing-mei an encounter with modern Chinese femininity. On the contrary, if anything, her twin half-sisters embody the old China that she so clearly sought out to look for. As Jing-mei muses, they are the missing link between her and her mother: "Together we look like our mother. Her same eyes, her same mouth, open in surprise to see, at last, her long-cherished wish" (288). And through this encounter with her half-sisters, who serve as direct transplants from the old China that her mother's stories depict, Jing-mei starts to resume her confrontation with her Chinese roots: "And now I know what part of me is Chinese. It is so obvious. It is my family. It is in our blood. After all these years, it can finally be let go" (288). Thus, the meeting with her half-sisters is the epitome of her recovery of her mother's memory of China.

This section of the last chapter re-evokes the same theme as the vignette and the first chapter. Through this encounter with the sisters, the story of the loss and recovery for the "old woman" symbolically reaches full circle. The sisters are the lost swan that the mother remembers through a single feather, and Jing-mei is both agent and object of recovery at the same time. In this light, just like the swan is an embodiment of Chinese culture locked in the mother's memory, one that the mother is waiting to communicate to her daughter, the daughters are embodiments of Chinese culture waiting to be recognized as part of Jing-mei's life. There is a mirroring of the development from loss to recovery, one in which Jing-mei reverses time. This reversal of time, and her trip to China figures at times like a time travel, connects thematically the narrative beginning and ending of the novel. This interrelatedness between the first vignette "Feathers from A Thousand *Li* Away," the first chapter "The Joy Luck Club," and the last chapter "A Pair of Tickets" through the intertextual discussion of the role of memory as vehicle of ethnic identity, re-evokes and appropriates uncritically, questions of authenticity and origin.

Because of Jing-mei's belated memory, triggered by her experiences of and in China, the meeting with her half-sisters is a forceful example of the novel's mostly skewed treatment of female solidarity, one that, although it highlights the difficulties of transnational solidarity, only partly suggests that such solidarity between American and Chinese women can be achieved. In the same manner as the American-born daughters cannot recognize their mothers as "peers in struggle" against racism and sexism, the actual reunion between the American and the Chinese daughters relies on a foregrounding of national identity over individual identity. While Tan's novel does suggest that the conflict between mothers and daughters can be overcome, such as when mothers empathize with their daughters' desire for a content life, or through the inter-textual dialogue between the two generations that the chapters facilitate, it does not address the transnational sensibility needed in order to achieve such a union. In this sense, the tear-filled reunion of the half-sisters projects a premature notion of global sorority. In line with Shirley Geok-lin Lim's observation that global feminism often tends to be confused with "an international feminism coming out of the West" (2004, 8), the specific location from which Jing-mei meets her half-sisters does not articulate the obvious cultural differences and global inequalities which emerges from a world order that is based on global binary oppositions. Unlike global feminism, which was characterized by "its tendency to essentialize, homogenize, and centralize Western social and cultural concepts of women" (Lim 2004, 8), transnational feminism offers a more dynamic set of parameters, language and frameworks for a contemporary discussion of experiences of migration across times and places. What interferes with a transnational alliance of Jing-mei with her half-sisters is their representation in the novel not as individuals, but as stand-ins for the China Jing-mei knows from her mother's stories. The ideological appropriation of the half-sisters discursively privileges Jing-mei, the narrative voice of the chapter, and thus enforces a sense of power and privilege of the American daughter over the Chinese daughter, one that reiterates the power struggle she had with her mother. Under these circumstances, the meeting of the sisters, which is supposed to suggest a sense of unity and healing for Jing-mei, can only be in part accomplished. The under-representation of a modern China, however, makes a transnational solidarity between mothers and daughters almost unimaginable.

CHAPTER FOUR

Coming Home, Coming Out: Mapping Gender, Ethnicity, and Sexuality in Mei Ng's *Eating Chinese Food Naked*

In contemporary feminist theory and practice, the concept of 'home' is a textual trope of multiple meanings: home as the opposite of the public and political sphere, as highly targeted by Marxist feminism; home as catalyst of difference between white and women of color feminism, as manifestation of minority cultures within the U.S.; and home as a geo-political room within society, as a microcosm of culture.[38] For many Asian Americas writers, the concept of a homeplace also encompasses issues of diaspora, immigration, and socialization into American society. Most importantly, the homeplace is an expression of a person's sense of belonging, whether this sense of belonging is self-defined by the individual or super-imposed by the various communities with which the individual interacts. For instance, when Asian Americans are asked "Where are you from?," the underlying implication is often that they do not look American. The question about the homeplace thus often conjures up racialist and racist assumptions about foreignness and operates with an originary moment of entrance into the homogenously defined American society which equates cultural identity and national identity. The question about the home country applies most frequently to first-generation immigrants as they confront the casual question "But where are you *really* from?" (Singh and Schmidt 2000, 7 original emphasis), a question that is implicit both of the homogenous definition of American society and of the racist mindset of the person who asks the question and who relies on stereotypical modalities of what *real* American might look like.

In Mei Ng's novel *Eating Chinese Food Naked* (1998), the young Chinese American daughter protagonist Ruby Lee experiences this tension between

---

[38] In *Yearning: Race, Gender, and Cultural Politics* (1990), bell hooks, for instance, argues that African American women create through their construction of a secure "homeplace" a "site of resistance" for cultural emancipation of their community. At the same time, transnational feminists use the trope of "homeplace" as location for diasporic cultures and their writers who do not fit into the paradigms of white mainstream feminism.

being at home and not being at home on several levels. During a temporary stay at her parents' house in Queens, she becomes aware of the complex interconnectedness of ethnicity, gender, and sexuality in her life as she confronts her unresolved conflict with her parents, her unequivocal ethnic consciousness, her ambiguous gender consciousness, and her homoerotic attraction to other women including her own mother. I use the term *mapping* in the chapter title to evoke the spatial framing of the ongoing process of Ruby's identitiy negotiation. In specific relation to Ruby's sexual awakening, the term *mapping* refers to the debated location of her sexual orientation within or outside normative boundaries and denotes the juxtaposition of coming home to her collective identity as opposed to coming out as an individual with her own personal definitions of ethnicity, gender, and sexuality.

In its depiction of a young Chinese American woman's quest for a homeplace, Ng's novel follows the general trend in Asian American literature to depict protagonists' quests for a stable and secure location within U.S. society, a home, that is, that offers a sense of agency. Most particularly, Ruby's temporary homecoming in which she crosses the lines between the multiple locations of her Chinese American identity, her heterosexual and homosexual desires, and her identification with and independence from her own mother are strongly reminiscent of her internalized ambivalence about persisting ideals of womanhood in both Chinese American and mainstream American societies. Emphasizing Ruby's discomfort with the idea of adopting a home in either of these cultures, Ng's novel defines the homeplace as an incarcerating burden to Ruby's individuality and autonomy. Although Ruby plans to stay with her parents only temporarily, her arrival at their house has a sense of desperate definiteness to it: "Ruby was fighting mad to be home again (she felt coerced, as if someone or something had twisted her arm behind her back)" (15).

This chapter analyzes the mutual interconnectedness of gender, ethnicity, and sexuality in *Eating Chinese Food Naked* by looking specifically at the novel's bi-fold treatment of the commonplace notion of "home": on the one hand, Ng's depiction of the cultural tensions between first- and second-generation Chinese immigrants raises issues about the construction of a cultural home for Asian Americans in the U.S.; on the other hand, by emphasizing sexual identity as incoherent with and often contradictory to existing classifications of ethnic identity, Ng's novel extends the metaphorical concepts of home to a juxtaposition between imposed sexual normativity and sexual coming-out. By setting Ruby's ongoing identity mapping in a deeply-rooted mother-daughter conflict, Ng makes Ruby's negotiation of a homeplace even more difficult.

I have structured the larger part of this chapter along the two different concepts of home that the metaphors of "coming home" and "coming out" imply. In order to be able to emphasize the ways in which the mother-daughter conflict further complicates Ruby's identitiy negotiation, I have organized individual discussions of ethnicity, gender, and sexuality with the risk of suggesting a clear-cut fragmentation between gender and ethnicity on the one hand and sexuality on the other. I do not mean to over-emphasize the novel's treatment of sexuality with respect to Ruby's *triple* marginality as it were. On the contrary, my separate discussions of the two different notions of "home" seeks to uncover the complexity and confusion which the protagonist's attempt to find a home within these divergent definitions of self entails. Furthermore, my discussion of Ng's use of food as performative act of gender and ethnicity as well as of sexuality seeks to analyze the novel's conflation of generically different, but finally not so dissimilar, metaphors that describe the processes of "coming home" and "coming out."

Homeplace in Feminist Theory

In their seminal essay "What's Home Got to Do With It?," Biddy Martin and Chandra Talpade Mohanty extend the metaphorical meaning of homeplaces from "concrete, physical anchoring points" (90) to specific and self-specified locations of feminist theory and practice, both in the context of American and global societies. Mohanty and Martin take their cues from Minnie Bruce Pratt's autobiographical narrative "Identity: Blood Skin Heart" (1984), a forceful example to their observation of how geographical and geo-political spaces within a city or community reflect and are interdependent with a woman's identity politics. Mohanty and Martin stress that the text's "movement away from the purely personal, visceral experience of identity suggested in the title [of her essay] to a complicated working out of the relationship between home, identity, and community calls into question the notion of a coherent, historically continuous, stable identity and works to expose the political stakes concealed in such equations" (89). Mohanty and Martin's intervention that the personal is not only in interaction with the political, but also with the geo/demographical, also reverberates in their definition of a feminist identity that emerges out of the tension between two interlocking concepts: "being home and not being home. 'Being home' refers to the place where one lives within familiar, safe, protected boundaries; 'not being home' is a matter of realizing that home was an illusion of coherence and safety based on the exclusion of specific histories of oppression and resistance, the repression of differences even within oneself" (2003, 90).

The importance of a homeplace, both the cultural link to the "place of origin" and the sense of belonging to the U.S., is a central aspect in Asian American literature. The variety of issues related to topical appropriations of the concept of cultural and national home are intricately connected to the social experience of "Otherness" many Asian Americans confront, ranging from the diverse immigration exclusion acts pronounced by the U.S. government, the interment of Japanese Americans resulting in conflicts over property repatriation and South-East Asian diaspora and immigration to the U.S. on the one hand to the experience of imperialism in nation-states such as the Philippines and military interventions in Korea and Vietnam, and neo-colonial global capitalism in Malaysia, Cambodia, and Taiwan on the other hand.[39] In the face of these various genealogies of struggle and histories of oppression in the U.S., the depiction of the homeplace as anchoring point within American society continues to resonate richly in Asian American literature. One need only think of the immense value the female characters in Kim Ronyoung's *Clay Walls* (1987) and Gish Jen's *Typical American* (1992) put in the establishing of a home and their struggles to find a place of residence that enables them to do so.

For second-generation immigrant children of Asian American parents, the maintenance of a sense of home and a sentiment of belonging to their parents' countries of origin is even more complex than the negotiation of a homeplace that the first-generation attempts. As Peggy Levitt and Mary C. Waters assert in the introduction to their collection of essays, *The Changing Face of Home: The Transnational Lives of the Second Generation* (2002), when analyzing the experience of the American-born generation of immigrant parents, important questions need to be kept in mind: "What role does racial discrimination play in the second generation's maintenance of ties to their parents' sending countries? And what role does transnationalism play in how the second generation develops racial and ethnic identities and copes with racial discrimination when it occurs?" (18). Andrea Louie's essay in that collection interrogates specifically the relationship of American-born Chinese American participants in the "In Search of Roots" Program in the San Francisco Bay area, a program whose very existence is referential to the complex and often ambivalent relationship between American-born Asian Americans and their Asian "home"-cultures including the ties within their extended families. Louie argues that due to the prominent stereotypical images of Chinese and Chinese Americans in mainstream American culture, the American-born generations of Chinese Ameri-

---

[39] For critical discussions, see, for instance Elaine H. Kim's "Home Is Where the *Han* Is: A Korean-American Perspective on the Los Angeles Upheavals" (2000); and Jacqueline Doyle's "'A love Letter to My Motherland': Maternal Discourses in Jessica Hagedorn's *Dogeaters*" (1997).

cans have difficulty discerning "authentic Chineseness" and identifying the culturally skewed perspectives that inform their own investigations of their Chinese origins (323).

Louie's observations also relate to the problem of second-generation cultural identification in Ng's novel. Ruby's homecoming to her parents' house and family laundry is doubly confusing: on the one hand, the Lee home is the location of the parents' diasporic relationship to China, their home country. This aspect is particularly confusing since the parents' sense of home refers to a place their American-born daughter has never been to. On the other hand, her parents' house is the home of Ruby's Chinese American cultural ties, the place where heavy Chinese food and the stereotypical Chinese laundry seem to be the main anchoring points of her parents' settlement in the U.S. Their lifestyle, however, has little in common with the life Ruby envisions for herself. Ruby considers the U.S. her home, not China, and, like Kingston's and Tan's protagonists, she is aware of the cultural differences between the generations of her immediate family. In their behavior, language and life style, Ruby's parents are more Chinese in contrast to the Western life Ruby leads. She thus resents coming home because she considers her parents' way of life as anchored in Chinese traditions, the same traditions she seeks to liberate herself from when she moves away in order to become "a regular American girl" (25). Her temporary return to her parents' home thus reconnects Ruby with the culture of first-generation Chinese Americans: "The screen door slams behind you and you find you're no longer a visitor but a resident again" (17). Not only does Ruby resent becoming a resident of her parents' home, even the idea of going to see them is bothersome to her. Her excuses for not coming home more frequently during her college years are plentiful, including her refusal to take the subway from Manhattan to Queens. Such discomfort is implicative of Ruby's resistance to any confrontation with her Chinese "Other.

The novel elaborates on this "Otherness" by juxtaposing Ruby's parents' immigrant settlement with Ruby's more *progressive* living arrangements, first with her boyfriend Nick and later in a women's boarding house. It is interesting that Ruby associates her parents' home with both a culturally different and at the same time socially inferior status. This conflation of ethnicity and class makes it even more difficult for her to establish a sense of belongig. Most specifically, the family laundry, stereotypical marker of the family's Chinese American heritage, stands in clear opposition to her American metropolitan life in Manhattan. In Ruby's orientalist perception, marred by her attempt to deliberately distance herself from the poor immigrant background her parents' house reminds her of, the house she grew up in "wasn't even a house but four rooms behind a laundry" (25).[40] In other words, Ruby perceives her home and her parents' laundry as location of Chinese culture within American society and associates them with China, an unfamiliar mystified place to which her father threatened to send his disobedient children: "China and the bogeyman, so they became one and the same" (41). Her rejection of her Chinese origin is also apparent in Ruby's conflict with her Caucasian boyfriend Nick. It is after Nick calls attention to Ruby's "Chineseness" that she finally breaks up with him for good (236). Yet, whereas Ruby rightfully protests Nick's racism, she herself falls into stereotyping Chinese Americans as specimens of an exotic culture. Ruby's orientalist approach becomes especially evident in her characterization of her parents' house as a metonymic representation of an exotic Chinese culture that fails to translate into mainstream American society.

At Her Mother's House

In line with feminist practices of considering the mother-daughter relationship as nucleus of feminist consciousness and female solidarity, home also plays an important role in the context of the relationship between Ruby and Bell. Because the domestic space is the place where mother-daughter relationships resonate most forcefully, many female authors chose the domestic space as a setting for their narrative representations of mother-daughter relationships. I am thinking here in particular of the following examples: 124 Bluestone Road in Toni Morrison's *Beloved* (1987); the country home in the Deep South in Alice Walker's "Everyday Use;" Esperanza's identity quest within her family in Sandra Cisneros' *The House on Mango Street* (1984); Angel's taking refuge in her grandmother's house on the reservation in Linda Hogan's *Solar Storms* (1995); Merle Woo's act of writing a letter to her mother in "Letter to Ma;" and Trinh T. Minh-ha's characterization of the grandmother's home as location of cultural memory in "Grandma's Story." These works recover the creative potential of female subjectivity by suggesting that the literary performances of identity are intricately linked to cultural performances in the home and can enact political gestures that impact the domestic and the public sphere in equal measures.

In her book *In Her Mother's House: The Politics of Asian American Mother-Daughter Writing* (1999), Wendy Ho observes that daughters in Asian American mother-daughter writing often re-investigate their cultural ancestries with empathy and understanding by placing themselves into the homeplace

[40] I borrow the idea of inter-familial orientalism from Sheryl A. Mylan, "The Mother as Other: Orientalism in Maxine Hong Kingston's *The Woman Warrior*" (1996).

their mothers created. In Ho's analysis, the homeplace in Kingston's *The Woman Warrior*, Tan's *The Joy Luck Club*, and Fae Myenne Ng's *Bone* is a refuge where daughter protagonists can safely come to terms with their identities as Asian American woman in the U.S. and where they can begin to formulate their ethnic and gender consciousness. As complex as the identity negotiations of the daughters in those books are, they eventually do assume a home within the cultural homeplace their mothers constructed. In fact, it is *in* their mothers' houses, as Ho emphasizes, that the daughters' identity negotiations come to a successful completion. In this sense, argues Ho, Kingston, Tan and Ng emphasize the homeplace and the mother-daughter relationship as strategic locations of ethnic and gender emancipation of Asian American women. The mother's house also serves as location for the identity Mei Ng depicts. In *Eating Chinese Food Naked*, the mother's home is also the location of Ruby's complicated identity negotiation, the place where she explores her ethnic belonging, her formulations of womanhood, and her sexuality. However, the mother-daughter relationship in Ng's novel foregrounds the tension between Ruby and the ethnic, gender and sexual model of womanhood which her mother embodies. In fact, the interconnectedness of ethnicity, gender and sexuality raises issues about Ruby's mapping of a homeplace in ways that Ho's discussion does not address fully.

Within the patriarchal construction of the nuclear family, mothers and daughters are caught within the strictures of oppression, lack of autonomy, and of mutual objectifying. As numerous feminist critics have argued, the daughter's identity formation entails a complicated process of negotiating between loving identification with the mother and resentment of the closeness that binds her to the image of womanhood conveyed through the mother, an assumption that lies at the center of my project here. As my discussion of Kingston's *The Woman Warrior* and Amy Tan's *The Joy Luck Club* in the previous two chapters illustrates, this oscillating pattern between intimate attachment and fierce detachment determines the daughter's gender consciousness. As I have pointed out in significant detail in the previous chapters, these patterns shape the narrativization of the mother-daughter relationship both in terms of the stylistic choices the individual authors make as well as on the level of thematic representation female solidarity, including the politics of location of narrative discourses of identity such as the politics of transnational memory. Entangled in a similar interplay of symbiosis and separation, mother and daughter in *Eating Chinese Food Naked* alternately seek and shun the close relationship to each other. As a result, their attitudes towards the family's house, the physical location of their relationship, differ considerably. Whereas Ruby is keen on trying to find her own apartment, Bell struggles with the idea of having to let

Ruby go her own ways: "Bell tries to check the relief she felt each time Ruby came home and said the apartment wasn't quite right for her" (201). Throughout the novel, the subtle hints at their ongoing conflict over the controversy about Ruby's moving out are indicative of the complex relationship between Ruby and her mother. Thus, when Ruby returns home after graduating from college, although only temporarily, she feels as if she had lost a bet with her mother that she would be able to make it on her own: "The words 'You win' popped into Ruby's head, although she hadn't been aware that there had been a fight going on" (16).

In Asian American immigrant families, the mother is indeed linked closely to the establishing of cultural homeplaces. As Rajini Srikanth observes, "[h]ome, as the site to which one can turn and return for a collection of all those things with which one is familiar – language, food, social traditions, ceremonies and cultural values – is increasingly identified with the woman" (1994, 151). Shrikanth's assertion illustrates that diasporas are always gendered and that women's roles in diasporic communities, as Gayatri Chakravorty Spivak suggests in her analysis of women's lives in a transnational world, reinforce and at times even amplify in the diaspora the gender patterns that were prevalent in their home countries. In "Diasporas Old and New: Women in the Transnational World," Spivak urges us to consider the specific gendered positions of women in relation to "(1) homeworking, (2) population control, (3) groups that cannot become diasporic and (4) indigenous women outside the Americas" (1996, 246) that all put into sharper focus the question of "place" within diasporic communities. In the same vein, as Srikanth's observation about the domesticated role of women in diasporic communities exemplifies, the status of women as preservers of the diasporic 'home' culture is also largely connected to heterosexual and conjugal relationships that enact patriarchal family structures.

Perhaps it is this domestication of women via the example of their mothers that rejects Ruby. The Lee family, so the novel seems to suggest, perpetuates such oppression in the subordinate position of woman/wife vis-à-vis her husband. Ruby's perception of her mother as silent obedient daughter – "and she knew not to argue with [her father] anymore (29)" – matches her observation that her mother is a silenced victim within her own marriage. By the same token, Franklin's verdict in response to Ruby and Bell's travel plans to go on a trip to Florida advocate a definite binding of the mother to the homeplace: "Your mother belongs here. In this house. Your mother's not going anywhere" (203). In this light, Ruby imagines the homeplace to which she returns to be the place of her mother's confinement to a strictly domestic space. As far as Ruby's conflict with her mother is concerned, it is important to remember that her resentment at identifying with Bell stems from her inability to think beyond the gender role her mother occupies within the domestic homeplace. This domestication of the mother and her suppression under the patriarchal ruling of the homeplace trigger in Ruby the urge to become different from her mother and lead her to claim a location for her identity formation that does not underlie the gender oppression her father exercises over her mother.

The ethnic background of her family's implication of strict patriarchal gender roles adds further to Ruby's inability to distinguish between her mother's status within the family and Chinese American womanhood in general. Typical of mother-daughter relationships in Asian American literature at large, Ruby considers the cultural origins of her family as main impediment to the mother's lack of autonomy. Because the mother, as Helena Grice observes, serves as "a mediator of the ancestral culture" and thus "often represents mother-land" (72), the daughter's ambiguity about her cultural origins and her psychological struggle between independence from and identification with the image of womanhood the mother represents merge. Ruby sees a connection between her mother's Chinese upbringing and the domestication Bell endures. The novel supports Ruby's cultural distance from her mother in that it invites deeper introspection into the dynamics of traditional families of Chinese origin and in that it characterizes Bell's life as emblematic of all Chinese women. A flashback episode about how Bell's father arranged the marriage between her and Franklin reviews the history of arranged marriages within Chinese culture. Another story in the same chapter alludes to the Confucian principles of Chinese societies as it sketches Bell's transition from under her father's to under her husband's authority.

Ruby's attempt to liberate herself from the sexist and misogynist ruling within the patriarchal Chinese American family in which she grew up urges her to envision a home that is not in any way related to her mother's home, a home that she believes is so clearly governed by her father and, so it seems, that does not allow for Bell to make her own choices in life. When Ruby moves out of her mother's house, she also symbolically moves away from the image of womanhood her mother conveys. Therefore, Ruby envisions a new homeplace free from the constraints she projects onto her mother. Upon moving into a women's boarding house, she ponders: "She liked her apartment bare. If her mother came to live with her, the place would get all cluttered. They would have to get a big place; her mother would have her own room and Ruby would have her own room and the two rooms wouldn't be right next to each other" (19). Ruby insists on different rooms for her mother and herself, *room*, of course, used in Virginia Woolf's sense of *A Room of One's Own* (1929) as feminist trope of female agency. She thus distinguishes herself from the feminist agendas her mother's room fosters, mainly because of the differences in ethnic and gender identity she perceives between herself and her mother. Although Ng's novel shares Virginia Woolf's claiming of a room for feminist development, it maintains that mother and daughter need to be located in different rooms, and, more importantly, that the mother be excluded from the daughter's room. The exclusion of the mother from Ruby's room is indicative of ideological differences within pan-Asian feminist theory and practice, as Esther Ngan-Ling Chow asserts in her discussion of Asian American activism within the feminist movement of the 1970s and 1980s (1994). It is also testimony to the heterogeneous constituency of an Asian American feminist consciousness, of the cultural differences within the Asian American community, of the generation conflict and of the intervention of fragmented selfhood. Furthermore, it raises issues about the possibility of constructing a feminist heuristic that encompasses all the diverse fragments within both Asian American and mainstream American feminist thought. The psychological dimensions of the mother-daughter conflict between Ruby and Bell amplify these differences within Asian American feminist representation. Whereas Bell's confinement to a domesticated space that is ruled by her husband's demands and burdened with his frustration with his low-class status within American society, Ruby's room in a non-conventional women's co-habitat boarding house marks her entrance to modern, progressive, independent womanhood.

Coming Home, Coming Out

Perhaps the most interesting moment of the novel's depiction of the interconnectedness of ethnicity, gender and sexuality is the concurrence of Ruby's coming home with her *tentative* coming-out.[41] This level of Ruby's being at home / not at home in her sexual identity raises particularly interesting issues about personal identity negotiations in the face of the largely homogenous constituency of Chinese American communities on the one hand and of mainstream American culture in the other. In the case of Ng's novel, Ruby is pretty much left to herself with her coming to terms with her sexual orientation. The novel does not depict a strong LGBT community in ways that Lydia Kwa's *The Place Called Absence* (2003) and Catherine Liu's *Oriental Girls Desire Romance* (1997), for instance, do.

[41] I am certainly aware of the contradiction, and maybe poor word choice, the concept of a tentative coming out implies, but I do believe that it encompasses the dynamic of Ruby's ongoing negotiation of her sexuality in relation to her hetero- and homo-erotic fantasies and encounters.

Ng's novel is one of several interesting examples of Asian American sexual coming-of-age stories of female young adult protagonists. Like other novels, including Gish Jen's *Mona in the Promised Land* (1996) and Julie Shigekuni's *A Bridge Between Us* (1995), Ng's novel depicts a young female protagonist's sexual awakening as part of her subject formation. Investigating how the parameter 'sexuality' further complicates identity mappings, recent scholarship emphasizes readings of sexual identity and sexuality in the literature of Asian American women. In "Gender and Sexuality in Asian American Literature," Sau-ling C. Wong and Jeffrey J. Santa Ana assert that "the interconnectedness, mutual constituency, and operational simultaneity of race/ethnicity, gender, and sexuality" are multiple constructions of the complex claims to social, political, and ideological visibility contemporary Asian American authors make in their writing (171). Such complexity, argues E. J. Levy, is not only evoked "as a result of passing as straight while feeling different" but indicates the dual conception of passing as heterosexual and passing as women, women being "an identity which is itself an artificial construction" (3-4). Being of Asian descent, a woman, and gay indicates three socially constructed categories, each with its own normative definitions and whose in-group/out-group polarization lacks congruency for those who endure the tripartite of ethnic, gender, and sexual marginalization. By positioning a multiply charged authorship at the core of her writing, Ng emphasizes the need to define sexuality as parameter of a complex identity mapping that is equally difficult in mainstream American society as it is in Asian American societies. Such a literary performance is central in queer writing and pivotal to its "political practice based on transgressions of the normal and normativity rather than a straight/gay binary of the heterosexual/homosexual identity" (1), as David L. Eng and Alice Y. Hom define it in the introduction to their book, *Q&A: Queer in Asian America* (1998).

Contrary to Gloria Anzaldúa's assertion in *Broderlands / La Frontera* that "the queer of [a person] is in all races" (102), homosexuality continues to be a minority within ethnic minority cultures. The multiple fragmentation that Asian Americans experience as they are torn between conforming to gender normativties within their ethnic groups and coming out with definitions of their own sexuality challenge the homogeneous constituency of Asian American communities. To be able to assume home within the Asian American community often requires not coming out. In *Asian American Dreams: The Emergence of an American People* (2000), Helen Zia reports on suffering under the exclusion from her Asian Americans activist group on the basis of her sexuality. According to Zia, the group members agreed that "[h]omosexuality is not part of [their] community" but "a symptom of white, middle-class self-indulgence"

(228). Not only did members of that group make it very clear that homosexuality was not part of the issues they were trying to articulate in their combined efforts to achieve equal rights for Asian Americans, they also specified that Zia's lesbianism would cast a shadow over the (straight) activists and would possibly diminish their impact against racism. Longing to be accepted by her activist community, she thus denounced her homosexuality. In order for Zia to be able to assume home within the Asian American community, she had to hide the fact that she didn't feel at home in the heterosexual life that is the norm within that community. This differentiation between her ethnic and her sexual "homes" makes apparent the difficulty of formulating one single "home" that does not draw on binary exclusivity.

A similar pattern of disguise and secrecy intervenes not only in public life, but also "at home" i.e. in relation to family and relatives. Karin Aguilar-San Juan notes: "going home involves entering a closet of furtive whispers and private pain" (McCann and Kim 267). Due to the intolerance of family and friends, Aguilar-San Juan contends, going home is for many Asian American gay men and lesbians a time when they cannot be authentic, a fact through which the familiar space of home acquires a contradictory meaning.[42] Aguilar-San Juan specifies: "It seems that for many Asian Americans, home is a place where "Asianness" originates, a place made more compelling by the negotiation of an Asian American presence elsewhere. Often, we look to the future with anticipation, hoping the next time we go home, we can be out" (ibid. 267-68). The home in itself thus becomes a place where a person cannot be at home within his or her sexuality.

This appropriation of a heterosexuality, or even a-sexuality, within the homeplace is one of the extended metaphors 'home' and 'house' imply in *Eating Chinese Food Naked.* Ng uses the trope of 'home' as incarcerating location of compulsory heterosexuality. In particular, the novel uses the images of 'home' and 'house' as extensions of the closet metaphor that denotes unacknowledged sexual orientation. When Ruby is torn between whether or not to commit more fully to her relationship with Nick, her boyfriend of four years, "all the walls in the house seemed to press too close to her and she had to go out walking" (160). Ruby's other amorous encounters are also always located in closed-in spaces such as a café in down-town Manhattan or a kitchen at a friend's house party, and every time Ruby backs out of the flirtatious interac-

---

[42] In contrast, Alice Y. Hom asserts in an empirical study of Asian American parents with lesbian daughters and gay sons that some parents, instead of considering homosexuality "a white disease," connect their children's sexuality to images of gay men and lesbians in their countries of origin (177).

tions with the man and the woman she meets, she leaves the room in order to escape the circumstance of the individual situation.

Perhaps the most complex implication of home as extended metaphor of Ruby's sexuality is implied in her relationship with her mother. In particular, Ruby's sexual desire for Bell contributes to the complicated negotiation between acceptance and refusal of her sexuality. As far as her depiction of Ruby's erotic yearning for her mother is concerned, Ng challenges the validity and absoluteness of patriarchal institutions that are prevalent in the nuclear family. In response to a reader's comment on her fiction as being "grim," Ng explains: "That's the kind of aesthetic I relate to. I don't like a happy Hollywood ending. I'm more interested in that sick world, that twisted-up stuff that's underneath family relations" (Cryer). Ng's writing thus seeks to subvert prescriptive social norms on all fronts. In addition to the cultural tensions within the immigrant Chinese American family, Ng depicts the daughter's homoerotic desire for her mother in her short story "This Early" and in her novel. In both cases, the protagonists fall in love with a heterosexual woman who is living in an unfulfilled relationship with her male partner. Whereas in "This Early," Ng attributes to the protagonist's female lover a symbolic, maternal role e.g. by placing her photo next to the photo of her own mother, her depiction of mother love in *Eating Chinese Food Naked* is much more obviously charged with the daughter's sexual desire.

Early on in the novel, Ruby's sexual/conjugal desire for her mother appears to be a reaction to Bell's unhappy marriage. At age six, when Ruby realizes how "lonesome" her mother is, she reasons that Bell's discontentment is "her father's fault" and decides to save her mother from having to further endure Franklin's tyranny: "she was dreaming about marrying her mother and taking her away" (18). This sentiment of being able to give the mother what the father is unable to provide still pertains in the present setting of the novel: "Now Ruby is twenty-two and still wanted to take her mother away" (19). Ruby's planned trip to Florida against the father's consent is not dissimilar from an elopement or a "twisted Freudian honeymoon" that is meant to liberate the mother from her domestication and the sexual demands of the father (Morin). Similarly, Ruby feels she has been unfaithful to her mother when she leaves the bed she shares with her mother and sneaks down into the basement to have sex with her boyfriend Nick.

Ethnic Foodways and Cultural Homeplaces

Like sexuality, foodways are also an extension of the symbolic meaning of home in Ng's novel. What is particularly interesting about Ng's use of ethnic foodways is that it ties together aspects of gender, ethnicity, and sexuality. The interconnectedness of these modalities is best described in Ruby's appropriation of food as a means of negotiating her own sense of home. In the context of ethnic American writers' agency and visibility within the dominant mainstream American culture, food and eating belong to the literary tropes that underscore the ethnic and cultural diversity of the U.S. Sau-ling C. Wong, for instance, notes that "eating practices are shaped to an extraordinary extent by culture and can thus serve as elaborate mechanisms for encoding and expressing social relationships" (1993, 18). Accordingly, Wong reads food culture in Asian American literature as a "necessity" that arises out of people's "ability to cope with the constraints and persecutions Asian Americans have had to endure as immigrants and racial minorities" (1993, 25). At the same time, however, Wong acknowledges that food, because it is not "inherently or statically 'ethnic'" (70), needs to be considered as "performance" of a person's identity in the sense of Susan Kalcik's definition of food as "performative act of ethnicity" (Kalcik 38).

Many American-born Chinese American writers characterize the difference in the generation-specific foodways between first-and second-generation immigrants as a narrative ploy. In *Ethnic and Regional Foodways in the United States: The Performance of Group Identity* (1984), Brown and Mussell define foodways as determined by boundaries of group identity: "Foodways bind individuals together, define the limits of the groups' outreach and identity, distinguish in-group from out-group, serve as medium of inter-group communication, celebrate cultural cohesion, and provide a context for performance of group ritual" (5). The culture specific implications of performative foodways are an important factor in understanding the cultural differences between first- and second-generation immigrants. Negotiating the local and global aspects of their diasporic cultures, the second-generation Asian American protagonists often expresses their yearning for entry into American society in their hunger for American foods.

In this vein, food can be, for the American-born Asian Americans, not only an encoded mechanism of their group belonging to the immigrant culture of their ancestors, but rather a parameter of individuality that also implies their distinction from the shared collective cultural consciousness of the first generation immigrants including their parents. Their alienation from the foodways of the older generation marks their integration into the dominant, 'non-ethnic'

American society. Or, as Wilfried Raussert's classification of foodways as performative acts in Asian American women's writing suggests, there are three critical tropes that emerge:

> [I]n the first place, they can help provide an insider's understanding of cultural processes at work within minority groups: as such, these tropes are designed to point out the ethnic and racial dimensions behind artistic productions, while – ideally – avoiding forms of essentialism. They can aim at exposing the intercultural tensions and dynamics underlying the literary and social relationship of mainstream and minority culture(s). Finally, they may link literary texts to transcultural experiences peculiar to individual existences in cross-cultural contexts. (183)

All three of these tropes are relevant for my subsequent discussion of Ng's use of food as a metaphor to negotiate Ruby's expressions of her ethnic, gender, and sexual identity.

Mei Ng's novel engages Chinese food as central means of communication within the immigrant family. Instead of verbal communication, Bell's cooking and serving of food is a symbolic interaction with her family. Food also characterizes the changes in Bell and Franklin's relationship, especially in the juxtaposition between Franklin's courtship with a perfectly shaped melon and his constant criticism of Bell's cuisine once they are married. Moreover, Ruby and her siblings interact with their parents almost exclusively through the sharing of meals: her brother Van invites the family to a barbecue after a year-long falling-out with his parents; her sister Lily is in constant transition between her own apartment above the family laundry and shared meals at her parents' dinner table; and finally, Ruby's temporary stay at her parents' house is framed by the constant planning and preparation of opulent "authentic" Chinese meals. But Ng does not depict these events as community celebrations. Instead, each of these moments in the novel emphasize the multiple personal positions from with the individual members of the family participate in the events and in which way the performative acts of the meals resonate differently with each family member.

Instead of characterizing the sharing of a meal as a community act, Ng's novel illustrates to which degree the family's collective foodways are made up of contradictory food performances by the individual, encoded with different cultural understandings, which acknowledges the conflict between individual and group identity. This is particularly evident in the mother-daughter relationship between Bell and Ruby. Given that food is detrimental to the conflict between identification with the collective cultural heritage and self-asserted autonomy, the process of Ruby's identity formation inevitably also includes her ambivalence about Chinese foodways. As Brown and Mussell hold, the categorization of foodways along ethnic parameters is a common practice of distinguishing between different cultures: "Mainstream Americans frequently use foodways as a factor in the identification of subcultural groups and find traditional dishes and ingredients of 'others' who eat differently from themselves a set of convenient ways to categorize ethnic and regional character" (3). In relation to her parents, for instance, Ruby feels more closely connected to Anglo-American culture and lifestyle, including food ethics, than to Chinese culture. A traditional Chinese crab dinner is an act of celebration for her parents while it is a traumatizing experience for Ruby, an experience that provides evidence of her alienation from Chinese culture. Accordingly, Ng's novel depicts the process of Bell's preparing the meal through Ruby's distance and cultural alienation from her parents' typically Chinese customs: "[Bell] dumped the crabs into the pot and poked them with a chopstick when they tried to climb out. The clacking of their bodies against the pot was terrible" (40). Although Ruby, then thirteen, partly sabotages her father's festive crab meal – although he ordered her to get only female crabs, Ruby also comes home with a few "boy crabs" (40) – her role as obedient daughter foresees that she partake in the preparation of the meal. Once the meal is ready, Ruby immediately distances herself from the ethnically charged foodways her parents represent. As if in order to counter her contribution to the preparing of a traditional Chinese meal, Ruby rushes to the nearest-by grocery store to get American comfort food. She "left the kitchen and practically ran around the corner to Jack's. She stood in front and ate a handful of Sno-Caps" (41). Not only are the Sno-Caps a sweet recompense for her viewing of the terrible ongoings in her mother's kitchen, they are also a token of her access to American foodways. Ruby's attempt to escape the eating practices of her family is thus indicative of her discharge of Chinese culture.

At the same time, the novel discursively "others" the mother through the detailed description of her exotic food practices. Ng's novel's emphasis on the parents' "authentic" Chinese cuisine as a main characteristic of their foreignness is a clever strategy to amplify the cultural difference between mother and daughter. In her essay "Authentic or Not, Its' Original," Meredith E. Abarca argues that the rhetoric of authentic ethnic foods, whether carried by insiders or by outsiders, implies a sense of essentialism that precludes any form of cultural heterogeneity (2). Abarca thus proposes the term "original" foods, a term that defines foodways as an expression of ethnic identity but of personal identity, whether that be more informed by a person's individual or collective sense of self. Similarly, Sau-ling Wong emphasizes that there is a fine line between the depiction of foodways as heritage of diasporic cultures and the intentional sensationalizing of ethnic foodways as othering spectacle. While it is true that "eating practices are shaped to an extraordinary extent by culture and can thus serve as elaborate mechanisms for encoding and expressing social relationships (Wong 1993, 18), depictions of foodways, when out of context, can also promote the curious gaze of cultural outsiders. Frank Chin's intervention of the concept of "food pornography" (qtd. in Wong 1993, 55) as an indication for the social interest in ethnic foodways comes to mind here, as well as Sau-ling Wong's discussion of the food pornography and food prostitution (1993, 55-65).

In this context, Ruby's accounts of her parents' exotic foodways are indicative of her perceived cultural differences between her and her parents, differences that seem to come across as essentialist notions of self versus other. The very attempt to construct the parents as holders of an authentic culture expressed through their foodways places them in a category that is not only different from the U.S. mainstream but as one they will never be able to overcome.

Food and Sexuality

Not only are elaborate meals the occasion for reunion und reconciliation between the estranged family members, food also has a gender hierarchy attached to it, as the novel's juxtaposition of Franklin's tyrannical demands for specific meals with his demands for sex implies. Eating is both a symbol of cultural performance as well as a reverberating image of sexuality. In *Appetites: Food and Sex in Post-Socialist China* (2002), Judith Farquhar quotes a proverb from the Chinese philosopher *Mencius*: "Appetite for food and sex is nature" (1). In her interpretation of this proverb Farquhar points out the biological and semantic parallels between sexual appetites and appetites for food. Similarly, Mary Douglas argues that "[l]ike sex, the taking of food has a social component as well as a biological one" (61). In this vein, Ng's novel performs depictions of sexuality through foodways in similar ways as it aesthetizises Ruby's ethnicity and gender consciousness through metaphors of food and eating.[43]

As far as Ruby's attempt at establishing a sense of home is concerned, Ng's novel uses food and sexuality as mechanisms of expressing the compli-

---

[43] Wenying Xu argues a similar point in *Eating Identities: Reading Food in Asian American Literature* (2008).

cated process of untangling the many facets of her identity.[44] The omniscient narrator of the novel depicts Ruby's appetites for food and sex as various, often as contradictory. Through the symbolic use of food, as I argue in the previous sections of this chapter, *Eating Chinese Food Naked* evokes the ambiguity of Ruby's ethnic consciousness. To the same extent, Ng's use of the eating motive circumscribes Ruby's heterosexual practices as well as her homoerotic desires. The novel candidly elaborates on the smells, savors, and tastes of sexual intimacy. Especially interesting, is Ruby's sequence of dreams about eating a roasted dog and having sex with her mother. The sex dream ends with Franklin disturbing the intimacy between mother and daughter. After this dream, the novel narrates a flashback into Ruby's childhood, where she learns about the eating ritual of a culture where people give the foods they grow to their friends and neighbors instead of eating them themselves. Linking the appetites for food and sex, Ruby repeatedly reflects on the prohibitions of eating one's own foods: "You weren't supposed to eat your own yams. Or your own dog. Or your own sister or mother. Your own yams, your own sister, your own mother you may not eat. Other people's sisters, other people's mothers, you may eat" (169). In the context of Ruby's dream, eating one's mother refers to Ruby's sexual hunger for Bell, eating here being a metaphor for oral sex. By putting eating dogs and eating one's mother into the same category of prohibited behavior, Ng juxtaposes unusual eating habits with unconventional sexual desires and characterizes both as practices of exotic subcultures. Such analogy is indicative of the marginalization of homosexuality within mainstream cultures and underscores the same interconnectedness of ethnicity, gender, and sexuality in the context of the mother-daughter relationship as Ng sketches in reference to the construction of a homeplace and the implied cultural mechanisms of foodways.

The exoticism about Chinese culture, the patriarchal ruling of nuclear (Western and Chinese) families, and the debated ambivalence innate to the mother-daughter dyad determine Ruby's ideological alienation and spatial distancing from the homeplace. Embracing the limited scope of Ruby's prejudiced perception of her mother, the novel operates with a polarized opposition between Bell's domestication and alleged inability to move freely and Ruby's constant movement between Queens and Manhattan, between different jobs as an office temp, between the parents' house and the family laundry. I have to put Bell's inability to move freely into perspective because its very observation relies on Ruby's unfamiliarity with the daily whereabouts of her mother. It is not until the very end that Ruby learns about Bell's endless strolls and walks

44 By means of compassion, see Janie C. Har, "Food Sexuality, and the Pursuit of a Little Attention" (1993).

through their neighborhood. One might argue that the same restlessness is indicative of Ruby's ongoing identity mapping and the complicated process of untangling the many strands of her ethnic and gender consciousness.

Furthermore, this opposition suggests Ruby's mobility within American society as supposed to her mother's lack of freedom. The latter aspect underscores Ruby's identity negotiation e.g. by using Bell as projected foil serving as a backdrop for Ruby's attempted individuality and liberation. Such narrative strategy inevitably undermines the subjectivity of Ruby's mother. Because the daughter narrator in *Eating Chinese Food Naked* entirely *owns* the discourse, Ruby's "intensely protective" attitude toward her mother contributes further to the patriarchal "othering" of her mother (Karpen). Her undisputedly benevolent and sympathetic intentions to re-imagine her mother in a life-context free from the father's suppression creates a breach between her and her mother from which Ruby arises as subject and her mother as object. Given Ruby's alienation from the cultural homeplace, this polarization between the inferior mother and the superior daughter is closely related to Ruby's attempted disassociation from her Chinese origins and from her mother's low status both in Chinese and in American culture.

The novel's ending suggests that in order to accomplish a successful mapping of her identity, Ruby needs to claim her individuality at the expense of her collective belonging. Ng constructs this distance in Ruby's decision to plot her life anew: by moving out of her parents' house and into an "all-women's building" Ruby, now single, chooses a form of co-habitation that subverts normative structures that rely on the patriarchally governed nuclear family (215). Contemplating the freedom of her newly painted walls and smooth wooden floors, she draws upon her mother's kitchen as negative example of comparison to her own home:

> Until that moment, she had never realized how much she hated the green linoleum of her mother's kitchen, green with gold swirled into it like a crazy marble cake. She had swept and mopped that floor so many times without realizing just how much she hated it. She went to the door and locked it, the leaned heavily against it, as if someone were chasing her. (220)

In contrast to Ng's earlier depictions of homeplaces as metonyms for Ruby's ambiguous identity mapping, this new home becomes a refuge to Ruby's sense of self because it implies her individuality and autonomy and grants space for Ruby's individuality.

By placing Ruby into this new home, Ng sketches a scenario in which Ruby can juggle the simultaneity of her ethnicity, her gender, and her sexuality. The novel ends with Bell's message on Ruby's answering machine quoting a family recipe Ruby asked for. This final scene is pivotal to Ruby's new attitude toward collectivity. Ruby realizes that her mother also maintains her own individuality, as implied, for instance, in Bell's long solitary walks about the neighborhood. With this realization Ruby begins to grant subjectivity to her mother which she was unable to do while she was too closely connected to Bell. Finally, whereas food was one of the ethnic markers of her family's Chinese heritage that Ruby resented the most, her decision to enroll in cooking school and become a chef enhances the performative aspects that food can have as an expression of identity in a non-essentialist manner. Her request for the family recipe that Bell recites thus implies that she renegotiates her family's Chinese foodways. With Bell's instructions on tape for the preparation of a traditional meal, the novel fuses the topics home, mother-daughter relationship, and foodways one last time. This fusion also suggests a new beginning for the formation of Ruby's collective ethnic, gender, and sexual consciousness.

Although mother and daughter are separated physically, there is a glimpse of hope at the end of the novel, hope that mother and daughter might find a definition of a homeplace that encompasses the many different aspects of female experience and that espouses these differences as fundamental premise for its location of a feminist consciousness that bridges the gap between ethnic and cultural diversity as well as multiple definitions of gender and sexuality. Again, this final possibility has to do with homespaces. Once settled in her new home, Ruby takes her laundry to a shop run by an Ecuadorian-American family business. The shop owners, who tend to the family business, are about the same age as Ruby's parents. For the most part, Ruby feels quite uncomfortable in the presence of the laundry women, as her urge to help the woman with the maintenance of the shop and her plead to the women to accept the moderate tip she offers suggest. What is particularly interesting about this encounter is Ruby's awareness that laundry shops are not essentially Chinese, which is what she had grown up believing. Her discovery of the demographic changes within the multi-ethnic communities and the diversity of diasporic peoples in the U.S. deconstructs her earlier assumption that national origin determines once and for all a person's performance within American society.

One of the novel's most convincing moments of Ruby's agentic transformation occurs in this laundry. While Ruby wonders about the cultural origin of the couple, there is a news report on TV about a major catastrophe that shattered an entire neighborhood. Whereas the location and origin of that catastrophe remain unidentified in the novel, this image of "people standing next to piles of rubble that just a few hours ago had been their homes" (250) addresses very explicitly the importance which people accord to their homes as places of security and comfort, especially when their homeplaces are in jeopardy. The loss of the homeplace in the TV report also mirrors Ruby's displacement and her complicated identity negotiation which makes it difficult for her to reach a sense of "at-home"-ness.

Finally, her sympathy toward the laundry owner hints at the possibility of a feminist solidarity that reaches beyond cultural difference and emphasizes the need to acknowledge the interconnectedness of women of different ethnicities, gender and sexuality and their experiences of oppression in the American and global capitalist societies. It is in that other laundry that Ruby's quest for a homeplace comes to an end as it connects to issues of transnational feminist solidarity.

CHAPTER FIVE

Transnationality and the Mother's Body in Nora Okja Keller's *Comfort Woman*

"Your body must be heard"—Hélène Cixous

My discussion of Kingston, Tan, and Ng in the previous chapter focused on the discursive representations of identity, memory, and home as recurrent tropes in Asian American literature in general and mother-daughter relationships in particular. My discussion of Keller's novel in this chapter introduces the second aim of my project: the representation and discursive construction of Asian American communities. While subsequent chapters treat the construction of literary and national communities, my analysis of Keller's *Comfort Woman* emphasizes the construction of academic communities in Asian American critique. I argue that Keller's novel, because it depicts the interconnectedness of Korean, Korean American, and American histories, lends itself well for a discussion of how transnational feminism has recently shaped the field of Asian American studies. These elements are evidenced in Keller's depiction of a mother-daughter conflict that emerges out of the daughter's need to come to terms with the historical relevance connected to her mother's body.

While attending a symposium on human rights at the University of Hawai'i in 1993, Korean American author Nora Okja Keller became captivated by a talk by a surviving comfort woman who had served as a forced sexual laborer during World War II (Hong 2002). Keller immediately recognized this testimony as an indication of a hidden part of Korean history, and her incredulity that "people didn't know about this" (Hong 2002) inspired her to address the legacies of the comfort women in a fictional narrative. Initially, Keller wrote the narrative of Akiko, the part of the novel that deals with female oppression in Korea. In an interview, Keller explains why she felt the need for the narrative perspective of a contemporary Korean American daughter to complement Akiko's narration: "I did the mother's narrative first, and it wasn't until I was almost finished with that that I realized that we needed to be brought up to date with the daughter's narrative. […] After that was done, I added the framework and put it all together" (Burlingame 2). Although Keller does not really expand on what this adding-on of a contemporary perspective does for the novel, it certainly puts into perspective Akiko's narratives that reconstruct female agency along with Korean national sovereignty. Beccah's perspective is crucial because it links Akiko's narratives to the contemporary American perspective on third world women. This interconnectedness of the different narrative perspectives is what makes the novel's treatment of the female body particularly compelling.

The Comfort Women Debate

Although the actual movement for redress for Korean comfort women initially operated along nationalistic parameters, critics have noted extensively the transnational character of the comfort women movement. The 1996 "Comfort Women of World War II: Legacy and Lessons" conference, organized by Margaret Stetz and Bonnie Oh, has propelled transnational interest in the issue of comfort women to the forefront of Asian American feminist studies. Similarly, Stetz and Oh's anthology *Legacies of the Comfort Women of World War II* (2001) characterizes the comfort women issue in its full dimension. The recent upsurge in the comfort women movement, inaugurated through the public appearances of the surviving comfort women of World War II and their disclosure of the atrocities they endured as sexual slaves in Japanese military camps in Korea, draws our attention not only to the women who now speak out, but to the cultural appropriation of the comfort women issue as more broadly a feminist issue. While many Korean feminist scholars and artists have utilized the comfort women issue as a vehicle for their critiques of militarization and Japanese colonialism, the ramifications of the movement have also reached and continue to shape feminist theory and practices, including Asian American feminism, in the U.S. In fact, more and more critics draw attention to the specific American context in which contemporary comfort women issues are being mediated.

In line with her analysis of the "peculiar protocols of inclusion and representation" of "Asian/American" women in *Compositional Subjects: Enfiguring Asian/American Women* (2002, 3), Laura Hyun Yi Kang's recent essay "Conjuring 'Comfort Women'" examines the multiple challenges the issue of Korean comfort women poses, issues of "of nomination, of identification, of representation, and of knowledge production" (Kang 2003, 26). In order to disentangle identification from representation/reparation, Kang stresses the hyphen in her analysis of the multiple positionings of Korean-American comfort women, namely in the context of "'Korean' postcoloniality, 'American' nationality, and 'Asian American' racial formation" (28). Each of these positions, argues Kang, place the comfort women within different critical debates, and combined these debates offer a multifaceted picture of a very complex issue. Like Kang, Kandice Chuh, in a recent essay that appeared alongside Kang's essay in a special issue of the *Journal of Asian American Studies* on comfort women, locates the matter of the comfort women at the entry point of Asian American feminist thought into ongoing discussions of transnationality. Chuh's essay focuses on the "claiming of 'comfort women' as an Asian American issue" (Chuh 2003, 9) and analyzes in what way this approach might promote "the advancement of the racialized and sexualized practices of the intersecting modernities of Japan, Korea, and the United States" (10). Drawing on Kang's research, on the findings of Lisa Yoneyama's studies on the politics and ideologies that are implicit in collective acts of remembering the past (Yoneyama 1999), as well as on Leti Volpp's interrogations of the racialized female body (Volpp 1994), Chuh presents the comfort women issue not only as a topic in Asian American studies but as an ongoing debate in the general world order of postmodernity.

That the issue of the comfort women is also entrenched in discourses of power/privilege is important in my analysis of Keller's literary representation of the comfort women in her novel. The novel narrates the stories of a surviving comfort woman and of her American-born daughter. Keller's fictionalized narration of the comfort women issue, as Kandice Chuh cautions us (Chuh 2003, 9), is a literary/epistemological appropriation of the general comfort women debate that differs from the representation of the people who actually experienced sexual violence under Japanese imperialism. This distinction between lived experience and literary representation is important in the context of Keller's novel, as it foregrounds the issue of transnational representation. At the same time, to bear in mind the metacritical consideration this distinction calls for also points to a critical moment in the framing of Asian American studies "as a purveyor of knowledge" (Chuh 2003, 8) with specific consideration of the critical sensibilities staked out by transnational feminist theory and practice.

Similarly, Pamela Thoma locates the "Comfort Woman" conference—the very conference that initiated a comparative methodology of the various trends in contemporary study of the comfort woman issue—at the crossroads of global feminism and transnational feminism. While the comfort women debate runs the risk of being absorbed by global feminist discourses that have obscured for the sake of promoting a Westernized model of women's liberation the specific location from which women maintain their agency, transnational feminism—to cite Inderpal Grewal and Caren Kaplan's very appropriate definition—"articulate[s] the relationship of gender to scattered hegemonies such as global economic structures, patriarchal nationalisms, 'authentic' forms of tradition, local structures of domination, and legal-juridical oppression on multiple levels" (Grewal and Kaplan 1994, 17-18). With its emphasis on the complex interconnectedness of global capitalism and militarism as shaping factors of women's experience of sexual oppression, the matter of the comfort women, and its reception in multiple feminist discourses throughout the world, amounted to the emergence of what Kaplan calls "anti-racist and anti-imperialist feminism": "[It] must articulate differences in power and location as accurately as possible. It must also find intersections and common ground; but they will not be utopian or necessarily comfortable alliances. New terms are needed to express the possibilities for links and affiliations, as well as differences among women who inhabit different locations" (Kaplan 1992, 116).

This generalization of the comfort women issue, despite its intrinsic connection to a more transnational heuristic, is also subject to discourses of power and privilege. While the matter of surviving comfort women in the United States liberates the discussion of sexual imperialism in Korea from a strictly nationalistic perspective, the specific appropriation of the comfort women matter as an American issue is facilitated by strong American nationalism. Lisa Yoneyama has characterized this adoption of the comfort women issue as an American concern as problematic by pointing out the ideological underpinnings that produce such discourses of "Americanization" of the comfort women issue. As Yoneyama argues, the "Americanization" (Yoneyama 1999, 57) of the movement for redress for comfort women, that is, the emphasis on the U.S. government's role as political liberator and legal mediator in the matter of ongoing negotiations between Japan and the surviving comfort women who sue for financial compensation, operates with strategic discourses that portray America as the "defender of the free world" (58). This more or less blatant notion of American essentialism in the comfort women issue is connected to a general "Westerncentrism" (79) of movements for redress globally and, with its implied elevation of the West over the rest, makes next to impossible a radical anti-colonial and anti-racist world order. After all, as Tina Chen contests, it was "U.S. cold-war hegemony justice which supported the suppression of [the surviving comfort women's] repatriation efforts against Japan, the refutation of their testimony concerning the brutalities inflicted upon them, and the Japanese government's refusal to offer an official apology" (Chen 116). At the same time, continues Yoneyama, there appears to be a second aspect of the Americanization of the comfort women issue, namely through the legal representation of the Asian immigrants and their claims to historical justice within the American judicial system. Because more and more lawsuits against the Japanese government come from California-based legal representatives, asserts Yoneyama, the comfort women issue is transformed from being a traveling memory of Japanese war atrocities to an Americanized topic that features U.S. mainstream cultural discourse (Yoneyama 1999, 60). According to Yoneyama's observations, the paradox lies in the fact that the comfort women issue risks being absorbed by U.S. mainstream cultural discourse, the same discourse that promotes its visibility on a national, and, as Chuh and Yoneyama equally emphasize, even on a global level.

While Chuh's and Yoneyama's essays share the concern that the comfort women matter undergoes strategic misappropriation and decontextualization in its ubiquity in the joined discourses of transnational Korean American, Asian American, and mainstream American feminism, critics have also pointed out the possible contributions the comfort women issue can make to a widely-anchored critique of global capitalism and militarism. Lynn Thiesmeyer, for instance, places the comfort women issue within a global economy driven by militarism and sexual tourism, both catering to and being promoted by U.S. enterprises and institutions (Thiesmeyer 1996). Thiesmeyer links the distinction between abuse and seduction to a prevailing discourse of orientalism toward Asian female bodies in Western cultures. Exploring the pedagogical potential for implementing the comfort women issue in women's studies curricula in the United States, Margaret Stetz argues in essay that was published in *Radical Teacher* that an acknowledgment of "the ongoing history of sexual exploitation of Korean women in and around U.S. military bases in Korea" (Stetz 2003, 20), alongside an in-depth discussion of the comfort women system under Japanese imperialism during World War II, does lend itself to an analysis of the postmodern global world order and the specific role that the United States plays in it.

These three larger trends in the debate on Korean comfort women, namely the consideration of the comfort women movement as a point of intersection between Asian American and transnational studies; the Americanization of the movement for redress for comfort women; and the emphasis on the interconnectedness of sexual abuse, militarism, and global capitalism, play out significantly in Keller's novel *Comfort Woman*. The issues become most apparent in the context of Keller's construction of a narrative plot that centers on a mother–daughter conflict, thereby foregrounding cultural differences within Asian American communities beyond discourses of heterogeneity. Within this setting of a complicated mother–daughter dyad, Keller's novel operates with cultural productions that digress from what Lisa Lowe has identified as "the master narratives of generational conflict and filial relation" (Lowe 1991, 26), thereby challenging concepts of Asian American identity as uniformly syncretic.

Keller's emphasis on a complex and rather distorted mother–daughter relationship between the Korean immigrant Akiko and her American daughter Beccah epitomizes, in a sense, the multiple positionings the comfort women debate encompasses. The central theme of the novel, the need for the two women to be able to communicate with each other, is not a mere narrative strategy that devolves into sentimentalism, but one that sketches the challenges of intercultural understanding. As Patricia P. Chu points out, Asian immigrant mothers in many Asian American novels serve for their Americanized daughters as a "mystic, essentialist force of nature; as witnesses and victims of a backward, oppressive, ahistorical culture; as feminist tricksters and critics of American Orientalism, and as the empowering sources of Asian American feminist consciousness" (Chu 2000, 22). While recognizing the potential for an "East–West understanding and cooperation," Chu also cautions that the binary narrative structure of Asian versus American voice "may trivialize or sentimentalize the Asian mothers' stories" (Chu 2004, 77). While Chu reads Keller's novel in light of Yoneyama's critical attention to the Americanization of the comfort women issue, Samina Najmi positions *Comfort Woman* within the tradition of the *bildungsroman* and war literature and argues that Keller, by fusing these two genres, achieves a subversive "gendering and Asianizing" of them (Najmi 2005, 210). This ambiguous location between, or better yet, at the intersection of, the two critical terrains (Americanization versus Asianization) epitomizes the multiple discourses that have emerged around the comfort women debate.

Language versus Body

One such decisive moment of a transnational feminism as opposed to a global feminist discourse occurs at the end of Keller's novel, when Beccah connects with her mother Akiko and with her Korean heritage by spreading her mother's ashes:

> I opened my mother's box, sprinkling the ashes over the water. I held my fingers under the slow fall of ashes, letting it coat my hand. I touched my fingers to my lips. "Your body is mine," I told my mother, "so you will always be with me, even when your spirit finds its way home. To Korea. To Sulsulham. And across the river of heaven to the Seven Sisters. (212)

There are different ways of reading this passage. The "idealized symbol[ic act] of mutual nurturance" (Chu 2004, 74) seems to be reminiscent of the physical and symbolic reunion between the mother and the unborn daughter, the very prenatal union that psychoanalytical feminists have discussed extensively (Rich 1976; Kristeva 1977; Irigaray 1981). In Adrienne Rich's terms, this "amniotic bliss" is the quintessential union between mothers and daughters: "Mothers and daughters have always exchanged with each other—beyond the verbally transmitted lore of female survival—a knowledge that is subliminal, subversive, preverbal: the knowledge of flowing between two alike bodies, one of which has spent nine months inside the other" (Rich 1976, 220). The above quotation from *Comfort Woman* can be read as a reversed amniotic relationship between the mother and the unborn daughter: the daughter's body absorbs and literally carries the mother's body; the mother's dead body substitutes for the daughter's unborn body, and the box that the daughter carries symbolizes the maternal womb, location of this initial amniotic bliss.

Such "preverbal" identification with the mother, however, obscures the role of language as a medium of cross-cultural identification and as a potential obstacle between Beccah and her mother Akiko. Instead, this reunion implies a resolution of Beccah's ambivalent relationship with her mother at the expense of the Akiko's subjectivity, since the daughter in this passage not only speaks to, but speaks for the deceased mother and thus, in contrast to the objectified remains in the box, manifests her subjectivity and personhood. In addition, this emphasis on an amniotic relationship between mother and daughter essentializes the female body by foregrounding the biological aspects of motherhood rather than the social and cultural representations of womanhood. Keller's construction of a preverbal, amniotic condition between mother and daughter as the ultimate reconciliation between two women is therefore unsatisfactory.

This emphasis on a preverbal mother–daughter relationship in the final passage is particularly striking since language plays such an important role throughout Keller's novel. Akiko's narratives in particular exemplify the importance of speaking out against Japanese colonialism in Korea and against sexism in the form of the pornographic fantasies Akiko's husband (a Christian missionary) forces onto her (body), and most importantly, they exemplify a non-Western, counter-monolithic historiography that accounts for the sexual assaults on her in a Japanese military camp in Korea. Throughout the novel, Keller characterizes language and the desire to speak as subversive acts against sexual oppression and the imposed silence on rape victims. Akiko's accounts of the brutality with which the soldiers in the "recreation camps" mistreated the comfort women, and her personal narratives of her own endurance of forced prostitution serve in the novel as empowering testimonials of personal resistance to and deconstruction of the institutionalized muting of the many victims. In the specific context of Akiko's survival of her traumatic experience as a sexual slave, the act of speaking is also a vital step in her ongoing recovery from trauma. Her ability to speak about the atrocities she witnessed and endured defines her psychological capacity to deal with her trauma. Why, then, does the novel end in a preverbal relationship between mother and daughter that entirely leaves out Akiko's voice? Can a reconciliation that is limited to a physical and corporeal level between mother and daughter still sufficiently invoke a viable discourse of matrilineage? Or is the final scene the ultimate triumph of the daughter's American discourse in perfect American English over the mother's immigrant Korean American voice? These are the questions I keep in mind when I argue in this essay that Keller sees the female body as a form of communication that integrates the corporeal level of human interaction not as an essentialist parameter of "race" or of women's "nature," but as a political medium that speaks out against rape and other forms of oppression of the female body. Through depictions of rape as a universal, non-culture-specific issue, Keller constructs a mother–daughter relationship in which the daughter finds a way to identify with the mother despite the fact that the mother remains, for the most part, a cultural "other." I use the debate of the movement for redress for comfort women as a frame for my discussion of Keller's novel and its attempt to offer a both/and narrative of the oppressed female body. In so doing, I position the novel within discussions of global gender inequities, at the same time taking into consideration the different instances for which the comfort women issue has been utilized in past and ongoing debates in feminist studies globally. At the same time I emphasize the different aspects of power/privilege that play out in various cultural productions and that different feminist movements have adopted in their claiming of the comfort women issue as a major component of their self-representation.

Many critics have read representations of the female body as cultural texts.[45] In Asian American studies in particular, critics have long noted a fascination with and over-emphasis on the "oriental body" and the concomitant production of misrepresentations and misappropriations of Asian and Asian American cultures in Western (feminist) scholarship. As far as the intersection of the preverbal and the maternal is concerned, Gayatri Chakravorty Spivak's critique (1987) of Julia Kristeva's study *About Chinese Women* (1977) offers the earliest and most avid criticism of orientalism in feminist theory. In "French Feminism in an International Frame," Spivak criticizes Kristeva's exploration of the allegedly maternal basis of Chinese language and the Chinese literary tradition and its tendency to "authorize [...] the definition of the essentially feminine and the essentially masculine as non-logical and logical" (Spivak 1987, 138). Kristeva characterizes Chinese literature through the "dependency on the maternal," the "absence of clear-cut divisions between the

---

[45] I am thinking here in particular of Judith Butler's *Bodies that Matter: On the Discursive Limits of "Sex"* (1993) and the edited collection by Katie Conboy, Nadia Medina, and Sarah Stanbury, *Writing on the Body: Female Embodiment and Feminist Theory* (1997).

order of things and the order of symbols," and the "predominance of the unconscious impulses," all of which she attributes to a cherishing of the "pre-Oedipal phase" (Kristeva 1977, 56). By claiming that "ancient China was [...] the best known and most highly developed matrilineal society" (Kristeva 1980, 139; qtd. in Hattori 1998, 123), Kristeva applies a "positive" orientalism, one that elevates Chinese culture over Western cultures (Hattori 1998, 122). Kristeva's positive orientalism is not only problematic on the basis of its one-dimensional definition of Chinese literature, its inscription of the maternal as a quintessential attribute of Chinese culture marks it as a "sexualized" counterpart of Western discourses (Chow 1991, 5).[46] Kristeva's definition of Chinese culture as essentially feminine and her use of a typology that echoes the maternal, prelinguistic, and unstructured characterizes China and, by extension, Chinese women, as dependent, immature, and inferior to Western women. By characterizing Beccah's reconciliation with her mother through a preverbal union, Keller's novel runs the risk of inscribing the same positive orientalism onto the mother–daughter relationship of two Korean American women. Out of context, the ending passage in Keller's novel might reduce womanhood to a biological condition that neglects the social construction of gender. Because it "insulates subjectivity from social practices and discourses" (Abel 1990, 184), this psychoanalytical paradigm of the mother–daughter dyad precludes any prospect for advancement of women's rights and human rights issues.

Em-body-ing Matrilineage

At first glance, Keller's representation of a Korean American mother–daughter relationship as a preverbal union invokes orientalist depictions of Asian women in Western representations and Western discourses. This reversed amniotic relationship, in which the daughter speaks to and for the muted mother, emphasizes the body and is thus reminiscent of what Tomo Hattori calls "psycholinguistic Orientalism" (Hattori 1998). However, the construction of an amniotic relationship between mother and daughter at the end of the novel stands in opposition to Keller's reconstruction of female agency and the visibility of "minority issues" through a polyvocal narrative discourse. In this discourse, the atrocities a woman's body endures are intimately connected to a woman's need to speak.

In Akiko's narratives in particular, language exposes the abuse of the female body as sexual commodity for Japanese soldiers. Sold into a military

[46] See also, Leslie Bow's *Betrayal and Other Acts of Subversion: Feminism, Sexual Politics, Asian American Women's Literature* (2001); and Patti Duncan's *Tell This Silence: Asian American Women Writers and the Politics of Speech* (2004).

camp at a prepubescent age as her sister's "dowry" (18), Akiko (this is the name the soldiers gave her in the camp) at first becomes a servant to the comfort women, and later serves as a comfort woman herself. After two years in the camp, Akiko is able to escape and eventually leaves Korea and emigrates to the United States. However, she cannot escape the haunting memories of her traumatic experiences of repeated sexual abuse:

> Whenever I stopped for a beat, for a breath, I heard men laughing and betting on how many men one comfort woman could service before she split open [...] I heard the counting reach one hundred and twenty-four before I could not bear to hear one more number. [...] I heard the grinding of trucks delivering more men and more *military supplies*: food, rations, ammunition, boots, and new women to replace the ones that had died, their bodies erupting in pus. (64-65, emphasis added)

Once the women's genitals were swollen shut, they were abandoned in the woods as "disposable commodities" (147).

The sexual abuse of women in Japanese military camps makes apparent the correlation of wartime sexual violence against women and political warfare. Reiterating Ruth Seifert's assertion that "rape is not an aggressive manifestation of sexuality, but a sexual manifestation of aggression" (Stetz 2003, 139), Stetz argues that governments under which "women are being violated, dominated, humiliated, and treated as chattel as serving its political interests" (Stetz 2003, 140) use systematic sexual violence in order to exercise imperial power. Keller addresses this aspect in Akiko's story about Induk, the woman who was the camp's Akiko #40 before her. In terms of a chronological lineage, Induk is the first of three women to speak out against the sexual oppression of the comfort women. Her speaking out against the military "invasion" of the female body and of Korea is an act of political emancipation for her body and for her nation: "In Korean and in Japanese, she denounced the soldiers, yelling at them to stop their invasion of her country and her body. Even as they mounted her, she shouted: I am Korea, I am a woman, I am alive. I am seventeen, I had a family just like you do, I am a daughter, I am a sister" (20). On the one hand, Induk's verbal defense saves her temporarily from the soldiers' sexual attention: "The men left her stall quickly, some crying, most angrily joining the line for the woman next door" (20). Through her brutal death, her body symbolically being "skewered from her vagina to her mouth" (20-21), on the other hand, she also becomes what Elaine H. Kim defines as an "unconventional martyr" for Korean sovereignty (Kim 1994).

Because it denotes a precondition for the communicability of the political issues the female body represents, *Comfort Woman* characterizes language as inseparable from the female body. In the narratives of Akiko's trauma as wartime sexual slave, Keller represents the female body as unmistakably political because it is regulated by sexism and colonialism and, as the soldiers' commands of "close mouth" and "open legs" (16) suggest, because the abuse of the female body is based on patriarchal impositions of silence and anonymity (Cheung 1988). This commodification through the exchange of the female body for rape and sexual abuse implies the eradication of the victim's subjectivity and individuality. Akiko, for instance, is named after the comfort woman whose identity and stall in the camps she inherits: as Akiko #41, her new identity, she replaces the deceased Akiko #40, and once her virginity was literally auctioned off to the highest bidding soldier, she becomes a "free for all" (21) military commodity. To speak of these atrocities, as numerous comfort camp survivors have done publicly since 1990 (So-hee Lee 2002) and whose stories inspired Keller's interest in this dark chapter of Korean national history (Young Oak Lee 2003), is to break the forced silence that colonial Japan, Korean society, and Western societies have imposed on the victims of this crime. As Kali Tal notes, "The raped female body is quite literally assumed to be 'unspeakable,' since rape has historically been constructed as a crime not against a person, but against property (belonging to the fraternity of fathers, brothers, husbands)" (Tal 1996, 155).[47] Since Induk's story makes up part of, and is thus symbolically integrated into, Akiko's narratives, Akiko perpetuates this counter-monolithic discourse. Her narratives thus promote female and national freedom in honor of Induk's martyrdom. By logical extension, Keller's writing about the loss of individuality through rape and sexual molestation restores the memory of a portion of history that has been largely suppressed by Eurocentric, patriarchal, and colonial discourses. In her depiction of rape as a means of political warfare, Keller thus re-establishes identity for the female bodies whose fates remained occulted and obscured because of their "unspeakable" status as rape victims.

On the other hand, as King-kok Cheung astutely argues in *Articulate Silences* (1993), silence itself can also be a subversive rhetorical strategy for agency. Cheung suggests that since the emphasis on voice and logocentrism leaves out the possibility of adapting silence as a rhetorical strategy, women writers' use of silence as counter-discourse deconstructs the binary opposition between voice and silence and the power definitions that are generally associ-

---

[47] Similarly, not until 1996 were wartime rapes recognized as crimes against humanity; earlier, they had been categorized as "crimes against honor" and were therefore not considered for separate legal redress (Setz 2003, 141).

ated with it. Cheung's claim that "silence, too, can speak many tongues" (Cheung 1993, 1) is important in the context of Keller's novel as it frees the concept of self-expression and communicability from the strictly verbal domain and invites what Theresa Hak Kyung Cha calls "other recitations" (Cha 2001, 81).

The communicability of the political female body, however, comes with obstacles. Akiko's ability to speak about her past is limited by trauma and the complexity of verbal trauma recovery. Trauma is difficult to heal, not only because the traumatic experience cannot be undone, but also because the actual "trauma is not experienced at the time of its occurrence but later as a haunting presence" (Kilby 2002, 217). Since trauma does not occur in the here and now, it is difficult to understand it in general. Explaining that trauma constitutes a double wound, Cathy Caruth specifies:

> the wound of the mind—the breach in the mind's experience of time, self, and the world—is not, like the wound of the body, a simple and healable event [...] so trauma is not locatable in the simple violent or original event in an individual's past, but rather in the way that its very unassimilable nature [...] returns to haunt the survivor later on. (Caruth 1996, 4)

Comfort Woman addresses the problematic that trauma is not easily communicable; in fact it is often not graspable for the person who experiences it, much less for others. Keller elaborates on two major questions in the context of recovery from trauma: "How can we come to know trauma, and how can we know the other's trauma?" (Cowie 2000, 191). The novel's discourse displays this problematic. I agree with Jodi Kim's assertion that by "(re)inserting into our collective memory the complicated and haunting legacy of the Japanese conscription of Korean women as sexual slaves" and by "complicat[ing] the very revision she imagines by employing a narrative strategy in which the trauma ultimately escapes or refuses adequate representation or resolution," Keller's discourse challenges and subverts "modernity's masculinist colonial discourses" (J. Kim 1999, 62). I would argue, however, that this problematic of understanding trauma becomes further complicated because it is located within a mother–daughter relationship that hosts its own difficulties. Recovery from trauma and the mother–daughter dyad share certain similarities: both can not be entirely reconstructed, neither physically nor verbally. At the same time, both influence the interaction between mother and daughter, as their relationship oscillates between identification and alienation. This interconnectedness of the complicated mother–daughter relationship and the problematic of recovery from trauma make Keller's novel particularly interesting, especially if one were to read recovery from trauma in the context of transnational communication.

Hence, the many mutual misconceptions and misunderstandings typical of mother–daughter relationships make Akiko's communication of traumatic experiences to Beccah even more difficult. Akiko and Beccah face dissonances in their ethnic and gender consciousnesses that are typical of the conflict between first-generation immigrant mothers and their American-born daughters. Beccah considers her mother to be stuck in Korean culture and unable to integrate into American society. One of the reasons for their conflicts is that Beccah resents the notion of becoming her mother's legacy. Through disobedience and disrespect, Beccah seeks to distance herself from the image of womanhood that her mother conveys in relation to mainstream American culture. Even as Beccah and Akiko start a new life together in Hawai'i after the death of Beccah's father, they never truly bond. As Akiko's employer and manager Reno reproaches Beccah after Akiko's death: "You was her daughter, dah one come from her own body. But you nevah knew shit about her, did you?" (203). Reno's reproach alludes to the amniotic, prenatal relationship between mother and daughter. However, contrary to Reno's argument that sharing the same body guarantees an intimate bond between mother and daughter, Beccah can relate to her mother only with considerable difficulty. This difficulty in mustering compassion and empathy also becomes apparent in the lack of communication between Akiko and Beccah. Neither woman can relate to the other her life story. For instance, only after Akiko's death does Beccah learn about the origin of her mother's trauma and of her unorthodox behavior, such as the fits of melancholy and anger in which her trauma continues to manifest itself. Similarly, Akiko has trouble understanding Beccah's complex identity as a mixed-race child. Moreover, two women never talk about Beccah's sexual molestation by her father. Hence, just because the two women once shared the same body does not guarantee that they feel a strong sense of allegiance toward each other. In fact, maybe their confrontation of the complex psychological dynamics of the mother–daughter relationship makes this mutual identification even more unlikely.

Despite the lack of verbal communication between Beccah and Akiko, Keller constructs a permeable sense of union between the Korean-born mother and her American-born daughter. Interestingly, the one topic they are most reluctant to talk about—the sexual abuses they endured—eventually offers a basis of mutual identification. For instance, Beccah's own experience of sexual molestation by her father offers a possible basis of identification with Akiko's life. In this occurrence of a shared experience, the cultural difference between first- and second-generation immigrant women does not interfere. Therefore, as

Elaine Kim argues, Keller's novel does not operate with a nationalist Korean American discourse but inscribes into the mother–daughter relationship a female solidarity that reaches across cultural and national boundaries:

> I invoke *Comfort Woman* here for the ways it connects Korean and Korean American women by establishing the centrality and subjectivity of the raped Korean mother and the molested Korean American daughter. As lower-class females, the one a raped World War II military prostitute and the other a mixed race incest victim, they are both "illegitimate." The two women exist in excess of patriarchy, state nationalisms, and their cultures. Keller represents the raped and abused woman as someone who becomes the subject through rape rather than being merely subjected to its violation. (E. Kim 1999, 9)

While I refute Kim's suggestion that the women reach a sense of agency through rape (I would argue that they maintain their agency despite the experience of rape), this prospect for a feminist solidarity across cultural differences places the novel within a framework of transnational studies. Despite the obvious cultural differences between the Korean immigrant mother and her American-born mixed-race daughter, the novel evokes a transnational sense of community among Korean American and Korean women by emphasizing the common experience of sexual abuse and trauma.

Any discussion of body politics needs to address at one point or another the problem of essentialism in relation to the female body. In part, I wish to invoke here biophobic essentialism, as in discourses that seek to make plausible the validity of sexist gender norms by emphasizing the biological differences between women and men, thus nullifying the necessity of treating gender as performance.[48] Taking issue with orientalist misappropriations of Asian bodies

---

[48] In the specific context of motherhood and the mother–daughter relationship, the body is the essential union between mother and daughter: before birth, in their shared experiences of biology throughout their lives, and in the specific context of the daughter's anticipated role as mother and the mother's experience as daughter. The body has also been, and often continues to appear as, an indicator of racial difference and marker of ethnicity. Skin color, physiognomy, and, as far as the sexual body is concerned, penis size and alleged physiological anomalies of the vagina have been interpreted as indicators of racial difference and, related to the racial tensions that were contemporaneous to such studies, as "scientific proof" for the racialist and racist observations of the black man's tendency to sexual predation and the black woman's enhanced libido.

in Western culture in particular, Asian American writers and critics have been challenging, and most recently recognizing the subversive potential of, images in mainstream American culture that operate with a "stereotypical desexualization of Asian American men and hypersexualization of Asian American women" (Wong and Santa Ana 1999, 173). There is, as transnational feminist theory points out, a persistent interest in Western feminism in issues of sexual oppression of third world women. Amal Amireh and Lisa Suhair Majaj, for instance, assert in *Going Global: The Reception of Third World Women Writers* (2000), that "[w]hereas First World feminists have tended to focus on sexual oppression and on the cultural dimensions of 'patriarchy,' Third World feminists often seek to address political and economic oppression" (Amireh and Majaj 2000, 8). This emphasis on third world women's different experience of sexuality works along the rhetoric of singling out the generic opposition between Western women and third world women, a practice that often implies hierarchical structures in the level of emancipation in which Western women came across as more liberated than non-Western women. Mohanty's observation of a promotion of one-dimensional images of third world women in Western feminist discourses summarizes well this tendency to promote Western exceptionalism: "Universal images of the Third World woman (the veiled woman, chaste virgin, etc.), images constructed from adding the 'Third World difference' to 'sexual difference,' are predicated upon (and hence obviously bring into sharper focus) assumptions about Western women as secular, liberated, and having control over their own lives" (Mohanty 2003, 42).[49] In the specific context of sexual oppression, this notion of the oppressed "other" women paints a picture of Western women as having control over their bodies.

Still, *Comfort Woman* is not so much about correcting one-dimensional representations of Asian women's bodies as it is about universal issues of sexual domination of the female body. Keller characterizes the female body, and most specifically the abuse of the female body, through issues of feminist consciousness that are non-culture-specific. Rape and other forms of sexual abuse are prevalent issues in many contemporary societies, no matter what the cultural background of the individual occurrences of these forms of sexism and sexual domination. On the contrary, as George Hicks argues, the violation of women's rights is a cross-cultural matter (Hicks 167). If anything, as Hicks emphasizes, the West has been complicit in the various institutionalizations of sex workers that cater specifically to the military. Such is the subject of Kel-

---

[49] Lata Mani's work (1989) on the transnational reception of *sati*, widow-burning in India, has generated discussions about the multiple cultural paradigms that feminist theory and practice need to acknowledge when discussing cultural difference and cultural practice.

ler's second novel, *Fox Girl* (2002), which is set in part an American military town in Korea and in part in a tourist town in Hawai'i. In both places, the commodification of the female body for sexual exploitation on the one hand and sex work as a vehicle of upward social mobility on the other hand emphasizes the global power structures that underly sexual labor. It is in the context of such global power structres that the representation of the female body as sexual enterprise gains further relevance.[50]

The subversive use of the female body is a powerful leitmotif that unites not only the individual narratives but also the feminist agendas of Akiko and Beccah. This subversive language of the body becomes the medium for the matrilineal heritage that connects Korean comfort women with Akiko's and Beccah's experiences as Korean American women. For instance, muted by the imposed silence in the Japanese military camps, the comfort women use body language as alternative means of communication. Akiko remembers: "But we were clever and creative. [...] We taught ourselves to communicate through eye movements, body posture, tilts of the head, or—when we could not see each other—through rhythmic rustles between our stalls; in this way we could *speak*, in this way we kept our sanity" (16, emphasis added). The same bodies that are being objectified as sexual commodities thus regain and manifest subjectivity through the use of body language as subversive means of articulation not only of pain, but also of resistance and survival. In other words, Akiko understands that the body can be an alternative means of communication, one that enables the women to maintain a sense of solidarity with one another and to "tell" one another that they were still alive. This language of the body is thus a form of communication that enabled the women to communicate sessential information and interhuman bonds.

Akiko also uses this "language of the body" with her newborn daughter, the same touches and gestures with which she communicated her love to her mother on the mother's deathbed: "I touch my child in the same way now; this is the language she understands. [...] This, not the senseless murmuring of useless words, is what quiets her, tells her she is precious" (18). Akiko's reliance on a language of the body, however, "isn't meant simply to overcome the language barrier between the two" (Chen 125). On the contrary, this touch between mother and daughter echoes the same alternative communication that Akiko learned in the military camp. Thus, by reenacting her relationship to her own mother, Akiko's touch invokes the collective Korean American heritage that informs their matrilineage.

---

[50] See, for instance, my essay entitled "Hooked on the American Dream?" for a detailed discussion of this issue.

Speaking the Body, Hearing the Body

While matrilineage, as Keller's novel exemplifies by the two cases of deliberate betrayal Akiko experiences (first her sister sells her to the Japanese military in order to secure her own dowry, and later, the woman who is taking care of her after she escapes the camp figuratively sells her to Akiko's abusive soon-to-be husband), while certainly not always automatically benevolent, it is nonetheless a driving force in the relationship between mother and daughter. It certainly plays a vital role in Akiko's attempts to reconnect Beccah with Korea, and by extension, with herself. Her frantic search for the lost umbilical cord when Beccah was a newborn (97) and her ritual of feeding her daughter tiny portions of dirt from the garden in order to help her get rooted (221) are reminiscent of the acute interrelatedness of the body and the land that Induk protests while being raped. All of these forms of communication promote a language of the body that is reminiscent of the subversive body language Akiko acquired in the camps. To the same extent that this language of the body offered hope and consolation to the women who were forced to work in the camps, this language is also designed to ensure the bond of love between Akiko and Beccah. Performing her ritualistic language of the body on her little daughter, Akiko marvels: "And each night, I touch each part of her body, waiting until I see recognition in her eyes. I wait until I see that she knows that all of what I touch is hers and hers to name in her own mind, before language dissects her into pieces that can be swallowed and digested by others not herself" (22). This ritualistic language of the body, rather than speech, is Akiko's chosen means of communication; she characterizes it as "language I know is true" (21).

It is this language of the body, then, that Beccah adopts in her reconciliation with her mother in the final passage of the novel. Beccah's touch is reminiscent of the nonverbal communication that Akiko uses to initiate her daughter into their collective matrilineage. When Beccah says, "Your body is mine" (212), while her mother's ashes are coating her body, she places herself within an existing matrilineage that celebrates the female body as a subversive means of communication. Despite Keller's emphasis on the physical interaction between the mother's and the daughter's bodies, their relationship is not one that echoes the prenatal amniotic bliss between mother and unborn child. Instead, the physical reunion signifies the healing of Akiko's sexually abused body, and through the use of the body as subversive means of communication, also its triumph over the silencing by the abusers. The same applies to Beccah's reunion with her mother at the end of the novel. Beccah's symbolic adaptation of bodily communication celebrates Akiko's clever rebellion against sexism and imperialism.

Beccah finds out after her mother's death about Akiko's true past. Akiko left a tape, which, as Beccah muses, was primarily an offering to Akiko's mother rather than to Beccah, despite the fact that the recording is in English. On this recording, Akiko narrates the atrocities she endured during the two years in the military camp. Overwhelmed by the impact of her mother's narrative, Beccah is unable to process the information: "I could not view my mother, whom I had always seen as weak and vulnerable, as one of the 'comfort women' she described. Even though I heard her call out 'Akiko,' the name she had answered to all her life, I could not imagine her surviving what she described, for I cannot imagine myself surviving" (194).

Still the heritage Beccah enacts is never told face to face, never spoken, as it were, only communicated through the body and the performance of the ritual of the dead body. The ubiquitous corporeal imagery throughout the novel bridges the individual narratives and thus reunites mother and daughter symbolically. The interplay of death and survival unites Akiko's and Beccah's stories and provides variations on the theme of reproduction and lineage. Akiko, for instance, defines Induk's death as the moment of her own death: "The corpse the soldiers brought back from the woods wasn't Induk. It was Akiko 41; it was me" (21). In this rendition Akiko alludes to the fact that the female bodies in the recreation camps were interchangeable. What is important, though, is that she also refers to the common fate of Korean women not only under Japanese colonialism but under Korean patriarchy as well. In the same chapter, Akiko revisits her death from a similar vantage point. In the opening lines of the chapter, Akiko places her death at an early point in her life, beginning with her first experience as a sexual slave: "I was twelve when I was murdered, fourteen when I looked into the Yalu River and, finding no face looking back at me, knew that I was dead" (15). She also locates her fate at the center of misogynist Korean society, again with death as leitmotif: "I am trying to remember exactly when I died. It must have been in stages, beginning with my birth as the fourth girl and the last child in the Kim family, and ending in the recreation camps north of the Yalu" (17).

Death and rebirth are also sequential links between the individual stories. A large section of the novel consists of sequences where one chapter ends with a person's death and the following chapter begins with a birth. For instance, the first chapter, told by Beccah, ends with the news of her mother's death, and the subsequent chapter, told by Akiko, starts with Beccah's birth. Akiko remembers the arrival of Beccah after a series of miscarriages: "The baby I could keep came when I was already dead" (15). This sequential recurrence of alternating renditions of death and birth constructs a permeable matrilineal discourse. As do the ghost story of Induk's continuous presence in Akiko's and Beccah's lives (J. Kim 1999), Akiko's shamanism (Chiu 2003), and a strong mirroring of the geographical and geopolitical landscape complementary to Akiko's and Beccah's identity formations, this appropriation of the death/birth theme at the center of the novel's discursive strategy is indicative of the need for alternative means of articulating rape and trauma on the one hand, and unwritten history and matrilineage on the other.

Not only does it illustrate the cultural differences between first- and second-generation immigrant socialization in the U.S., the birth/death leitmotif also serves as a metaphor for the act of storytelling. Like her mother, Beccah, too, needs to find other means of expressing and recording her difficult relationship with her mother, her relationship to her Korean ancestry, and her life as an ethnic minority in the United States. Beccah does so by adopting the metaphorical use of death and rebirth that characterizes Akiko's narratives. After Akiko's death, Beccah finds a tape recording her mother made with instructions for a traditional Korean burial. With Akiko's chants in the background, Beccah explores a box of her mother's memorabilia that opens up new possibilities for her understanding of her mother. With the chant of the dead in the background, Beccah discovers a document issued by the American Embassy in Seoul that, for the first time in the novel, reclaims Akiko's real name: "Dear Mrs. Akiko (Kim Soon Hyo) Bradley" (173). This letter, although it announces the possible death of Beccah's aunts in Korea, is also a rebirth for Akiko's name and identity before she was forced into sexual slavery. In the chapter that follows this rebirth, Akiko assumes her narrative agency for the first time under her Korean name Soon Hyo. At the end of that chapter, Soon Hyo prepares the box of memorabilia that later becomes the urn for her cremated body. In this box, she puts the dried stump of the umbilical cord that once united her with her daughter, while claiming their Korean names: Soon Hyo and Bek-hap. With Akiko's claiming of her daughter's name, Beccah also experiences a kind of rebirth: she is no longer the name her Anglo-American Christian father gave her—a name her mother can only pronounce as "Rohbeccu" (116)—but she becomes the name her mother intended her to be: "Bekhap, the lily, purest white. Blooming in the boundary between Korea and America, between life and death, this child, with the tendril of her body, keeps me from crossing over and roots me to this earth" (166-67). Although Beccah never assumes the Korean name her mother gave her—her narratives never display the name Bek-hap as chapter titles—she assumes the role her mother interprets into the symbolic meaning of her name.

All these reminiscences of Akiko's construction and maintenance of a narrative discourse that echoes her adaptation of a subversive means of communication reverberate in the final scene of the novel in which Beccah claims her mother's body. Like her mother, Beccah uses her body to communicate her matrilineage. She thus connects her personal discourse to her mother's use of "other recitations" of matrilineage in general and of female survival of sexual oppression in particular. In one of Beccah's first narratives, she describes how difficult it is for her, a journalist for a Honolulu newspaper, to write her mother's obituary. Although she usually uses a simple, formulaic format, "Name, age, date of death, survivors, services" (26), it becomes impossible for her to write her mother's obituary: "I did not have the facts for even the most basic, skeletal obituary. And I found I did not know how to start imagining her life" (26). Later accounts of Beccah's tormented relationship with her mother make clear the reasons for her inability to put her mother's life and death into words. The persistent obscurity about Akiko's life in Korea, her frequent retreats into a trance, her exorcism of ghosts in order to protect herself and her daughter, all these aspects of Akiko's behavior terrify Beccah during her childhood and alienate her from her mother's "exotic" customs and behavior. When Akiko tries to introduce Beccah to the presence of Induk's spirit, Saja the Death Messenger, Princess Pari, or the Heavenly Toad, Beccah either becomes frightened or dismisses her mother's concerns entirely: in both cases, however, Beccah seeks comfort in mainstream American culture, which offers her logical explanations for all the supernatural phenomena her mother conjures up and where she can find reassurance in the "normalcy" of her American childhood, such as school outings and afternoon play dates. The fact that her mother's life was incomprehensible to her makes it difficult for Beccah to commemorate her mother's death with words. In contrast to this inability to speak her mother's death, Beccah is able to *speak* her mother's body. Instead of composing one of her formulaic obituaries such as those that appear in a standardized format in mainstream American newspapers, she performs a matrilineal ritual of claiming the mother's body and its history, and, by so doing, makes Akiko immortal.

This, however, is a very abstract notion of expressing grief, since Beccah celebrates her mother's death and rebirth at once. As the leitmotif of sequential deaths and rebirths throughout the novel suggests, Beccah's embodiment of her mother's legacy keeps alive Akiko's body and the political implications her body bears. This moment emphasizes Beccah's *double agency*, which, in Tina Chen's definition, foregrounds the constructed nature of Asian American identity while "attending the complex negotiations between always already articulated roles and emerging paradigms of performance encourages a consideration of how such roles both limit and make possible the emergence of self-reflexive strategies of enactment" (Chen 5). Focusing on these strategies of enactment, as Chen continues, facilitates a better understanding of the performance and impersonation of Asian American identity (7). In the specific case of Beccah's performance and enactment of her Korean heritage, Keller's novel thus connects the seemingly exotic rituals and practices Akiko performed with Beccah's commemorative ritual while she listened to the tape her mother recorded with the instructions for a traditional funeral. And while Beccah resented her mother's performance as shamanistic, she now performs the same ritual, thereby claiming her connection to her mother's agency.

This claiming of the mother's body at the end of Keller's novel is a reproduction on the level of women's rights and the political struggle of imposed concepts of female gender rather than an expression of the physical reproduction from mother to daughter. Beccah's claiming of her mother's body needs to reach beyond the boundaries of culture and ethnicity. For instance, Beccah's celebration and commemoration of her mother's death cannot be put into the language of newspaper obituaries; and because Beccah does not speak Korean, she cannot lament her mother's death with the chants Akiko recorded on the tape. Instead, Beccah uses the language of her body as an alternative discourse for both the American and the traditional Korean verbal commemoration of death she is barely able to perform. Beccah's handling of her dead mother's body, the body that has been raped by Japanese soldiers, American doctors, and Akiko's husband, is emblematic of Beccah's coping with patriarchal institutions in her own life: it echoes her own suffering inflicted by an abusive father; it also foreshadows her emancipation from conventional role models that prescribe what a woman ought to have or do. By claiming her mother's body, Beccah also claims the communicability of the body in the same ways that Akiko and Induk have used their bodies in order to break imposed silences, thereby adopting a discourse that transgresses Eurocentric models of a speech/silence binary. Moreover, not the maternal image of the body and prelinguistic interaction between mother and daughter, but the body as legacy of the inscriptions of patriarchy and colonialism are at the core of matrilineality in Keller's novel. In contrast to Kristeva's characterization of Chinese women through the appropriation of the pre-Oedipal, pre-linguistic relationship, Keller inscribes into the mother–daughter relationship aspects of corporeality which articulate women's struggles for survival and agency.

The novel's discourse makes particularly apparent this complex interrelation of trauma and the mother–daughter relationship. Keller's novel is different from other novels that operate with polyvocal narrations and whose dialogicity remains merely invoked and is never fully constructed, but rather relies on the reader's willingness "to explore the dialogic potential between the monologues" (Souris 1994, 103). In fact, the novel also treats Beccah's experience of sexual abuse by her father as rather unspeakable in the sense that Keller does not write it out openly. She depicts Beccah's experience through the frame of a recurring nightmare: "But when he rolled me into the sweater, binding my arms behind me, my father opened his eyes not on the demons but in me. And the blue light from his eyes grew so bright it burned me, each night, into nothingness" (2). The intertextuality of the sets of first-person narratives, however, amplifies the hidden message of Beccah's own experience of sexual abuse and thus connects her to the experiences of the comfort women.

The mother's and the daughter's narratives are thematically and discursively interconnected. Both offer countercultural manifestations of personal and political liberation from a Korean and a Korean American perspective. The novel's discourse of interlocked narratives emerges out of two necessities: the need for communication between mother and daughter in order to secure their collective matrilineality, and the need to cope with trauma and to articulate internalized pain and suffering in order to counter imposed silences that initially made the traumatic experience so unforgettable. While many Asian American mother–daughter narratives that explore the sense of alienation between the first-generation immigrant mother and her American-born daughter favor the daughter's perspective and give priority to the daughter's narrative agency (Grice 2002, 37), this is not the case with Keller's novel. As becomes evident from the title *Comfort Woman*, a euphemism for women who were sold into forced prostitution to "comfort" Japanese soldiers, Akiko's experience of sexual slavery in Japanese internment camps in Korea is at the center of the novel.

There is a similar interdependency that also determines Beccah's identification with Korean women in general. While her encounter with Korean traditions alienates her from her mother, her awareness of political crimes against women's bodies in the military camps provides a meeting ground for her collective gender consciousness. Because rape and trauma are universal forms of oppression regardless of a woman's sexual orientation, ethnicity, nation, religion, class, or age, women's protest against rape and other violations serves as a bridge that unites feminist struggles beyond the difference rhetoric of mainstream U.S. feminist theory and practice. Although it seems at first that Akiko's rape is much more sensationalized than Beccah's, Akiko also retains ownership of her body in her use of her body as a means of communication with her fellow camp inmates and later with her own daughter. In addition, her body performs rituals of Korean shamanism that, as Reno indicates, are a clever strategy to earn money. Akiko is thus not only a victim: she is a clever, subversive, and independent woman who survived times of struggle, both in Korea and in the U.S.

However, there is a difference in representation between Akiko's and Beccah's traumatic experiences. This difference is closely linked to their experiences of Korean culture and is thus emblematic of the cultural-political locations from which they speak. In fact, all three women, Induk, Akiko, and Beccah, represent different vantage points and appropriate Korean national identities differently. Their need to speak emerges from specific culture-political contexts: Induk's screaming and shouting is an act of nationalistic emancipation. Her voice, as the novel's convergence of Induk's and Korea's experienced penetration exemplifies, is the voice of an invaded and colonized country. Akiko's voice also displays some of this nationalistic character, but it incorporates the experience of immigration and diaspora as well. Akiko's need to speak is located in her longing for the diasporic home country before it was dominated by Japanese colonialism, especially given the sexual submission and cultural marginalization she has seen in the United States. Finally, Beccah's voice is mostly removed from the nationalistic and diasporic discourse of Induk's and Akiko's verbal agencies. Instead, her location in the United States stands for a transnational perspective on Induk's and Akiko's discourses of nationalism and diaspora.

In essence, Keller's novel connects to the idea that the comfort woman debate cannot be successfully addressed in a context that does not acknowledge the transnational character of the comfort women issue both during World War II and in contemporary attempts to find public closure and in the context of the global sex trade in general. As Pamela Thoma argues in her discussion of the "Comfort Women of World War II" Conference, the transnational character of contemporary Asian American feminist practices holds "significant messages about alternative communities" (Thoma 32). The emphasis in ongoing debates about the comfort women issue, as Lisa Yoneyama's essay articulates so astutely, is on the liberation of the movement for redress from strictly nationalistic contexts at the same time as it propels the notion of collaborative feminist practices crucial in the shaping of the world-system of postmodernity. The question of empathy and identification between mother and daughter, as well as the general discussion of Korean, American, and Korean American identity politics in Keller's novel, is in line with Thoma's assessment that the comfort women issue pertains equally to Asian American studies and to transnational studies. This interconnectedness between Asian American cultural production and transnational identity-reception offers the possibility for a both/and approach that locates Asian American studies and transnational studies within each other's realms.

In that it portrays a compassionate identification with and passionate agency for the rights of sexually abused women, Keller's construction of a basis for mutual understanding and identification is emblematic of a transnational feminist heuristic that is "looking for points of contact and connection as well as disjunctures" (Mohanty 2003, 243) among women globally. As Kandice Chuh points out, "Keller's novel arguably calls for an interpellation of individual readers into subjects who identify with 'comfort women' as a designation of a tradition of women who resist patriarchal oppression" (Chuh 2003, 19-20). In this sense, *Comfort Woman* thus suggests that transnational feminist solidarity is possible, even necessary, and that this solidarity is not only beneficial to all women, but that it is also the most effective strategy for deconstructing patriarchal domination.

By depicting issues that are linked at the same time to Korean nationalism and Asian American cultural production, Keller's novel "mak[es] impossible teleological narratives of identity formation" (Chuh 2003, 14). On the level of Keller's literary agency, this interconnectedness of Asian American and transnational studies takes on yet another interesting perspective. If one were to consider Keller's choice of depicting such a highly political and controversial topic, one cannot help but note the different levels of agency her book utilizes. What is particularly interesting in the context of the comfort women debate is that Keller is part of this transnational agency because she assumes "historical responsibility" for the unwritten history of Korean comfort women and puts the unspeakable into words" (Koo 132). Yet despite the obvious link between the systematic rape of Korean women and the military invasion of Korea, Keller's novel is not a nationalistic protest novel that seeks solely to restore the identities of the anonymous rape victims. In *Comfort Woman*, a woman's ability or inability to speak about rape and trauma is strictly nonessential. In other words, Keller's novel is not only about Korea. It is about the oppression of the female body in general. By adding the daughter's Americanized perspective to Akiko's narratives, the novel speaks from complementary perspectives that both promote women's personal voices and unite them symbolically for the purpose of reaching a common goal.

CHAPTER SIX

Translation and Agency in Amy Tan's *The Bonesetter's Daughter*

Like her previous three novels, Amy Tan's forth novel *The Bonesetter's Daughter* (2001) depicts a seemingly unbridgeable gap that divides the Chinese American daughter from her matrilineal heritage. In her portrayal of the lack of communication between a daughter and her Chinese immigrant mother – a scenario she also depicts in *The Joy Luck Club* (1989) and *The Kitchen God's Wife* (1991), and to a similar degree in the encounter between the Chinese American woman and her Chinese half-sister in *The Hundred Secret Senses* (1995) – Tan focuses on language barriers within the immigrant family that mark the experience of the first generation as distinctly different from the experience of the American-born second generation. In *The Bonesetter's Daughter*, this difference becomes most apparent in the mother's limited command of English and her daughter's unfamiliarity with the Chinese language. While the inability to speak Chinese is not central to Ruth's identity as a Chinese American woman, it is the main point of contention in her relationship with her mother. Most specifically, the absence of a common language that mother and daughter share is emblematic of the cultural difference between the two. But more importantly, the inability to read Chinese renders Ruth unable to read her mother's life story. Therefore it becomes especially difficult for Ruth, the daughter, to relate to and preserve the matrilineal heritage that her mother LuLing recorded in an autobiographical narrative written in Chinese. Given her mother's progressing Alzheimer Disease, this written legacy, intended to communicate to her daughter the details about herself personal and collective past, is the only means by which the daughter can find out about her collective past. By addressing through the mother-daughter conflict the process of literary translation and the reception of "foreign" texts, Tan's novel raises important issues about the dynamics of the cross-cultural translation and their resonance within the complicated mother-daughter relationship. While the depiction of the daughter's who discursively "other" their mothers is a common phenomenon throughout Asian American literature, Tan's gesture of framing the mother-daughter relationship by issues pertaining to cross-cultural translation adds a fairly unexplored perspective to Asian American literature.

Translation is a concept that many immigrant writers use to denote the states of transition between immigration and acculturation. The term 'lost in translation' which Eva Hoffman uses to describe her transition from Poland to the U.S. applies especially well to the distorted relationship that overshadows the mother-daughter dyad Tan depicts in *The Bonesetter's Daughter*. In Tan's novel, the mother's dementia and the daughter's chronic laryngitis further complicate the cross-generational and cross-cultural communication between mother and daughter. In this chapter I read Tan's novel as exemplary treatment of the problem that pertains to cross-cultural translation of non-English texts by Asian authors and their difficult transference into a Western, English-speaking readership, especially as far as issues concerning their gender and ethnic identity are concerned. By focusing on the daughter's ineptitude in translating the mother's manuscript from Chinese into English, Tan's novel addresses the problematic of cultural transference in the transnational context that is characteristic of the relationship between first-generation and second-generation immigrants. I argue in this chapter that the daughter's need to work with the text in order to be able to participate in the matrilineal tradition she inherits (in the form of the manuscript her mother wrote for her) and her attempt to reconstruct the mother's narrative are indicative of the cultural alienation from the culture in their "home" country that second-generation immigrants encounter. While translation figures as a symbolic act of cross-cultural communication in general (Simon 134), Tan's novel epitomizes the complex dynamics of a transnational mother-daughter relationship between a Chinese immigrant mother and her American-born daughter by exploring the act of translation both in its literal sense of transliteration as well as in its figurative sense of transference. With the example of the "*un*translatability"[51] of the mother's life story and the daughter's reliance on a first-generation immigrant, male mediator, Tan's novel challenges the idea of an undistorted matrilineage between mothers and daughters and thus invites a renegotiation of prevalent classifications of ethnic American literature that depict mother-daughter relationships. As far as the daughter's need or ability to recover the maternal voice within her own discourse is concerned, *The Bonesetter's Daughter* characterizes the use of language and cross-cultural communication between mother-daughter as significantly different from other Asian American texts: in Maxine Hong Kingston's *The Woman Warrior* and Tan's first novel *The Joy Luck Club*, the mother-daughter conflict is either about the ambivalence between self and other or

[51] See Spivak's use of this term in "The Politics of Translation," 195.

about the dialogic interconnectedness between the mothers' and the daughters' sets of stories. And unlike Nora Okja Keller's *Comfort Woman*, where the mother-daughter relationship is complicated by the silence that overshadows it, *The Bonesetter's Daughter* depicts mother-daughter relationship in which the communication between mother and daughter does not work because of language boundaries: mother and daughter *do* speak to each other but the daughter does not fully understand the mother because they do not have a language in common in which they are both equally fluent.

"The Days of No Talk"

At the center of the relationship between Ruth and her mother LuLing is a linguistic power struggle over. The first hint of a power struggle between mother LuLing and her daughter Ruth in Tan's *The Bonesetter's Daughter* are Ruth's "days of no talk" (10). The days of no talk are connected to a tragic incident when six-year-old Ruth throws herself down a slide, "head first, arms straight out," despite her mother's warnings (77). Seriously injured after her foolhardiness, Ruth silently feeds on her mother's worries about her health. She refuses to speak, despite being tampered and spoiled during the time of her convalescence. By remaining silent, Ruth achieves to get the attention she wants from her mother, a single parent with numerous jobs: "It was comforting to be a baby again, well loved, blameless" (80). As the above quotation illustrates, her refusal to speak, however, is not a sign of her pain and trauma, but rather signifies a subversive strategy through which she manipulates her mother. In particular, her inability to speak allows her to be a child again instead of assuming responsibilities, such as phone calls to banks and stores, which her mother cannot tackle with her limited command of English,. Thus, long after her physical convalescence, Ruth prefers to remain mute, "afraid all the good things that were happening might disappear" (80). Yet upon her daughter's schoolteacher's advice, LuLing makes Ruth talk again, not in the conventional sense, but by teaching her to use a chopstick with which to scribble letters into a tea tray filled with sand. With this new means of communication, Ruth experiences incredible "power with words" (85). Because the tea tray marks her as 'special,' she becomes a fortuneteller for her curious schoolmates. But more importantly, Ruth derives a sense of authority from the fact that her mother, who encourages her to practice with the chopsticks, "was asking her opinion on all kinds of matters" (84).

The use of the tea tray makes Ruth equally powerful vis-à-vis her mother as her perfect command of English did before the accident. While Ruth initially resists the idea of writing words into sand, she soon appreciates the power she thereby exudes. Since her mother now always agrees to the things she scratches into the sand, Ruth scribbles the word "doggie," thinking her mother might eventually buy her the pet dog Ruth has always wanted. Unknowingly, Ruth had scribbled the nickname LuLing got from her nursemaid in China. Therefore, LuLing believes that her daughter is a medium for her long-passed nursemaid Precious Auntie with whom she never reconciled after an emotional dispute. By using Ruth as a medium, LuLing continuously asks Precious Auntie for forgiveness and for guidance in her present life, a fact that leads Ruth to believe that her mother is haunted by her past. Frightened by her mother's reliance on this ghost she addresses by using Ruth as her medium, Ruth, once out of her wits, randomly scribbles meaningless characters into the sand, not knowing that she actually produces a Chinese character. LuLing takes this as a sign for a true miracle, thinking that Precious Auntie guides the hand of her daughter, who does not speak, much less write, Chinese. When Ruth, to set an end to all this, eventually starts speaking again, LuLing believes that yet another miracle manifests itself before here eyes and that Precious Auntie cured Ruth. This childhood trauma inflicted onto Ruth by her accident and her encounter with her mother's communication with her aunt's ghost reappears annually in the form of chronic laryngitis, her days of no talk, which Ruth has begun to cultivate as meditative time of introspection. The novel depicts this incident by offering a flashback into Ruth's childhood in order to explain where her ritual of retrieving annually into a stage of silence stems from.

Translating for the (M)Other

During her "days on no talk" (10) in the novel's present setting, Ruth discovers a manuscript in her writing desk drawer, the manuscript her mother wrote in Chinese and asked Ruth to translate into English. This is how the topic of translation is being introduced in the novel. At the same time, the discovery of the manuscript is the starting point for Ruth's flashbacks of childhood experiences with her mother. These experiences all revolve around the issue of translation. Similar to the task of translating her mother's manuscript that was hidden in her writing desk, her entire childhood is marked by her role as her mother's translator, the one who explains to her mother how public life in American society works.

The reader learns this through another flashback into the times before Ruth's accident on the playground. One issue of her past that resonates into the present relationship between Ruth and her mother is her LuLing's insufficient command of English. Every time her mother calls her name, this issue comes up: "'Lootie! Lootie!" Why had her mother chosen a name with sounds she couldn't pronounce?" (50). Ruth hates LuLing's difficulty with the English language, so much so that she tells her classmates that LuLing "is not [her] mother" (77). Ruth does not want to be identified with her mother's linguistic inaptitude. In line with Bakhtin's definition of language as "borderline between self and other" (282), Ruth's dissimilation from her mother's language is emblematic of her "ideological becoming of a human being is the process of selectively assimilating the words of others" (Bakhtin 341). This desire to distance herself from her mother persists into Ruth's adult life. And while she admits that she is starting to look more and more like her mother, "she wasn't like her mother in other respects, thank God" (17). Ruth remembers:

> LuLing got into fights mainly because of her poor English. She didn't understand others, or they didn't understand her. Ruth used to feel she was the one who suffered because of that. The irony was, her mother was actually *proud* she had taught herself English, the choppy talk she had acquired in China and Hong Kong. And since immigration to the Unites States fifty years before, she had not improved either her pronunciation or her vocabulary. Yet her sister, GaoLing, had come to the States around the same time, and her English was nearly perfect. She could talk about the difference between crinoline and organza, name the specific trees she likes: oak, maple, gingko, pine. To LuLing, cloth was classified as 'cost too much,' 'too slippery,' 'scratchy skin,' and 'last long time.' And there were only two kinds of trees: 'shady' and 'drop leaf all the time.' (49, original emphasis)

Ruth identifies her mother's fragmented English as ethnic marker that casts LuLing as eternal foreigner in the U.S. and places her at the margins of American society. Thus, Ruth's rejection of her mother is based on her disrespect for the peculiarities that determine LuLing's status as minority woman.

Voice, and agency, as my discussion of Nora Okja Keller's novel in the previous chapter suggests, are important issues within Asian American communities. In *Boundaries of the Self: Gender, Culture, Fiction* (1987), Roberta Rubenstein proposes that "[I]f women are typically muted within their own cultures even when they constitute a demographic majority, then women of ethnic minority groups are doubly muted. Both gender and ethnic status render them 'speechless' in patriarchy" (8). In *The Bonesetter's Daughter*, Rubenstein's observation in part also applies to LuLing's difficulty maintaining a voice in American culture. It is interesting to note that while LuLing already encounters a doubly-muted position within American patriarchy, her daughter Ruth contributes to this muting by engaging in a linguistic power struggle with her mother. Throughout the novel, their use of different languages is emblematic of the different cultural affiliations they attribute to themselves and each other. In the context of Ruth's search for individuality and her attempted disconnectedness from her mother, the linguistic barriers of their mother-daughter relationship symbolize such emotional distinction. The fact that Ruth speaks English impeccably and her mother does not culminates in a linguistic power struggle between mother and daughter. In public life, where English is the language of the dominant culture, LuLing is dependent upon her daughter's translations. Although Ruth resents serving as her mother's "mouthpiece" (50), she exercises at the same time a certain power over her mother when she is correcting LuLing's pronunciation or grammar. Similarly, Ruth resents learning to speak and write in Chinese, in fact, she perceives it as "punishment" for correcting her mother's spelling on banners and sales signs she writes for numerous stores (57). Since LuLing's competence of Chinese diminishes the feeling of superiority that Ruth acquires from criticizing her mother's bad English, she does not allow her mother to teach her Chinese calligraphy, her mother's mastery.

Through this power struggle, Tan's novel depicts differences between the mother's and the daughter's socialization into American culture. This issue of power and priviledge is also reflected in the different gender consciousness between first- and second-generation immigrant women. Both issues combined are reflected in the novel's treatment of the question of cultural authenticity, most forcefully in the general assumption that language defines cultural belonging. For instance, Ruth assumes that her mother does not fully belong to American culture because of her immigrant English. Although Ruth knows, from her experience as a ghost writer, that eloquence can also be trained and that different text demand different jargons and registers, she does not accept her mother's form of English as a language variety but considers her mother's English one of the main aspects that she would like to diassociate from. By pitting Ruth's and LuLing's voices against each other, Tan's novel, consciously or unconsciously, points out the limitations of identitiy politics that emphasize monolingualism. The need for more pluralistic, heterogeneous and counter-hegemonic definitions of identity, a need that is implied in the emergence of different cultural voices in the novel, also evokes tensions that are prevalent within U.S. feminist theory and practice. One of such tensions pertains to the classification of American literatures along a distinction between mainstream and minority discourses and authors respectively. These questions appear throughout Tan's novel and thus make relevant critical conversations about cross-cultural translation in a transnational context. But not only is *The Bonesetter's Daughter* a forceful example of Tan's interest in depicting language and writing as plot elements, the novel also implies that the processes of writing and translating are akin to the identity negotiations that occur in mother-daughter conflicts. That such negotiations are never devoid of power becomes evident from the linguistic power struggles that Ruth leads against her mother. Thus argues Nancy Willard when she observes in her review of Tan's novel that "The characters Tan cares about the most are those who use the power of writing to preserve the past and the art of translation to revise it." In other words, by emphasizing the role of writing as a medium of identitiy formation, Tan creates a hierarchy among her protagonists.

Translation Studies

The linguistic power struggle between Ruth and LuLing privileges the translator's responsibility toward the text and agency in the relationship between translator and translated. This is a common topic in translation studies at large. In *Rethinking Translation: Discourse, Subjectivity, Ideology* (1992), Lawrence Venuti critiques prevalent assumptions about translation as an "invisible practice" (1) and calls for a "rethinking of translation that is philosophical, but also political, engaged in questions of language, discourse, and subjectivity, while articulating their relations to cultural difference, ideological contradiction, and social conflict" (6). In his discussion of the discourse, subjectivity and ideology of translation both as a critical practice and as an academic field, Venuti refers to and cites extensively poststructuralist critics such as Walter Benjamin, Paul de Man, Jacques Derrida and the work of Gilles Deleuze and Felix Guattari, whose scholarship repositions translation as well as literary production in general. Following Benjamin's investigation of the responsibility and agency of the translator, as discussed in his essay "The Task of the Translator" (1923), Venuti acknowledges the creative process that shapes a translation, grounds it in its socio-cultural and ideological context, and thus elevates translation from a practice of mere transmission of content and meaning to one of literary creation. In essence, Venuti's contribution to translation studies lies in the critical analysis of the dynamics that shape translation: the reconsideration of translation beyond "the binary opposition between 'original' and 'translation'" (6) on the one hand, and through his juxtaposition of translation and literary creation on the other hand.

Much in line with Venuti's appeal for a poststructuralist approach to translation, Sherry Simon's study, *Gender in Translation: Cultural Identity and the Politics of Transmission* (1996), pinpoints the gendered position that the practice of translation has maintained throughout history. Simon's study does two things. On the one hand, Simon illustrates the gendered aspect of translation by referring to the networking possibilities that translation offered women in the early feminist movements in the U.S. as well as across Europe by offering women the possibility to engage in social movements and to giving them access to the pen in general (2). On the other hand, her study delineates the affinities between translation theory and feminist theory, such as by defining "translation as a process of mediation that does not stand above ideology but works through it" (8). Simon comes to the following conclusion:

> Both feminism and translation are concerned by the way "secondariness" comes to be defined and canoncized; both are tools for a critical understanding of difference as it is represented in language. The most compelling questions for both fields remain: how are social, sexual and historical differences expressed in language and how can these differences be transferred across languages? What kinds of fidelities are expected of women and translators - in relation to the more powerful terms of their respective hierarchies? (8)

Similarly, scholars in translations studies have been increasingly devoting attention to the role of the translator in the context of globalization, hybridity, and postmodernism. Studies such as Susan Bassnett and Harish Trivedi's *Post-Colonial Translation: Theory and Practice* (1999), emphasize the complexity of translation in the transference, through the act of translation, and in the production of literary texts. Their scholarship, much in line with the interventions of Homi K. Bhabha and Gayatri Chakravorty Spivak in postcolonial studies and their reverberations into the field of literary criticism, contribute to what Bo Pettersson has called the "postcolonial turn in literary translation studies" in an essay of the same title.

The translations of ethnic women's texts affront the interconnected issues of gender and ethnicity that the original texts articulate. The role of the translator is thus not simply to translate a text linguistically and technically but to acknowledge and reflect in the translated text a whole range of cultural spaces. Gayatri Chakravorty Spivak notes that the politics of translation requires that the translator "surrender to the text" (1993, 183) and that the inability to do so implies that "the translator cannot engage with, or cares insufficiently for, the rhetoricity of the original" (1993, 181). Spivak's idea of surrendering to the text reminds us that the translator needs to approach the text by critically engaging its multiple contexts, including the contexts of the conception, production, circulation and reception of the text. Spivak defines the ideal translator in the following terms:

> The task of the translator is to facilitate this love between the original and its shadow, a love that permits fraying, holds the

> agency of the translator and the demands of her imagined or actual audience at bay. The politics of translation from a non-European woman's text too often suppresses this possibility because the translator cannot engage with, or cares insufficiently for, the rhetoric of the original. (1993, 181)

Spivak thus proposes a concept of translation that is sensitive to the possible reception of the text, rather than to the meticulous transference of meaning.

In cross-cultural translations, this is a particularly prominent dilemma. Because texts are also carriers of cultural implications and because they are often read as cultural documents, cross-cultural translation also serves as a mediation between two cultures. Homi Bhabha, for instance, defines all cultural encounters as translation, thus foregrounding the creative activity that relies on the interaction of two cultural worlds. For Bhabha, the existence of a "third space of enunciation" between two cultures provides a site where cultural translation takes place (37). This "third space," as Bhabha argues in *The Location of Culture* (1994), "constitutes the discursive conditions of enunciation that ensure that the meaning and symbols of culture have no primordial unity and fixity; that even the same signs can be appropriated, translated, rehistoricized and read anew" (37). This in-betweenness, as Bhabha argues in the interview "The Third Space," shows affinities with the subject-object relation in psychoanalytic theory of identity. By the use of this psychoanalytic analogy, Bhabha comes to think of identification as "a process of identifying with and through another object, an object of otherness, at which point the agency of identification – the subject – is itself always ambivalent, because of the intervention of that otherness" (Rutherford 211).

All of the above discussions in translation studies also pertain to the relationship between Ruth and LuLing. Concepts such as the notion of surrendering to the text, the emergence of a Third Space, and agentic secondariness, characterize the mother-daughter relationship in *The Bonesetter's Daughter* through the vocabulary of translation studies and thus subsume the mother-daughter dyad under the theoretical framework of translation. In *The Bonesetter's Daughter*, this Third Space in which translation takes place is marked by the daughter's negotiation of her Chinese American identity and also reflects her ambivalence between identification with and independence from the mother. For Ruth, this Third Space does not offer liberation from the conception of culture as based on binary oppositions but rather constitutes a place of "unhomeliness"[52] as far as her psychological identity is concerned, and a place

[52] In *The Uncanny* (1941), Sigmund Freud denominates with the word "unhomely" or "uncanny" this innate ambiguity between alienation and familiarity when he gives a definition of "The species of frightening that goes back to what was once

of conflict and dissonance as far as her cultural identity is concerned. The complex role of the cultural translator is further complicated by the daughter's psychological ambivalence toward her mother. This interconnectedness of the daughter's cultural in-betweenness and her ambivalence about the mother is what makes a reading of the cultural translation in Tan's novel especially interesting.

Because she does not read and speak Chinese, Ruth's task of translating her mother's legacy confronts her with an entirely new and foreign referential world to which she is liked by heritage but of which she does not consider as a crucial part of her life in the U.S. This is a common phenomenon in the practice of translation. For instance, Samia Mehrez's proposes that translation is a process where

> the language of the Other comes to encode messages which are not readily decoded by the monolingual reader whose referential world continues to exclude, ignore, and deny the existence of the other referential worlds that are crucial to a more global rather than "colonialist," "imperialist" reading of the text. (Venuti 122)

This process of "defamiliarization," as Ken-fang Lee calls it, enables writers such as Kingston and Tan to "bring the 'newness' and the 'foreignness' into the wor(l)d" by cobbling together Chinese traditional story elements into an American context as well as into American literature (106). Lee's concept of "defamiliarization" explains well the circumstances under which Ruth approaches her mother's text. For instance, Ruth struggles with the defamiliarization of her mother's text and, resigning over her cultural alienation as monolingual speaker, puts her mother's manuscript away with the verdict that it is simply too difficult to "decipher" (13). This resignation is testimony to Ruth's marginality both to the word and the world that constitute the cultural frameworks of her mother's manuscript.

The concept of defamiliarization also raises the question as to why the need for translation arises in the first place. The problem at hand stems from the conceptualization of the U.S. as a monolinguistic nation, one in which English is the dominant language, especially in the public sphere. Ruth, who translates for her mother in all circumstances of American public life, has therefore

---

well known and had long been familiar" (124). In the case of *The Bonesetter's Daughter*, Ruth's confrontation of the hidden past, which is symbolized by the discovery of the mother's manuscript, brings back into memory the long-know conflict with her mother as well as the knowledge about her rejection of the unknown, that is, of her Chinese heritage. Similarly, Bhabha argues in *The Location of Culture* the "unhomeliness" pertains to the "extra-territorial and cross-cultural initiation" (9).

access to American culture in ways that her mother does not. In return, her mother introduces Chinese as a language in the private sphere, such as through her attempt to teach her daughter Chinese calligraphy, an attempt which Ruth perceives as her mother's ploy to assert her power. While Ruth's translation in the public sphere seems necessary for LuLing to be able to function in American public life, LuLing's translation in the private sphere appears to be an extravagance that Ruth does not seem to need. This discrepancy – the fact that English is worth being translated whereas Chinese is not – reminiscent of Shu-Mei Shih's intervention of an "asymmetrical cosmopolitanism," a concept that exemplifies the inherent power struggle in global feminist encounters: "non-Western intellectuals need to be knowledgeable about Western cultures and speak one of the metropolitan languages to be considered 'cosmopolitan,' while Western intellectuals can be cosmopolitan without speaking any non-metropolitan language" (93). This notion of an asymmetrical cosmopolitanism explains well the dynamics of Ruth's resentment of translating for her mother on a daily basis and further renders plausible her inability to translate her mother's manuscript. It also reiterates Gayatri Chakravorty Spivak's observation in "The Politics of Translation" that one "cannot translate from a position of monolinguistic superiority" (195).

The question of power relationships that Spivak's assertion implies also pertains to the circumstances of translation in *The Bonesetter's Daughter*. At the center of Ruth's difficult relationship with her mother is the fact that she resents being her mother's mouthpiece and translator. In particular, the progressing stages of her mother's dementia remind Ruth of the role reversal between her and her mother all throughout her childhood, when she was assuming responsibilities her mother was unable to meet: "She felt ten years old again, translating for her mother how the world worked, explaining the rules, the restrictions, the time limits on money-back guarantees. Back then she had been resentful. Now she was horrified" (65). While on the one hand, Ruth dreads the responsibility of serving as her mother's translator, her resentment also refers to her disrespect for her mother's bad English. In fact, Ruth thinks of her mother as inadequate and ignorant. For instance, one particular incident displays how Ruth's disrespectful attitude toward her mother is based on her assumption that LuLing's limited command of English indicates her lack of intelligence. At age eleven, Ruth thinks she got pregnant by her neighbor from using his bathroom. Against her mother's warnings, Ruth had sat down on the toilet seat; and when her precocious friend at school explains to Ruth that babies are made from semen in a man's urine, Ruth thinks she is pregnant. Ruth reasons:

> It made terrible sense, the part about the pee. That was why boys and girls had separate bathrooms. That's why boys were supposed to lift the seat, but they didn't, just to be bad. And that was why her mother always told her never to sit on the toilet seat in someone else's bathroom. What her mother had said about *germs* was really a warning about *sperms*. Why couldn't her mother learn to speak English right? (134, original emphasis)

Instead of questioning her friend's logic, Ruth immediately jumps to conclusions about her mother's poor pronunciation and blames her for the misunderstanding.

This power struggle between Ruth and LuLing is reflected in her attitude toward translating her mother's manuscript. Taking on the role of the translator, as Ruth has done so involuntarily throughout her life, means giving up her own agency for the sake of narrating her mother's story. The act of translation marginalizes Ruth's discourse and places her in an inferior and secondary position, a position of "secondariness" (Lee 106), which Ken-fang Lee characterizes as being "similar to the situation that a woman confronts in a patriarchal society" (106). Because she wants to underscore her American identity, she does not want to be identified as a kind of doubly-muted alien that her mother's identity as Chinese American identity implies. Since translation requires, as Ken-fang Lee goes on to argue, "not only literal transformation but also cultural and psychological interaction" (106), this conflict with her mother that is at the very basis of Ruth's inability of translate her mother's manuscript.

Moreover, Ruth's resentment toward serving as her mother's mouthpiece and translator are reminiscent of her own struggles against racism and sexism. Ruth's forceful claiming of a space within the dominant American society renders her unwilling and eventually unable to locate her agency within her Chinese American matrilineage from which she could narrate her life without relying on binary structures of identity formation. Yet, Ruth's essentialist notion that she is not her mother confines her to the same colonialist and imperialist approach to her mother's narrative that Samia Mehrez considers as central to the translator's experience of defamiliarization. While it is true that Ruth is different from her mother, the particular ways in which Tan's novel constructs this difference are worth exploring.

Translating and Afterlife, or, The Question of Canonicity

In "The Task of the Translator," Walter Benjamin proposes that the translation of a text signifies its value: for instance, the translation of a foreign text ensures its "afterlife"[53] (72) by enabling its canonization and larger dissemination. Benjamin's argument also implies that translation carries the importance of a definitive mechanism that singles out texts worthy of translation from those unworthy of translation. In other words, this implies that the translation of a text is also an attribute of worth. The question that remains, however, is: Who determines the worth of a literary text? Recent discussions of canonicity offer potential ways of approaching this question. Much like the canonization of literary texts itself, the singling out of text worthy of translation relies on established critical conventions and ideals of aesthetics on the one hand and the need to accommodate the increasingly present ethnic diversity of literary productions on the other. As David Palumbo-Liu points out in his discussion of literary canon formation during the heydays of multiculturalism, the extensive inclusion of so-called minority authors did comply with a much-needed revision of the criteria that ensure inclusion into the literary canon, but happened under the sole purpose of adopting texts into the canon that helped reiterate the relevance of already existing formal criteria. In other words, Palumbo-Liu and his contributing authors of *The Ethnic Canon: Histories, Institutions, Interventions* (1995) critique the inclusion of minority authors by arguing that the authors' minority status on the socio-cultural American landscape served as sole representational logic for inclusion. Therefore, and this is what *The Bonesetter's Daughter* exemplifies so well, the criteria that determine the worth of a text are not devoid of ideology. On the contrary, Ruth grows up under the assumption that her mother's spoken text, i.e. her verbal English skills, characterized by unidiomatic expressions, limited vocabulary, and a heavy foreign accent, is inferior to the standard American spoken and written texts, the very texts that her mother can oftentimes not understand without Ruth's intervention as an interpreter.

The same applies for Ruth's attitude toward her mother's written text, i.e. the manuscript she hid in a living room sofa. Neither the fact that the mother chose a hiding place for her manuscript nor the fact that this is the only written text besides decorative banners for stores in Chinatown that her mother ever produced convinces Ruth that the text at hand carries crucial importance. In the

[53] Marie-Therese Abdel-Messih applies the idea of an afterlife due to translation in her study of the Fayoum portraits of the Greco-Roman period, pointing out that a cultural translation of the semiotics of the portraits promotes their function of "traversing death" (8).

context of both Benjamin's and Palumbo-Liu's discussions of literary worth, Ruth does not recognize her mother's text as worthy of an "afterlife," neither through translation, nor through inclusion into the production of books that she participates in as a professional ghost writer. Ruth's refusal to decipher her mother's manuscript thus reflects her lack of appreciation for mother's text. Ruth does not deem LuLing's manuscript worthy of translation, especially not because of the effort it would take her to achieve a translation. Because these criteria are not objective, but are the result of a deeply-rooted chasm that characterizes their relationship as mother and daughter, the entire situation in which the issue of translation occurs in *The Bonesetter's Daughter* illustrates the enmeshment of psychological and ideological aspects of the power struggle between Ruth and LuLing.

Translation and Narrative Structure

The power struggle between Ruth and LuLing can also be felt on the level of the novel's narrative structure. For instance, the absence of an intertwined discourse between mother and daughter, such as in Maxine Hong Kingston's mother-daughter aesthetics, calls attention to the lack of communication between Ruth and LuLing. Similarly, the first long section of the novel is set in the present time and narrated by Ruth. Her flashbacks and her memories serve as a backdrop and almost as an explanation for the tensions between LuLing and Ruth. From Ruth's perspective, we get to know about the language barriers in the family as well as about the power struggle that she perceives between her mother and herself. Only after Ruth's narrative do we get to hear LuLing's life story. Her story, although equally long, is wedged in between Ruth's story, and is thus framed by it. The narrative of LuLing's life in China is the storyline of her manuscript in China. Because of the novel's structure, it appears as if Ruth was reading the translation of her mother's manuscript, a process that possibly mimics the reading practice that the audience of Tan's novel experiences. In this section of the novel the reader also recognizes the story that serves as the prologue of the novel, the one in which LuLing introduces her family genealogy with the enigmatic words "These are the things I know are true" (1). At first, the story of the prologue remains unidentified and out of context. Only much later into the novel does the reader realize that the prologue is also narrated by LuLing. This creates the impression that the narrator of the novel is Ruth, and that her mother's story is the story that Ruth reads. This impression emphasizes Ruth's perspective and, much unlike the alternating narratives of Tan's first novel *The Joy Luck Club*, discursively privileges Ruth's narrative agency by creating the impression that it is overall Ruth's story more than LuLing's.

The fact that the novel presents her mother's life story "after translation," as it were, also raises questions about LuLing's narrative agency. Even the novel's prologue, when read in connection with the long narrative of LuLing's life story in the second part of the novel, gives the impression of having been channeled through the act of translation, while at that point it is not clear who might have translated it. The very chapter titles of LuLing's story encompass the aspect of translation in a very literal manner. Whereas the chapters of Ruth's story are numbered and thus give the impression of a chronological sequence, the chapters of LuLing's stories all bear thematic chapter titles, such as "Heart," "Change," or "Ghost." The chapter titles themselves evoke the issues of translation, as they feature both the Chinese ideograph and below it the English translation for the concepts depicted in the chapters. Moreover, LuLing's narratives also contain episodes from Precious Auntie, all of which appear in the novel in italics. These episodes, too, imply a degree of transference, since Precious Auntie was unable to speak, and LuLing had to interpret her gestures accordingly.

Therefore, in contrast to LuLing's narrative, Ruth's appears to be much more monolithic. Her narrative stands side by side with her mother's, but her mother's offers a greater variety of languages and discourses, clearly discernable on the level of the novel's layout and structure. Also thematically does LuLing's narrative display a high awareness of her matrilineal agency and her responsibility to keep alive the memory of Precious Auntie. The circumstances of her writing, her progressing Dementia, require that she remember and record as much as she can about Precious Auntie. Furthermore, the fact that she writes out of a sense of shame for having failed to recognize Precious Auntie as her own mother make plausible her active incorporation of Precious Auntie's life story into her own. All of these evidences characterize the narrative situation and the context of LuLing's writing as a cultural narrative that seeks to maintain a collective sense of heritage instead of establishing the writer's individuality. Accordingly, the context of translation in LuLing's narrative is different from the one of her daughter's narrative, which, as far as the novel's narrative structure is concerned, has the effect that while both women are confronted with the task of translation, their personal quests determine their abilities to fulfill this task.

In the last section of the novel, Ruth seeks to recover the same matrilineal discourse that LuLing's narrative exemplifies. However, I argue that she only partly succeeds in doing so. For instance, the impression that Ruth's perspective in the novel is much more prevalent than her mother's is also discernable in the novel's ending. In the last section of the novel, a rather brief one compared to the two middle sections, Tan constructs a possible solution in Ruth's attempt to write out her own collectivity. Ruth sets out to write down her life story under the following premise: "It is for her grandmother, for herself, for the little girl who became her mother" (403). Moreover, the fact that Ruth for the first time, after having made a career as a ghost writer for new-Age literature, writes for her own course, using her own persona and voice to tell her life story, underscores the sense of unity and healing that the novel aims for.

Still, Tan's depiction of Ruth's acceptance of her matrilineal agency is only partly satisfying. Although Ruth begins to incorporate her matrilineage in her own writing, she nevertheless patronizes and objectifies her mother. By referring to her mother as "little girl," for instance, Ruth re-enacts the power struggle she fought with her mother during her own childhood, when LuLing's unidiomatic English called for the intervention of Ruth's linguistic authority. In addition, it is not quite clear how the Americanized daughter can relate to 'exotic stories' of the mother's life in China, a problem that Tan addresses in a similar fashion in *The Joy Luck Club*. Whereas Tan's novel foreshadows such idealistic reconstruction of a matrilineal discourse, its division into distinctly separated narrative agencies for the mother's and the daughter's stories precludes such discursive reconciliation.

Finally, Ruth's appropriating of her mother's stories and the recovery of her matrilineage for her own manifestation of an "authentic" literary voice might be just as problematic as her inability to transfer her mother's stories: in both cases, she runs the risk of accommodating a discourse marked by Orientalism. This can also be said of Tan's novel in general. By creating a "mother" narrative that stands in contrast, even in opposition, to the daughter's narration, and is even further commodified through the act of translation it has undergone, Tan marginalizes the narrative agency of the first-generation immigrant mother. Certainly, by leaving out any accounts of LuLing's life in the U.S. (all the reader knows of LuLing's American life is filtered through Ruth's perspective), Tan's novel reinforces the mutilation of the mother's voice in the U.S. as if as a Chinese American her voice must invariably be traceable to her Chinese life and recovered in her storytelling. At the same time, the fact that LuLing's narrative ends with her journey to the U.S. and describes only her life in China emphasizes the role of cultural translation even more. To the same extent as LuLing initially serves as a foil in for Ruth's cultural distinction from first-generation Chinese Americans, she remains a foil in Ruth's appropriation of her Chinese heritage. Thus, in *The Bonesetter's Daughter*, the diasporic condition of the first-generation immigrant cannot be represented be the daughter without Orientalism and stigmatization, without objectification and patronizing. In this regard, Tan's novel evokes Gayatri Chakravorty Spivak's assertion that the subaltern cannot speak because of the Western interference through translation and transference in her famous essay that asks the question "Can the Subaltern Speak?"(1988).

A translation of this manuscript, together with the short chapter "Truth" preceding the novel's account of LuLing's and Ruth's present lives, constitutes the mother's counter-voice and appears in the novel's middle section. Narrated by LuLing in the first person, this part shows little discursive congruency with the figural narration of the other parts. Whereas the reader's first impression of the mother-daughter relationship is coined by Ruth's blames and complaints, this second part makes up for the discursively imposed silence upon LuLing in the section where Ruth's perspective is dominant. Such insertion of the mother's story into the daughter's discourse -- Tan does the same thing in her second novel *The Kitchen God's Wife* -- decreases the subject-object narration the novel's first part starts out with in its empathy with the daughter's anger against her mother. With this narrative strategy, Tan epitomizes the socio-cultural implications of Ruth's silencing of her mother. Whereas in the U.S., Ruth "owns" the discourse and her mother remains silenced by her status as minority woman, this part of her narration (albeit translated and thus not represented in its original) reconstructs the mother's voice fully. In this narrative set in China, LuLing's voice comes into existence as legacy of the language her ancestors speak and to which Ruth is unable to relate since she is largely unfamiliar with Chinese traditions, including the Chinese language. Yet, given her mother's progressing Dementia disease, Ruth realizes that the translation of her mother's manuscript is the only essential means that can solve certain enigmas that have been haunting her mother and, by consequence, Ruth as well. But because she is unable to read her mother's life story, Ruth has to rely on a translator whose competence she trusts. Interestingly, Tan chooses a male Chinese American writer to become the translator of LuLing's memoir.

Translation and the Mother-Daughter Conflict

Placing the mother-daughter conflict at the center of the circumstances of translation also underscores the difference between the translation of written and oral texts and the different possibilities for recovery that they each hold. Translations of oral texts, as Ruth's role as her mother's mouthpiece exemplifies, project a sense of immediacy and urgency that distinguishes them from written translations, which can be postponed, or even delegated to another person. For instance, in *The Joy Luck Club*, Tan introduces bilingualism "as a game of translation" (Yuan 293), in which Jing-mei Woo "talked to her [mother] in English, and she answered back in Chinese" (23), and cautions of the potential mutual misunderstandings that occur in oral translation: "We translated each other's meanings and I seemed to hear less than what she said while my mother heard more" (27). The daughter's misunderstandings, as Yuan Yuan proposes, result from the fact that the mother's "China narratives become a text of culture" (293) and can therefore not be translated into the American context the daughter's are familiar with. In contrast, the translation of a written text "allows for later translation and mediation" (Dunick 14), as Ruth's postponement of the translation of her mother's manuscript implies. While translating American concepts from English into Chinese instills in Ruth a certain authority over her mother and thus adds to the chasm in their relationship, the immediate need for oral translation also forces her to adopt the much dreaded role as her mother's mouthpiece in the first place. In contrast, by storing away the written manuscript her mother had given her, Ruth can escape the responsibility of serving as translator temporarily. Finally, postponing the act of translation also enables Ruth to return to the manuscript at a time when she becomes aware of her mother's diminishing memory, at a time when she recognizes the importance of her mother's life story. Tan's emphasis in *The Bonesetter's Daughter* on the translation of a written text therefore illustrates to complexity of cross-cultural translation and defines it as a possible metaphor of mother-daughter relationships located at the critical intersection of ethnic American studies and transnational feminism.

The lack of interconnectedness between the mother's and the daughter's discourse of the novel reinforces this difference between mother and daughter. There is a clear division between the daughter's storytelling and the mother's story. Of course, one might note that the daughter's storytelling relies on her matrilineage, especially in the final section of the novel, but Ruth's narrative agency and dominant discourse of the novel certainly puts the mother's story in a more subordinate position. In addition, the book displays the mother's story after translation. Accordingly, the version of LuLing's manuscript printed as it appears in the novel is subject to mis-interpretations and manipulations through the process of transference. In the context of the novel's emphasis on the problem of cultural misinterpretations and the unreliability of language for authentic cultural representation, this division of the mother's voice from the daughter's is central to Tan's depiction of the challenges of incorporating transnational matrilineage into literary texts.

Unlike *The Joy Luck Club*, which offers first-person narratives from both the mothers' and the daughters' perspectives, *The Bonesetter's Daughter* works with two different narrative situations: in contrast to the omniscient perspective in Ruth's story, LuLing's story is a first-person narrative, one in which she narrates both her personal and her collective history. The use of a first-person narrative perspective gives LuLing the possibility to assert her identity through her storytelling. At the same time, this narrative situation also raises issues about the reliability of these stories: not only are first-person narrative perspectives always limited, the fact that LuLing's memory is failing her also makes her an unreliable narrator. This search for a way to reconstruct her life story on her own terms is also the main theme of LuLing's narrative. LuLing's story first and foremost reasserts her family genealogy. By writing down her life story, for instance, LuLing connects with her family's tradition of producing ink, the implement of LuLing's written legacy. The "secret family recipe" for ink LuLing mentions has been passed down from her great grandmother (176) as a token of female historiography. LuLing's story also pays tribute to Precious Auntie, LuLing's birth mother, who lost her husband very early into their marriage and stayed with her in-laws as a nursemaid under the pretense that LuLing was the daughter of the eldest brother-in-law and his wife. Having destroyed her vocal cords by swallowing hot ink out of grief over her family's disloyalty to her late husband, Precious Auntie does not have a voice. Body language, movement of the eyes, and most importantly the scribbling of short notes onto a chalkboard are her means of communication. This similarity between LuLing's relationship with Ruth and her relationship with her own mother emphasizes the voicelessness of women in patriarchal societies and asserts the existence of a matrilineal interconnectedness that Ruth can acknowledge only with difficulty.

The stories about the relationship between LuLing and Precious Auntie are very similar to the relationship between Ruth and LuLing. While LuLing's relationship to her own daughter is skewed by cultural difference, the mother-daughter narrative of LuLing and Precious Auntie isolates the psychological dimensions of the mother-daughter dyad. In this light, LuLing's story in the novel does not only provide the missing link for Ruth's (and the reader's) understanding of LuLing's past, it also exemplifies the psychoanalytical dimensions of the mother-daughter conflict. Leaving out the cross-cultural alienation and the (re-)negotiation of their identities which LuLing and Ruth experience differently, LuLing's narrative as a daughter is dedicated to affirming a collective matrilineal voice despite the patriarchal impediments on motherhood and daughterhood and emphasizes the family history that Ruth needs to learn about in order to be able to fully understand her own mother. In this context, the depiction of the mother's own experience as daughter, "long ago and far away" (179), focuses exclusively on the establishment of LuLing's gender consciousness. Growing up with the belief that her mother is her nursemaid, LuLing fails to see her mother beyond her inferior social stuatus within the family. Given Precious Auntie's marginalized position within the extended family, LuLing abhors the idea of being Precious Auntie's mouthpiece (208). During this fierce conflict with the woman whom she does not recognize as her mother, LuLing rejects Precious Auntie's parenting, "It's not for you to decide" (236), she protests and decides to marry into the family that killed Precious Auntie's father and husband. When Precious Auntie gives her a manuscript that contains all the things she is (literally) unable to say, LuLing discards it as unimportant.

> I looked at the first page. 'I was born the daughter of the Famous Bonesetter from the Mouth of the Mountain,' it began. I glanced through the next few pages. They concerned the tradition of her family, the loss of her mother, the grief of her father, all the things she had already told me. And then I saw where it said: 'Now I will tell how bad this man Chang really is.' Right away, I threw those pages down. I did not want Precious Auntie poisoning my mind anymore. So I did not read the end where she said she was my mother. (239-40)

By refusing to read Precious Auntie's manuscript, LuLing denies her mother the ability to speak up for herself and counter the wrongs that have been done onto her. LuLing's mutilation of her mother's voice is connected to the fact that she is unable to recognize her mother on the one hand, but also to her conscious decision not to read her story on the other. This combination between mistaking the mother and muting the mother also characterizes Ruth's relationship to LuLing.

While the relationship between LuLing and Precious Auntie focuses on the psychoanalytical dimensions of the mother-daughter relationship, the translation of LuLing's manuscript emphasizes cultural dimensions. These cultural dimensions, as I have tried to analyze in some detail in the previous section of this chapter, culminate in Ruth's frustration with the manuscript written in Chinese and her contestation that it is too difficult and time consuming to "decipher" (13). More importantly, however, Tan isolates the cultural aspects of the mother's narrative by locating its actual translation outside of the mother-daughter conflict. Instead, a male translator steps in, whose role it is not only to transfer it to the daughter but also to assess the story based on its authenticity and to thereby restore LuLing's cultural competence to her daughter. This male translator takes up the role of the father figure in the Oedipal triangle that replaces the mother-daughter dyad in the second part of the novel. Ruth entirely trusts Mr. Tang's insight into LuLing's life, mainly because she acknowledges his cultural connectedness to LuLing's own life. Like LuLing, he is a first-generation immigrant and knows Chinese culture in a way that is unfamiliar to Ruth. Hence, Mr. Tang "reads" LuLing differently: "Ruth realized that Mr. Tang translated for LuLing, as she once had. But he knew not to be concerned with words and their precise meanings. He simply translated what was in LuLing's heart: her better intentions, her hopes" (391). Yet, despite this appearance of a father figure to whom Ruth maintains a better communication than to her mother, the intervention of a male translator who helps restore the legacy of LuLing's matrilineal storytelling is quite extraordinary. Given the very definition of matrilineality as a form of cultural transmission from mother to daughter, it is difficult to argue that the intervention of a male translator does not distort the matrilineal inheritance from mother to daughter. The intervention of a male interpreter is especially interesting since the manuscript he translates is a reconstruction of LuLing's relationship with her own mother. Mr. Tan thus mediates between Ruth and LuLing and at the same time enables the successful transference of Precious Auntie's life story. In this light, Mr. Tan helps Ruth to overcome her emotional distance fom her mother. He also helps LuLing preserve the memory of her mother by making her life story accessible to those members of the Chinese American community who do not read Chinese, and thus gives the text he translates an afterlife. Mr. Tan's translation is testimony to the possibility of translating a text and "surrendering to this text." He is able to do so because he is not engaged in a power struggle with LuLing in ways that Ruth is. On the contrary, the fact that he is in love with LuLing explains his dedication to her and to her text. Through this intervention of a male translator, Tan's novel seems to suggest that translation across gender is more readily feasible than translation across culture.

"Surrendering" to the Other('s) Text

The fact that Mr. Tan translates across gender even positions the cultural difference between Ruth and LuLing into further spotlight. While it is only logical that Ruth, because she cannot relate to her mother's life in the U.S., will not be likely to be able to relate to her mother's life in China, the novel's emphasis on the cultural difference between mother and daughter raises issues about the possibility of a transnational solidarity. Furthermore, the novel's depiction of the encounter between Ruth and LuLing invites an exploration of the representation of China and Chinese women. For instance, the episode about the tea tray I quoted above, emphasizes language and the issue of translation with Ruth as medium, as well as exoticizing the mother. This further distances the two women from each other. Similarly, the fact that Ruth uses as her writing utensils the pen, the typewriter and the computer while LuLing only uses a brush also contributes to a cultural positioning that ascribes to the daughter a modern and to the mother an traditional writing culture. This practice of encoding the two women differently is pivotal to the novel's biased representation of the two women. This discrepancy can best be understood by reference to Yuan Yuan's definition of "China narratives." China narratives, as Yuan suggests, "have lost their reference to China" and "are related more to the present American situation than to their original context in Chinese society" (292). Following Yuan's definition, LuLing's production of calligraphy banners for Chinese restaurants and stores in the U.S. acquire a new purpose because it occurs in an American context and is also designed for an American audience. If we read her banners as "text[s] reconfigured within other contexts" (Yuan 292), the specific context of her relationship with her daughter attributes to her writing Chinese calligraphy the position of a marginalized discourse, one that is characterized, in particular, by the very fact that she produces them with a brush. As such, Tan's novel characterizes the relationship between Ruth and her mother's text as one that cannot exceed the power roles that are reminiscent of an East/West relationship in general.

As such, the ending of Tan's novel evokes a common problematic in the transnational encounter between Western and Chinese feminism. As Shu-mei Shih argues in an article on the labeling of women of the Chinese diaspora as feminist, Western conceptualizations of Chinese woman are often locked in discourse of difference. In Shih's observation, either "the Other woman is frozen in absolute difference (too difficult and too time-consuming to understand fully) or she is trapped in the earlier phase of the development of feminism (too familiar and thus either dismissed or condescendingly told what to do next)" (93). The development of the relationship between Ruth and LuLing over the course of the novel displays a transition from one of these extremes to the other. While sensitive to the issue of transnational translation, the novel only partly addresses the obvious cultural differences, thus enacting an essentialist depiction of Chinese women.

Nevertheless, in her emphasis on the written word, Tan makes a very original contribution to the discussion of orality in ethnic American literature. While many critics have focused on the oral tradition in non/Western text, and have thereby, as Lisa Dunick asserts, overlooked the *literary* potential of such texts, Tan's representation of the importance of writing and written legacies in particular offers a stark contrast to this tradition. While it is true that Ruth cannot read her mother's memoir, she at least understands and appreciates this memoir for the cultural legacy it provides for her. This understanding is in part triggered by Mr. Tan, the man who translates her mother's manuscript for her. He explains to Ruth the complexity of translation and mediating: "I don't like to just transliterate word for word. I want to phrase it more naturally, yet ensure these are your mother's words, a record for you and your children for generations to come. They must be just right. Don't you agree?" (342). Although Ruth does not offer a reply to Mr. Tan's rhetorical question, the reader knows from previous chapters about her ability to appreciate the "power with words" (85).[54] Ruth is also aware of the power that comes with her profession as a ghost writer for New Age literature, her ability to "make it sound sexy and easy to grasp" (46). And while being a ghost writer allows her to remain anonymous and thus ungraspable as a person, she is also frustrated by her lack of presence in the writing she produces, wishing for "*some* recognition" (43, original emphasis).

This appreciation of the "importance of original authorship" (Dunick 13) is the one thread that ties the three generations of women – Precious Auntie, Luling, and Ruth – together and comprises their matrilineal heritage. As the daughter of a famous bonesetter and ink maker, Precious Auntie inherits the "secret family recipe" (178) to make ink, a skill which enables her, like all women in her family (176), to produce ink. Through such knowledge, LuLing has access to the pen, a privilege that, as she points out, is uncommon for Chinese women of her generation. Luling comes to appreciate this power of the written word when Precious Auntie teaches her that "a person must think about her intentions" and learns to recognize Precious Auntie's intentions which, when she writes, "flowed from her body into her arm, through the brush, and into the stroke" (269). And in the face of her progressing dementia, she realizes that only a written record of her life story can serve as testimony of her cultural legacy. Both, the appreciation of writing as a medium of emancipation and as a performative act of identity, inspire Ruth's own writing. In the novel's epilogue, Ruth starts writing a story about her own life, much in the tradition of her mother and her grandmother. On her writing desk is a picture of Precious Auntie, reminding her to "[t]hink about [her] intentions" (402). While at the beginning of the novel, Ruth's intention is to distance herself from her mother, Ruth's, now her intentions are the recovery of her matrilineal heritage into her own story writing. As the final lines of the novel emphasize, Ruth's writing is "for her grandmother, for herself, for the little girl who became her mother" (403). With these lines, Tan sketches a recovery of Ruth's matrilineage, one that reconciles the breach between her individual and her collective identity. This sense of healing becomes evident from the fact that although the time of year when she usually retrieves into silence approaches, "Ruth still has her

---

[54] One example is when she scribbles alleged messages from Precious Auntie to Luling onto the sand tray or when she fears her mother might have tried to commit suicide in response to the hateful message Ruth write into her diary (159).

voice," a fact that symbolizes her completed identity formation and of her purpose: "Before, she never had a reason to write for herself, only for others. Now she has that reason" (401).

While Tan's novel does underscore the importance of recovering Ruth's transnational matrilineage and thus gives the novel a positive ending, it also exemplifies how purpose and meaning of a cultural narrative cannot be equally recovered through translation. Tan's depiction of a strong tradition of writing, one that projects an intact transnational matrilineage,[55] suggests that women of different cultural backgrounds share similar desires for self-representation and agency. At the same time, however, her emphasis on the untranslatability of the cultural circumstances from one culture to another demonstrates the limits of such transference. This also becomes evidenced in the fact that Ruth does not learn how to undertake the translation of her mother's text, but is still eager to claim the translated text as part of her identity as a writer. For instance, she learns from the context of her mother's story and its plot, which suggests that the cultural representation of China outweighs the critical awareness of the discursive construction of China in Tan's novel.

Translation and Feminist Solidarity

The ultimate question with regard to the mother-daughter relationship in *The Bonesetter's Daughter* is discerning how much Ruth learns from the experience of having to translate her mother's text. I would argue that Tan's ready-made solution at the end of the novel, where Ruth spontaneously adopts her Chinese heritage and starts writing "for her grandmother, for herself, for the little girl who became her mother" (403), precludes a discourse in which Ruth approaches her matrilineage with a transnational sensibility, that is, an awareness of the conceptualization of difference in the representation of women from different cultural backgrounds. Instead, the novel's ending seems to evoke the idea that the three generations of women are happily united in a bond of global sisterhood, one that forges similarities without paying full attention to the power dynamics at play at such a cross-cultural comparison. By so doing, Tan reduces the relationship between the three women to their gender roles, thereby disregarding the different politics of location as subjects as well as authors of each other's histories. The entire novel is very context-oriented and only partly reconciles the challenges and issues prevalent in transnational appropriation of

---

[55] Sheng-mei Ma speaks of a "matrilineage of female pain," one that "unfolds not only in terms of physical damage but in psychological hurt – Precious Auntie's life as a nursemaid to her own daughter, LuLing's immigrant awkwardness and reversal to dependency, and Ruth's childlessness and pseudo-stepmotherhood" (197).

gender. But discursively and conceptually speaking, Ruth never learns to truly engage her mother's text, and thus, symbolically, only partly accomplishes a successful negotiation of her Chinese heritage. To a certain degree, Ruth offers a forceful example to Shih's assertion that "[w]ith the power to arbitrate difference and similarity in such reductive terms, the Western subject can thus simply ignore that which otherwise needs to be learned with time and effort, namely, the history, experience, and representation of the Other woman in multiple contexts" (93). This tension between approaching her mother's text and approaching representations of Chinese women at large remains unresolved throughout the novel although it *does* seem to impact the narrative structure of Tan's storytelling. What Tan does exemplify is not only the complex dynamics of transnational exploration of matrilineage, but the artistry a narrative reconstruction of this exploration demands.

The complex enmeshment of matrilineage and transnationality, pitted against a translational context, characterizes Tan's novel as an example of what Waïl S. Hassan calls "translational literature:"

> Translational texts are performances of interlinguistic, cross-cultural communication, operating on several levels of mediation and contestation, alternating between autoethnography and the rewriting of metropolitan narratives from the perspective of impersonalized societies. (755)

Tan's *The Bonesetter's Daughter* exemplifies these characteristics both on the level of plot and on the level of structure. While Luling's manuscript in translation reads like "an original rather than like a translation" (Hassan 754),[56] the generic problems with literary (and cultural) translation are explicitly written into the structure of the novel, illustrated by the very fact that Tan cobbles together original and translated stories without differentiation. While Hassan's definition of translational literature circumscribes primarily the extratextual interaction between text and audience, Tan's novel incorporates this notion of a translational literature on an intratextual level, namely in its representation of the complex patters of interaction between mother and daughter. And while on the level of the novel's structure, the performance of the individual narratives suggests a sense of recovery, this challenge to bridge the cultural gap that the act of translation confronts remains prevalent. In the novel's epilogue, Ruth faces a photograph of her grandmother Precious Auntie, imagining what kind

[56] Hassan refers here to Lawrence Venuti's argument in *Scandals of Translation: Towards an Ethics of Difference* that "translation participates in the construction of cultural identities, not only by reproducing stereotypes of the source culture but also by reinforcing dominant discourses and self-images for the target culture" (Hassan 754).

of relationship she would have had with her: "Could her grandmother ever have imagined she would have a granddaughter like her [Ruth] – a woman who has a husband who loves her, two girls who adore her, a house she co-owns, dear friends, a life with only the usual worries about leaks and calories?" (401). By having Ruth speculate about her grandmother's projected astonishment at her granddaughter's life in the U.S., Tan forges a special, temporal, and ideological difference between the two women. Of course, one might argue that the difference between the Chinese grandmother and her American granddaughter is obvious, but precisely through this self-evident difference does Tan's novel reiterate the same cultural dichotomy that Ruth experienced with her mother. Tan affirms the cultural plurality among the individual women in Ruth's family, characterizing them as members of distinctly different cultures and thus evokes the "limits of translatability" (Hassan 755) of Ruth's matrilineage.

This ultimate emphasis on difference prevails in Tan's suggestion that while the content of the individual written legacies can never be fully recovered through the act of translation, the purpose of writing can. In the end, Ruth acknowledges that her idea of her matrilineage is biased and that there is no authentic reconstruction of her mother's voice. This enables Ruth to redefine her own position in relation to her mother and her mother's story, a position from which she can appropriate the act of translation for her negotiation of her ethnic and gender consciousness. Her agency as translator and the act of assuming the implied responsibilities suggest to Ruth ways of how to deal with her own identity. For instance, by adopting the role as writer of her matrilineage, Ruth demonstrates her awareness that cultural identity is not a fixed unity, but "is constantly enacted through practices of representation" (Simon 151). She thus comes to appreciate the symbolic meaning of translation as a vehicle of cultural manifestation of identity and difference at once, much in line with Homi K. Bhabha's intervention of translation as definitive moment of cultural representation, as defined by his "Third Space of enunciation." In the end, Ruth sees translation not as a burdensome task that evokes her negative memories of her mother's inability to function in an English-only world, she acknowledges that translation is a much more complex, but at the same time universal process of identity negotiation. As Sherry Simon suggests, translation is

> a rhetorical figure describing on the one hand the increasing internationalization of cultural production and on the other the fate of those who struggle between two worlds and two languages. Women 'translate themselves' into the language of patriarchy. Translation, as a tangible representation of a secon-

> dary or mediated relationship to reality, of a sense of exclusion from the codes of the powerful (134-35).

Not only does Tan's novel in this emphasis in Ruth's matrilineality suggest the importance of translation as a cultural act of recovery, it also positions the question of female agency in a new light. While Ruth initially operates with a notion of agency that reminds of Judith Butler's definition of the concept in *Gender Trouble* as characterized by its "question of how signification and resignification work" (184), she reaches by the end of the novel an understanding of agency that is less defined by its discursive constructedness. Such a shift in concepts can also be detected in Butler's work, as Kathy Dow Magnus argues in a comprehensive essay on Butler's notion of subjectivity. According to Magnus, Butler's later work, including *Excitable Speech: A Politics of the Performative* (1997), no longer considers subjectivity "purely in terms of the discourse that produces it" but embraces a more formative stance on agency: "No longer interpreting the 'Other' as a mere danger to subjectivity, she illustrates how subjective agency requires the support of intersubjective relations" (100).

In this vein, this recognition of the importance of the written word enables Ruth to restore her matrilineage. And this is the ultimate learning experience she has to master, the "importance of original authorship" (Dunick 13). As Tan's novel seems to suggest, the difficulty in cross-cultural translation, and in the transference of cultural identification between different generations and their distinctly different definitions of Chinese American experiences, lies in definitions of identity that are based on binary opposition and rigid boundaries rather than on assumptions that a person's authorial agency is not a state, but an activity; in the same light, matrilineage is not so much a matter of identity, it is a matter of identification.

CHAPTER 7

Between Imagined Communities and Imaginary Homelands: Gender and Nationhood in Vineeta Vijayaraghavan's *Motherland*

> A Self does not amount to much, but no self is an island. – Jean-Francois Lyotard

In the previous two chapters, I have pointed out the cultural tensions and ideological implications in depictions of mother-daughter relationships by contemporary Asian American women writers with specific regards to the context of academic and literary communities. By singling out a variety of tropes in transnational feminist theory as heuristics for my readings of the individual works, my project at large emphasizes the multiple locations of culture and identity to which the encounters between women of the same family but of different cultural self-identification belong. I have emphasized the literary recovery of matrilineage and the need for a transnational sensibility with which the authors navigate these encounters and conflicts in their narratives. I have also pointed out moments in the individual texts where this sensibility seemed somewhat amiss. This led me to the conclusion that contemporary Asian American women writers confront and negotiate in their works well-pronounced binary oppositions between East and West and, at times, represent these oppositions by characterizing the mother-daughter relationship through aspects of essentialism, informed by the daughters' incomprehension and impatience. To transgress such oppositional discourses, as my analysis of Nora Okja Keller's novel *Comfort Woman* and Amy Tan's *The Bonesetter's Daughter* in the previous chapters exemplifies, marks the beginning of a new era in Asian American critique, one that no longer grapples with the legacies of what Sau-ling C. Wong calls the "claiming America" (1995, 3) trope of the emerging endeavors of Asian American communities during the civil rights era to establish their space within the U.S., and consequently, on the level of discipline, within the American academy.

The work that I have cut out for the final chapter is to bring together some of the tropes that previous chapters have identified a point of contention within the mother-daughter relationships, tropes such as concerning the question of translation and agency, language and the body, memory and travel, and food and homeplace, and look at the fundamental driving force that lies at the base of these points of contention. I am here talking about the role of community, the establishment of a *sensus communis,* within heterogenous societies and the post-modern world order. While community is a subtext to all the previous chapters' discussions of identity, especially the ones on Keller and Tan, I have left out discussions of philosophical and political theory of community until now. Although the previous chapters of this book describe various encounters between the daughters as individuals and the communities in which they participate and with which they interact, these encounters occur primarily through the daughter's relationship with her mother. In this sense, the mother becomes an iconic figure in the daughter's imagination of the larger Asian American communities, and as in the case of Tan's work and Keller's novel, of an Asian community as well. While community plays an important role in the previous chapters, in particular in the context of ethnic and female communities and feminist solidarity, I will here pick up the question of community and nationhood. This chapter illustrates the discrepancy between community and nationhood as suggested in Vineeta Vijayaraghavan's novel *Motherland* (2001). I argue that Vijayaraghavan's novel offers us a host of challenges in our understanding of how community works in a transnational context and how, both in relation to the mother-daughter conflict as well as on the level of national conflicts, a feminist discussion of community forges important ground in postmodern conceptualizations of identity and belonging.

Communities and Homelands of the Global Imaginary

The increasing globalization of post-modern societies has claimed a high demand for new concepts and frameworks to theorize communities that are no longer bound to place but that are fluid in nature and often contradictory in kind. Two contemporary scholars of transnational feminist theory, Caren Kaplan and Inderpal Grewal, provide concepts that facilitate a better understanding of how to read globalization, its effects on community, and the contexts and issues within feminist and cultural studies that can be applied to discern the issues of power and privilege that shape myriad different kinds of transnational and diasporic experiences within these communities. In her book *Questions of Travel: Postmodern Discourses of Displacement* (1996), Caren Kaplan investigates the ideological reach of metaphors of travel, including those of tourism, nomadism, exile and locations in "traveling theories,"[57] that is, in the global circulation of knowledge. In particular, Kaplan looks at the continuities and discontinuities between these individual forms of movement and observes that what these forms of movement have in common can best be expressed through the term "displacement." Kaplan defines displacement not in

[57] Kaplan adopts this term from Edward Said's *The World The Text, and the Critic* (1983).

strict terms of diaspora and nostalgia, but as a discourse "to question modernisms of representation of movement, location, and homelessness in contemporary critical practices" (4). By characterizing displacement as an ongoing process, Kaplan takes cues from Jean-Francois Lyotard's assertion quoted in the epigraph of this chapter. Uncovering Lyotard's tendency toward "sweeping generalizations" (16), Kaplan urges that in such discourses of displacement, the term local "requires similar deconstruction" as do the terms difference and similarity.

Such heuristics also characterize the discussions of postmodern cosmopolitanism and global mobility in Kaplan's and Grewal's work, respectively, when they speak of a modern nomadism through which people can become native in a foreign land "while retaining their identity and power" (Grewal 43). Kaplan's notion of modern nomadism suggests, among other things, a potential of considering diaspora as not only associated with the loss of power and agency but within global patterns of mobility. These global patterns utilize already existing power structures which resist easy classification as mere "loss of the homeland," a classification with which diasporic communities are often associated. William Safran, for instance, proposes that the concept of diaspora is often used only in the context of forced exile, and that related discourses of return "solidify ethnic consciousness and solidarity" (91) in the temporary existence outside of the nation-state that previously defined a community's sense of belonging. Similarly, Ien Ang contends that it "is the myth of the (lost or idealized) homeland, the object of both collective memory and of desire and attachment, which is constitutive of diasporas, and which ultimately confines and constrains the nomadism of the diasporic subject" (5). In contrast to such existing notions of diaspora, Kaplan's investigation of nomadism also acknowledges the influences of global neo-liberalism on these patterns of hypermobility, thus repositioning diaspora at the center of all global movements and not only of the ones that are concerned with those pertaining to the lower working class.

While Kaplan's work traces displacement as metaphor for the multiple global circuits of Western cultural currency in general, other scholars offer investigations of how the U.S. in particular figures as a nexus within transnational cultural formations. In her book *Transnational America: Feminisms, Diasporas, Neoliberalisms* (2005), Inderpal Grewal examines the "conjunction of geopolitics and biopolitics in relation to the production of gendered and racialized bodies and subjects" (3) and the "imbrication of changing and contingent nationalist belonging with a transnational consumer culture facilitated by new technologies of communication, production and consumption" (13). In particular, Grewal looks at the multi-layered cross-fertilizations of consumer products including the novels of Bharati Mukherjee and Chitra Banerjee Divakaruni and the "Indian" Barbie that Mattel started circulating in the late 1980s. All of these circulations of consumer goods and the ideological economic master plan in which they occurred, contributed, proposes Grewal convincingly, to the formation of a transnational American identity, one that shaped the U.S. market in comparative measures as it shaped the Indian market. Based on these observations Grewal contends that "Americanness was produced transnationally by cultural, political, and economic practices, so that becoming American did not always or necessarily connote full participation or belonging to a nation-state" (8) but that it operated with an "imaginary coherence"[58] that informs the collective consciousness at the roots of Indian diasporic communities in the U.S. as well as communities in India that draw identification from the presence of global consumer culture, including American popular culture (49).

Both Kaplan and Grewal foreground the transnational components of the complex vectors that make up place in a postmodern, global world system. Their accounts of the displacements of traveling theories and the transnational production and global circulation of culture in the Indian communities do, respectively, also imply the importance to re-conceptualize community as a conjoining force of identification. Kaplan's and Grewal's work is symptomatic of a general concern in feminist and postmodern theory to examine the extent to which defintions of gender, race and class continue to be colonial legacies in contemporary conceptualizations of the global world order. As they do in their individual projects, so, too do Kaplan and Grewal forge new grounds into the study of gender in a transnational context in their co-edited collection of essays, *Scattered Hegemonies: Postmodernity and Transnational Feminist Practices* (1994). In that project, Kaplan and Grewal put under scrutiny the terrains and structures of cultural exchanges with the ultimate goal of teasing out the gaps and overlaps between feminist theory and studies of postmodernity outside of Western academic discursive practices in ways that Ien Ang and Gayatri Chakravorty Spivak have delineated successfully. I am thinking here in particular of Spivak's discussion of "old" and "new" diasporas and her conclusion that woman in diaspora is "the site of global public culture privatized" (251) as well as of Ang's adoption of Bhabha's "third space" metaphor in her argumentation that diasporic communities are characterized by a cultural "collision/collusion" that demarcates their innate "ambivalent in-between-ness" (16).

---

[58] Grewal borrows this term form Stuart Hall's "Cultural Identity and Diaspora," where he defines the concept of "imaginary coherence" as the "experience of dispersal and fragmentation which is the history of all enforced diasporas" (qtd. in Grewal 49).

Destabilizing the notion of community as it often prevails in relation to a person's sense of belonging begs the following question: how does community still function in a transnational era, or has the very concept of community itself become, as Btihaj Ajana proposes, "too fluid, too amorphous, and too problematic" (99)? In pursuit of answers to these questions, the final chapter of this book will explore the construction and negotiation of national and transnational communities. I have chosen for the exploration of this question Vineeta Vijayaraghavan's novel *Motherland* (2001), a novel that has not received any critical attention thus far. What I find worth exploring in Vijayaraghavan's novel are two things: first, the fact that it is set exclusively in India, while the other novels I have discussed in the previous chapters are mostly set in the U.S.; and the fact that the question of matrilineage arises out of the protagonist's experience of multiple female communities in India, whereas in the other novels I have discussed the question of matrilineage emerged solely from the daughter's conflict with her mother. It is from within this context that Maya, the young protagonist, revisits her relationship with her mother and her motherlands, both India and the U.S. Although the mother is not Maya's only or primary means of identification with the homeland, but that the grandmother and the female community of her relatives and kin function as a means of projecting a feminized image of India, thus exposing the young Indian American protagonist Maya a variety of challenges toward her understanding of her symbolic motherland, both the real and the imaginary one, and her place in it.

In line with Salman Rushdie's assertion that as exilic Indian writer he lives with "imaginary homelands, Indias of the mind" (10), I argue that *Motherland* configures the mother-daughter relationship as a site in which the imaginary homeland that Maya lives with resists easy classifications in terms of her sense of belonging. Maya's encounter with Indian culture and the discrepancy between the homeland she imagined and the one she actively experiences underscores the complex discursive constructedness of cultural and national communities, or more aptly, between communities of culture and communities of nation-ness.[59] For instance, while India grapples with the recent assassination of Rajiv Gandhi, Maya struggles to make sense of the many encounters with consumer culture within contemporary Indian culture. Following Benedict Anderson's argument in *Imagined Communities* (1983) that nationalism is being disseminated through "the convergence of capitalism and print technol-

[59] Benedict Anderson defines the concept of nation-ness, and by extension the concept of nationalism as well, are "cultural artefacts" that "became 'modular,' capable of being transplanted, with varying degrees of self-consciousness, to a great variety of social terrains o, to merge and be merged with a correspondingly wide variety of political and ideological constellations" (4).

ogy" (46), I am most interested in this chapter in Maya's negotiation of her identity, her experience of diaspora and return, and the related negotiation of her role as a daughter and granddaughter at a time of an increased attenuation to national discourses and ongoing globalization. In short, I am concerned with the question of how gender and national imaginary communities can reconcile nationalism and globalization in an era of hyper-mobility and the interconnectedness of Indian and Indian American communities, an era in which, as Maya suggests "Everyone has an American niece these days" (69).

Diasporic In-Between-ness

The novel starts with a declaration by the 15 year-old protagonist Maya that her trip to India in the summer of 1991 was a punishment for having gone joyriding with her high school friends, one of whom was the drunk driver: "I was shipped off to India that summer because of the death of a deer" (1), reads the first line of the first chapter, "Migration." With these lines, the chapter offers the first of several brief flashbacks to the causes for Maya's trip to India before reverting back to the present setting of the novel, her arrival at a regional airport in the state of Tamil Nadu, from where she rides with her uncle Sanjay and her grandmother Ammamma to the family home on a tea plantation, chauffeured by a driver from her uncle's company. In another flashback, Maya recalls the argument her parents had that led up to their decision to send her to India in order to teach her a lesson. This discussion over how to discipline Maya soon shifts into a conversation about the family's socialization into U.S. culture, displaying two distinctly different approaches: "My mother thought spending time with my relatives might teach me to remember where we had come from. My father thought where we had come from wasn't as important as dealing with where we were now" (5). What sounds at first glance like a mere parenting discussion on how to raise their teenage daughter also evokes the primary condition of diaspora that Paul Gilroy paraphrases as centered around the two modes of identification "where you're from" and "where you're at." These two moments, so Gilroy elaborates, emphasize the distinction between origin and present location, the first one privileging discourses that conflate national origin with cultural identity, and the second one trying to recover the complex interconnectedness of heterogeneous national communities (1990/91). While the father comes away as being more progressive, the novel follows the mother's assertion that origin prevails. The recovery of origin also sets the tone for Maya's trip to India.

Maya's trip to India amplifies her location in between discourses of where you're from and where you're at. In particular, the novel's striking adherence to symmetry is one of the features that place Maya in the in-between-ness of cultural entities and ideological paradigms, and thus create the novel's tension. For instance, already in the U.S., Maya is torn between her father's and her mother's ideal of how Indian American women should behave, her father being more sympathetic towards Maya's teenage escapades. In India, confronted with her origins, Maya encounters a number of cues about her identity, encounters that always appear "in pairs." For instance, her British cousin Madhu and her Indian cousin Brindha signify to Maya how young "Indian" women behave. Madhu exemplifies to Maya the extent to which Indian transnational identities in the U.S. and in Britain differ from each other, and Brindha offers to Maya an example of what growing up in India is like. Through Maya's juxtaposition with Madhu and Brindha, the novel thus emphasizes not only a difference between national and transnational communities but also among the specific transnational communities as well. Furthermore, Madhu's self-governed sexuality and sexual freedom stand in contrast to the marriage agreement that is being negotiated on Maya's behalf and the policed interaction between her and her suitor Suraj. In a different context, Maya's two caretakers, Ammama and Rupa, are both associated with a level of "traditional" Indian culture that Maya needs to learn to understand in order to be able to function within the family setting of her aunt and uncle's home. And finally, the traditional Indian rituals of cooking and burial offer a contrast to the global consumer culture and movie industry. Of course, in part Vijayaraghavan seems to want to offer an account of modern India that does not conform to the preconceived notions that the likes of Madhu keep, but to offer instead a glimpse of the cultural tensions and innate heterogeneity of modern India. But in the end, the main question that Maya faces with regards to her personal location in India also only leaves two options, as her aunt Reema explains to her: "You can come here and be a tourist, do whatever you like to do, or you can come here and be a member of this family, with responsibilities and obligations" (115).

The novel's attention to various nuances of traditional and modern Indian culture characterizes Maya's in-between-ness in transnational terms, in that it deconstructs the boundaries between East and West, presumably between traditionalism and modernity. In this sense, Vijayaraghavan's novel pursues a different trajectory from what Amy Ling has coined as "between worlds" trope of Chinese American women writers. In *Between Worlds: Women Writers of Chinese Ancestry* (1990), Amy Ling discusses the cultural location of Chinese immigrant and American-born Chinese American authors as both defined and rejected by U.S. culture and by Chinese culture. This double negation of space renders them invisible on the American and the Chinese cultural landscapes (20). In Ling's terms, being between worlds in essence means falling through the grit of cultural definitions both in the U.S. and in Asia. Unlike Ling, Elaine H. Kim proposes the concept of a "diasporic shift," that is, of the complex experience of hybridity, in Asian American literature (1992, xiii).

Vijayaraghavan's novel takes this notion of in-between-ness a step further by dismantling not just the two but various imaginary communities that construct American and Indian identity. For instance, the novel's juxtaposition of 'where you're from' and 'where you're at' in the first chapter briefly alludes to the multiple conceptual frameworks that constitute identity in the community of the Indian diaspora. Similarly, cultural diversity in India, both in terms of racial and class divisions between the likes of her uncle's family and the families of his co-workers and their Tamil servants but also within the upper middle class, which practices traditional customs at the same time as it participates in post-modern consumer culture, exemplifies the cultural complexity of the land of her ancestors and extended family. But even more so, this complexity is emblematic of Maya's identity quest and her search for her personal location within the motherlands that frame her sense of belonging. While both countries, India and the U.S., can be a home for her, the cultural heterogeneity of the two countries and her transnational negotiation of them makes it difficult for her to assume a definite sense of home. And because the two cultural identities are also constructed in relation to one another and thus are discursively intertwined, negotiating one culture always also entails redefining the other as well.

This linkage between and convergence of the processes of identification is akin to the dynamics of mother-daughter relationships. It echoes both on the level of Maya's relationship to her mother and to her grandmother as well as on the level of national and cultural identity "the ambivalence of identification in terms of national citizenships and belonging" that Francoise Lionnet and Shu-mei Shih define in *Minor Transnationalism* as a key moment in transnational identity politics (13). It also substantiates Aamir Mufti and Ella Shohat's claim for "a conceptual framework that refuses to separate the linked histories of race as well as the contemporary complication of communities within and across the borders of nation-states. [...] It is impossible to discuss issues of nation and gender in national isolation" (McClintock et al. 2-3).

At the same time, however, it is interesting to note that despite the novel's successful resistance to fall into orientalist classification of East and West, its reliance on symmetries and binary oppositions does reinforce an all too familiar conceptualization of Western modernity, one that espouses a clear distinction between past and present, center and periphery.[60] This is especially inter-

---

[60] In *Modernity at Large: Cultural Dimensions of Globalization* (1996), Arjun Appadurai locates this binary oppositionality at the center of modernity: "One of the most problematic legacies of grand Western social science [...] is that it has steadily re-

esting since the novel employs such binarity in order to emphasize Maya's Western approach. After all, in line with her mother's intent of making her daughter's trip to India a didactic and formative experience, Maya does transition from a rigid assumption of national identities to a more fluid concept of transnational and intersubjective conceptionalization of herself. For instance, her arrival is dominated by her assumption that the contrast between Indian and American culture is well pronounced. She exhibits such a notion in relation to her own body, such as when she is taking a shower in attempt to "peel away the Americanness that made [her] feel clumsy and conspicuous here" (35), and in relation to Indian culture, as becomes evident from her uncle's reminder "This isn't the frontier" (16) in response to Maya's comments on what she considers the pristine hillside of rural India. Through such comments, Maya's "India of the mind" becomes tangible for the reader, a fact that illustrates her in-between-ness and supports the novel's *bildungsromanesque* movement form innocence to experience.

Such adherence to binary oppositions also characterizes Maya's relationship to her mother. Much in line with her assumption that her mother's decision to send her to India for the summer is a punishment, Maya sees her mother her antagonist. Of course, this is somewhat to be expected of a 15-year old girl in the middle of adolescence and conforms largely to the kinds of childhood memories many daughters narrate in Asian American literature. But while in the works of Maxine Hong Kingston, Amy Tan, Mei Ng and Nora Okja Keller the fathers are largely absent and the mother-daughter relationships form tight units and binary oppositions in themselves, Vijayaraghavan's novel presents a father who is well invested in his daughter's teenage life, in fact so much so that Maya has a closer bond to her father than to her mother. With her mother away on business trips for extensive lengths of time, Maya and her father form a unit, characterized by mutual understanding and empathy, such as is the case when Maya's trip to India comes across as a "defeat" (5) both to Maya and to her father. By emphasizing the Oedipal triangle between Maya, her father and her mother, Vijayaraghavan's novel evokes strong affinities with the family feminist romance that many Western women writers adopt.[61]

While this antagonistic relationship between Maya and her mother underscores the psychological conflict with her mother in ways that characterizes the Western *bildungsroman*, Maya's encounter with multiple female figures during

---

inforced the sense of some single moment – call it modern moment – that by its appearance creates a dramatic and unprecedented break between past and present" (3-4)

[61] Marianne Hirsch discussed at length the predominance of feminist family romances as genre of mother-daughter writing, see chapter 4 in *The Mother/Daughter Plot*.

her stay in India contrasts the binary opposition she feels towards her mother. These female figures, including her grandmother Ammamma, her aunt Reema, her British cousin Madhu, her Indian cousin Brindha, and the family's servant Rupa embody possible role models for Maya. In particular, the fact that Maya used to live with her grandmother for several years, even thought during that time that Ammamma is her mother, when her parents immigrated to the U.S. alone, emphasizes her comparison between her real mother and the person she first imagined to be her imagined/remembered mother. And while the novel initially foregrounds the binarity between self and other in the relationship between Maya and her mother, for the most part it sketches Maya's interaction with multiple, and heterogeneous "others," various women of different cultural backgrounds.

Although the novel focuses on Maya's development, it does not present her surroundings as static. In other words, while Maya is central to the novel's plot development, she is not the only protagonist who is in constant negotiation of her identity. This is especially interesting since the narrative prespective always stays with Maya. Because she is the narrator, all of the events are filtered through her perspective. This is interesting to note because despite the fact that Maya is the novel's main narrator and focalizer, the reader also learns a great deal about the other characters' thoughts and feelings, for instance through their conversations with Maya.

Because Maya is aware of the various different notions of Indian identity, the novel does not fall into the trap of appropriating Indian culture through an orientalist framework, thus avoiding clear distinctions between Western individualism and Eastern collectivism. Instead, it addresses different cultural phenomena without locating them on either side of the East/West binary. For instance, Maya grew up believing that her mother left her in India with Ammamma for what she considers selfish reasons – the same approach she takes towards her mother's successful but time-consuming job as a business executive. What she does not know until this summer in India, until her grandmother tells her the long kept family secret, is that her mother fell into a severe postpartum depression after the death of her baby daughter. This is the first time that Maya learns about her twin sister, and about the toll this tragic event took on the relationship between her mother and Ammamma. In particular, this knowledge enables Maya to understand why her mother never wanted her own mother to come visit in the U.S. for any extensive period of time (210). More importantly, however, Maya learns that it was her grandmother's idea that her mother should come to India to give birth to her daughters. In the same chapter, Maya picks up on this sentiment, announcing closure to her identity conflict with her mother: "Here I had gained (however tenuously) a mother, a conscience, and the awareness that compassion often mattered as much or more than justice" (231). Hence, Maya's reconciliation with her mother and her understanding of her past sketches the transnational complexity of Maya's imagined community.

While Maya and her mother Kamala do reach a sense of mutual understanding, Maya realizes that the main solution to her identity quest is her appreciation of the intertwined histories of India and the U.S. that chart the map of her family genealogy. This sense of intertwined personal histories is embodied in her relationship with Ammamma. The novel speaks of "maps of the heart" – thus foregrounding the interpersonal relationships at the basis of the East/West encounters between Maya and her family. This is also the note on which the novel ends. Maya's last thoughts before returning to the U.S. are: "Maps of the physical world were changed all the time because history and memory ultimately trumped geography. With what Ammamma had given me, I had a suspicion that I, too, could surpass geography. I could live anywhere, be grafted and take root anywhere, and anywhere could be my home" (232).

Thus, Maya's sense of self shifts from a Westerncentric paradigm, epitomized by her experience of her arrival in India in terms Turner's frontier thesis, to a more transnational understanding of her location within different cultures and geographies. The novel ends with a very optimistic take on global mobility free from constraints of nationhood, much in line with Gloria Anzaldúa's assertion of living without borders[62] and Aihwa Ong's concept of *flexible citizenship*.[63] In this sense, community in *Motherland* exemplifies Anzaldúa's definition of borderlands as place of cultural encounters: "borderlands [are] physically present wherever two or more cultures edge each other, where people of different cultures occupy the same territory, where under, lower, middle and upper class touch, where the space between two individuals shrinks with intimacy" (*Borderlands* 9).

However, this notion of borderlands pertains to Maya much more than it does to the personal and cultural encounters between other female figures of the novel. In particular, the characterization of Ammamma as archetypal "Mother India" on the one hand and the servant Rupa's marginality within Indian national discourses exhibits that the concept of borderlands is not equally applicable to all women.

---

[62] In *Borderlands / La Frontera: The New Mestiza*, Anzaldúa argues that transnational identity in a global ear requires of a person to "live *sin fronteras*, be a crossroads" (217, original emphasis).

[63] Ong's book animates the scholarship on "migration, diaspora, and other transnational flows" (8) by emphasizing the ways ih which late capitalism coins the flexibilty of movement in a global era.

Origin and Belonging

The binary opposition that Vijayaraghavan's novel foregrounds also raises issues about the question of origin and belonging in this diasporic in-betweenness that characterizes Maya's identity negotiation. In line with Edward Said's definition of origin as a *passive* and beginning as an *active* mode of belonging (1975, 6), Maya moves through the course of the novel from a passive to an active sense of belonging. This active beginning also entails approaching the question of her national and cultural belonging in a new light. In "Displaced Relations," Makarand Paranjape proposes a reading of diaspora that emphasizes the discursive constructedness of the concept of belonging. Paranjape suggests that neither *belonging* nor *disbelonging* is "a given condition" (231) and that there is "neither pure belonging nor pure disbelonging" (233). In line with Said's notion of beginning and Paranjape's notion of belonging, Vijayaraghavan's novel presents a reciprocal relationship between the communities in the homeland and in the diaspora,[64] thus questioning the nostalgic connotation that diaspora as a cultural concept often carries. Without recognizing the reciprocal relationship between homeland and diaspora, the full scope of what Vijayaraghavan's novel does cannot be understood. This is due to that fact that the field of diaspora studies, for the most part, overlooks the transnational interconnectedness of communities in a global era.

As Vijayaraghavan's novel suggests, this attention to this interconnectedness of homeland and diaspora in an important intervention with which to approach the complexity of Asian American identity and the multiple discourses that shape Asian American critique. To apply the concept of diaspora without keeping this relationship in mind would hardly offer sufficient insight into the complexity of third and forth generation Asian American communities, nor would it make sufficiently visible the interconnectivity between the histories of Asia and the U.S. and the multiple encounters that shaped these histories in the past and continue to overshadow present cultural encounters. This is a general problem with the concept of diaspora as a cultural phenomenon. In particular, diaspora is always preoccupied with an originary moment of dispersal, whether this be an active beginning or a passive origin, and a moment of arrival, a singularly defined *telos*. In part, the terminology of diaspora is indicative of a double hauntedness, i.e. the quest for the nation state and the nation state's issues with receiving and accommodating diasporic people, but especially because it re-enforces the iconistic value of a nation state. Such asser-

[64] Paranjape even proposes that there are "competing notions of India" in diasporic writing (237).

tions govern William Safran's discussion of diaspora in his seminal essay "Diasporas in Modern Societies: Myths of Homeland and Return." But what Safran does not sufficiently recognize in his essay is a host of questions that emphasize the multiple meanings and nuances within the cultural currency that diaspora carries. For instance, the very concept of diaspora conjures up a host of questions: who gets to be called a diasporic people? At what point does voluntary migration become coerced diaspora? Who determines the legitimacy of diasporic discourses of a people? At the same time, diaspora often has been applied as a concept that defines the loss and disadvantage of those who left their homelands behind, often with the result of implicating nostalgic images of origin.[65]

As far as non-first-generation immigrant Asian American writers are concerned, these questions only tentatively evoke their own experiences of U.S. culture, of the diasporic cultures their ancestors embody, and of the Asian cultures their relatives in Asia represent. The prevalent emphasis on the nation-state with which the methodology of diaspora operates also idealizes the position of an imaginary and physical homeland and thus in a sense also reinscribes national boundaries into the cultural discourse. In particular, the issue of legitimacy and authenticity makes apparent rigid boundaries with which individuals or specific groups need to measure themselves in order to fit into prevalent concepts of a mostly masculinist and heteroreferentialist critical paradigm of diaspora. Due to the underlying preoccupation with essentialism, the dynamics of diversity, hierarchy, and heterogeneity within diasporic people and their cultural legacies often gain little attention. In this vein, David Leiwei Li proposes in *Imagining the Nation: Asian American Literature and Cultural Consent* (1998) that Asian American critique needs to move beyond "the inventive and interventional power of 'Asian America(n),' not as a thing in itself but as an insistent dialogue among dominant, ethnic, and diasporic communities" (17). And by maintaining such dialogues, Asian American critique overlaps with the field of transnational studies, that field that most recently deconstructed and reshaped the vocabulary and practice of Asian American critique.

---

[65] Makarand Paranjape interrogates this in "What About Those Who Stayed Back Home," an essay that examines the privilege of diasporic writing over nationalistic writing.

Between Womanhood and Nationhood

Maya's encounters between her imaginary homeland and the imagined community of India as a present-day nation also lead her to understand to which extent gender, race and class are parameters that influence national discourses. In particular, in conversation with her British cousin Madhu, who is a couple of years older than Maya, various comparisons emerge through which Maya becomes sensitive to racial and class differences in different societies, including, the U.S., India, and Britain. For instance, the two girls have a rather heated discussion about Indian diasporic identities. In this conversation, Madhu seems to be more aware of the class difference as a contributing vector to ethnic social diversity in Britain. In the chapter "The British Are Coming," Madhu argues that "What's race in the U.S. is class in Britain and in India" (104), a statement by which she inevitably picks up on the colonial implications of British-Indian relations that the chapter title may evoke.[66]

It is also in conversation with Madhu that Maya encounters most explicitly questions about her identity as Indian woman of the diaspora. Speculating about her personal choices of partnership, such as the issue of picking a partner whose ethnic heritage meets her relatives' approval, Madhu anticipates that "her life will be too incomprehensible for" her Indian relatives (122). In particular context of Madhu's formulations of her identity as independent from her Indian relatives, the proposal for an arranged marriage that Maya receives during her stay in India emphasizes transnational conceptualizations of femininity that she needs to figure out as part of her rites of passage. This is important because her personal negotiation of her identity as woman is intrinsically linked to conceptualization of gender in the context of Indian culture. In her aunt's statements such as "girls keep the family going" (69), Maya confronts prevalent discourses about women's cultural responsibilities towards the collective identity that position them within the nationalistic conceptualization of Indian culture at large. In this sense, one of the learning experiences Maya has to undergo is to figure out on her own terms which measure gender and national identity are underlying parameters that govern cultural identity.

Recent scholarship in transnational feminism has made accessible this understanding that the concept of nationhood cannot be addressed without looking at the implications of gender in the formation of national identities. In the introduction to the collection of essays, *Between Woman and Nation: National-*

---

[66] Although the exclamation "The British Are Coming!" possibly refers to a warning Paul Revere might have issued as a warning to the Americans against British invasion, I would argue that Madhu's arrival to India provokes a reading of the chapter title as referential to British colonization of India.

isms, Transnational Feminisms, and the State (1999), Norma Alarcón, Caren Kaplan, and Minoo Moallem argue that "the nation-state sharpens the defining lines of citizenship for women, racialized ethnicities, and sexualities in the construction of a socially stratified society" (1). The authors position their definitions of the nation-state and its impact on communities by drawing on Benedict Anderson's concept of imagined communities and Homi K. Bhabha's discussion of nationalist discourses. They propose that to consider race, gender and sexuality as imaginary communities, that is, as discursively constructed matrixes, defines the nation-state as discursive construction in Benedict Anderson's terms. In *The Location of Culture* (1994), Homi K. Bhabha contends that "the complex strategies of cultural identification and discursive address that function in the name of 'the people' or 'the nation' and make them the immanent subjects of a range of social and literary narratives" (140). Bhabha's definition of "counternarratives" of the nation, so argue the authors, "evoke and disturb those ideological maneuvers through which 'imagined communities' are given essentialist definitions" (7).

Women maintain a special position within this social formation of nationhood. As Alarcón and her co-editors specify: "Women are both of and not of the nation. Between woman and nation is, perhaps, the space or zone where we can deconstruct these monoliths and render them more historically nuanced and accountable to politics" (12). This contestation follows a general determination in transnational feminist studies to point out the limitations of modernity, whose formation was largely overshadowed by the "naturalization and essentialization of nation and woman" (13). In contrast, volumes like Alarcón's underscore the discursive constructedness of woman and nation, arguing that the naturalized cathexis of the two materializes in the discourses of normativity which coined the modern nation-state.

Maya's identity quest leads her to an exploration of this space between woman and nation, that is, between her maternal grandmother Ammama and her experience of modern India after the assassination of Rajiv Gandhi. Ammama's death toward the end of the novel marks the closure of an entire era in Maya's imaginary community of India: with Ammama, the family secrets and stories die, and Maya thus loses her closest connection to the country she was born in. After Ammama's death, Maya also experiences a shift in her relationship to the family's servant Rupa, a shift that ossifies in the incarceration of both girls and Maya's uncle's refusal to assist Rupa and the legal defense against the accusations of terrorism that incriminate her. And finally, the convergence of Ammama's death, the changes in the Indian political landscape and the changes within Maya's extended family, all three frame Maya's rite of passage from girlhood into womanhood. While in the U.S. she is already secretly dating a boy, Maya encounters in India images of womanhood that she needs to incorporate into her self-understanding as an Indian woman of the diaspora, including social norms and codes of dating in Indian communities, Indian popular culture and the Bollywood movie industry, and female sexuality. These encounters between the India Maya remembers or imagines and the 'real' India, such as the one that is maintained by the social norms of the upper-middle class families, are sometimes at odds with her younger cousin Brindha's fascination with Indian pop culture and the way it facilitates in-group alliances among the girls in her boarding school, and her older British cousin Madhu's sexual escapades in Britain and her trekking tour to Goa, a trendy tourist resort for the young and hip travelers. All of these encounters amend Maya's idea of India, one that she got from her mother's attempt to "re-create India from all things American" (67) after the family settled in New York. In a sense, all of her experiences of Indian culture, whether in the homeland or in diaspora, are mediated by female figures, including the family's servant Rupa and the female terrorist who killed Gandhi. This presence of female figures in Maya's experience of India shares affinities with Vijayaraghavan's conceptualization of India as inherently feminized space and Indian national identity as a way to offer gendered images of traditional and transitional social, political and cultural spaces.

On the level of topics, Maya's immersion into the family life of her relatives and kin coincides with the assassination of Rajiv Gandhi in 1991 by a female terrorist from the Tamil Tigers. This coincidence frames Maya's stay in India, starting with her arrival and the heightened security measures she has to undergo at the airport when entering the country, and ending with the arrest of the family's servant Rupa by the police and her accusation of being a member of the Tamil Tigers. Maya, too, is being arrested and thus identified as suspiciously alien to Indian national identity and as a potential accomplice to a terrorist group. But even before that, the relatives' worries about how much Maya knows about the present political situation in India foregrounds isues related to Indian national identitiy and thus places the novel under the light of discussions about traditionalism in India, both Muslim fundamentalism and Hindu nationalism, respectively. The convergence of gender and nationhood is especially striking in the way in which the novel thematizes the concept of *female* terrorists. While the information about Gandhi's assassination by a female terrorist is historically accurate, the excessive attention that the novel devotes to the idea of female terrorists suggests a fascination with the fact that women can be, and are, terrorists. The novel sensationalizes the idea of female terrorism in two ways: first by forcing the reader to rely on speculations as to whether Rupa is indeed a member of the Tamil Tigers, and possibly also a terrorist herself, and second, by encorporating this issue into the conversations of the upper-middle class male citizens. In both contexts, the novel offers a sensationalist approach to the notion of female terrorism by emphasizing the modifier female. What seems to be otherwise a category that primarily connotes deviance from a national sense of solidarity and allegience – terrorist – thus becomes a highly gendered category through the fascination with the modifier female. This is particularly jarring since the gendered image that the reference to female terrorists connotes not only highlights their lack of allegiance to the nation-state, it also infers their deviance from normative concepts of feminine spheres of domesticity and reproduction.[67]

The convergence of imaginary conceptionalizations of gender and nationhood, as Alarcón, Kaplan and Moallem propose in their discussion of the discursive space "between woman and nation," epitomizes the need in feminist theory and practice to investigate the ways in which gender informs concepts of nationhood and, reciprocally, the ways in which nationhood informs gender. With specific attention to Indian modernity, Nalini Natarajan draws such connections in her analysis of Salman Rushdie's novel *Midnight's Children*. In particular, Natarajan examines "the spectacle or visual effect of woman as it shapes the national imaginary, the way woman functions as sign in the imagining of community, the relation of these aspects of woman as sign and spectacle (as figurations of the beloved, mother, and daughter) to the failure of the secularization project that 'Indian' culture generally, and the Bombay cinema industry in particular, envisaged for itself in the early decades of Indian independence" (76). Natarajan's observations about the ways in which "woman function[ed] as a signifier in many ways in the contrary dialectics of stasis and change in the imagining of India" (79) also pertain to Vijayaraghavan's novel. These ways are defined as three distinct aspects of nationalism: "(1) the movement from regional to national in the 'modernizing' process, (2) the threat of communal or civic rupture within the body politic, and (3) the rise of fundamentalism" (79). Because these distinct aspects adequately relate to the plot movement of *Motherland*, I will offer in the following section a detailed analysis of Maya's encounters of the convergences of the two imagined communities, woman and nation, during her stay in India.

The movement away from the regional and toward a national reach of community is central to Maya's encounter with a gendered concept of nationhood. The person who embodies this is Rupa because she embodies the convergence of regional and national classification: on a regional level of Tamil Nadu, Rupa represents the dark-skinned working class to the established upper-middle class business families; and on a national level, she represents the Tamil

[67] I am grateful to Cara Cilano for calling my attention to this matter.

ethnic minority that, with the assassination of Gandhi, is being associated primarily with terrorist activities against the nation-state of India. In line with Natarajan's assertion that a "[w]oman's body is a site for testing out modernity" (79), Maya's growing awareness of the regional and national implications which Rupa represents occur in relation to the biopolitical implications that Rupa's identity carries. There are two incidents in the novel which conceptionalize Rupa within Indian nationalist discourses, and it is rather telling that both incidents have to do with her body. The first one occurs during Maya's outing into the wilderness, where she wants to go bathing in a lake and Rupa, who was told to accompany her, also jumps into the lake. Maya experiences this moment with Rupa as a moment of bonding, and reflects on how Rupa, while maintaining a physical distance to Maya, shares Maya's sense of liberation when bathing in the lake. Rupa even offers to take Maya to the lake after a heavy rain and to see its waterfall, an offer that seems to solidify the bond between the two women who just transgressed the boundaries of the social behavior deemed appropriate for them (126). Therefore, Maya has difficulty understanding why Rupa begs her not to touch her when Maya offers to pick the leeches off of Rupa's back, a gesture which she thought would reciprocate the help Rupa offered in picking the leeches off of Maya's body. What first starts off as a playful encounter between two young women soon becomes a cultural encounter framed by race and class hierarchies.

These hierarchies also pertain to the second incident, where Maya, Brindha and Rupa are being investigated by three agents from the Central Bureau of Intelligence for potential complicity in Tamil Tiger terrorist activities. Maya and Brindha's interaction with Rupa is another point of contention. While Maya's transgression of class boundaries in her relationship with Rupa is indicative of her unfamiliarity with Indian social codes of behavior, her and Brindha's fascination with Rupa's alleged connection to the Tamil Tigers borders mere sensationalism. Brindha, for instance has a collection of news articles on the key suspects in organizing the assignation of Rajiv Gandhi and pictures of the female suicide bomber bowing in front of the president, thus initialing the explosion. Moreover, she keeps in her boarding school locker an empty cyanide capsule, one that allegedly all Tamil Tigers carry with themselves in case of facing arrest or torture by the police.[68] While Ammamma is in the hospital after a stroke, 10-year old Brindha is being bestowed with the task, in order to keep her from worrying too much about her grandmother, of collecting the hospital bills and paying them with the money her father gives her each

[68] The novel makes clear, however, that Brindha's fascination with the Tamil Tigers echoes to a certain degree the national distress over the terrorist acts, such as the constant broadcasting and circulation of the same images that Brindha collects indicate.

time. Apparently, she also (knowingly or unknowingly) pays for the medication of a number of Tamil Tigers who are also hospitalized at that time, arguing defensively that she was only trying to follow her father's advice to help others (219). It is not clear whether the men whose medicine she paid are indeed terrorists – they are "Rupa's friends" (219) and the novel never explicitly clarifies whether they are being falsely accused or whether they are indeed active members of a terrorist group. But based on the fact that Rupa is Tamil and that the CBI have been raiding Brindha's stash of Tiger memorabilia the novel seems to suggest that Rupa and Brindha are guilty. Such, at least, seems to be the parents' impression. Still, it is not so much the accusation of Maya and Bridha for conspiracy in illegal behavior which reifies existing social hierarchies between Hindus and Tamils, it is Sanjay's explicit refusal to come to Rupa's defense. Maya's comments: "The agents were letting us go because Sanjay uncle had convinced them that we were different from Rupa, that we didn't have the same motivations, but that wasn't necessarily true. They didn't account for our fascination with danger, Brindha's and mine, with the forbidden and the unknown" (220).

Sanjay's lack of solidarity with the family servant becomes plausible when considered in juxtaposition with an earlier incident in the novel in which his co-workers debate about the psychological motivations that may lead to terrorism. As is Sanjay's assertion, so, too, do his fellow upper-middle class citizens foreground racial difference as main factor. In conversation about which young woman is more likely to become a suicide bomber, a fair or a dark-skinned one, one of Sanjay's co-workers maintains: "It's not the pretty ones who become killers, it's the dark, homely ones who don't have any other way of getting attention. Blowing up leaders is the only way dark-skinned girls will ever get their picture in magazines" (81).

Just as much as these politics of the body determines the discourse of the allegations against Rupa, it also epitomizes the nationalist discourses that determine the conceptionalization of gender. In a sense, the same politics that results in the racial othering of Rupa also results in the melancholic longing for traditional gender concepts. This is also what links the incident with Rupa to the novel's general conceptualization of Ammamma as embodiment of an intact Indian social order. Much in line with Natarajan's assertion that at the basis of nationalist discourses is a rhetoric which employs "'Mother India' [as] a site for the mystic unity in the face of fragmentation" (79). Ammamma represents.a social order which successfully resists diversification. This does not mean that Ammamma serves as the novel's most conservative figure whose traditional values the young generation cannot possibly embrace. While such is Madhu's belief, for instance, when she warns Maya that "Grandmothers are the worst. They don't understand that things change" (110), Maya sees her grandmother in less essentialist terms. Still, Ammamma plays a symbolic function that in Maya's identity quest, one which exemplifies the feminization of India suggested in the novel's title. For instance, the fact that Ammamma's death coincides with the end of the Gandhi era signifies the convergence of regional and national events that Natarajan detects as factors through which nationalist discourses gain momentum.

Similarly, the very fact that Ammamma is the keeper of the family secret is suggestive in this context. Ammamma symbolizes the familiy's tradition, not as a moral instance that counters modern conceptualizations of Indian culture, such as the ones that Maya needs to formulate in her own Indian American context, but as a more empathetic one. When she records the anecdotes that Maya tells her in order to help Maya regain her memory after she suffered from a concussion, Ammamma takes on the role of the recorder of both the collective family history and of Maya's personal memories. Nevertheless, it is the reliance on female mother figures and the implication of a heteronormative social order that ultimately facilitates Maya's self-discovery and leads her to adopt a notion of India as essentially feminized space. This becomes evident from her embracing of India as homeland, as maternal space: "That place was home even though here was where I had gained and lost a grandmother, gained and lost a friendship, a sister, a marriage proposal" (231). Unlike her cousin Madhu, who maintains that the experience of Indian culture facilitated through Maya's temporary stay with her relatives is "quaint and beautiful" but "not real" (103), Maya believes that the "maps of the heart" bind her to this feminized Indian culture. This is pivotal of Maya's sentimental adherence to an idealized homeland because it exemplifies her critical understanding of the transnational ties that can be maintained between cultures and continents.

While the novel ends on such an optimistic note in relation to Maya's identity quest as a young woman of the Indian diaspora, it does not support her suggestion on the novel's last page that place and identity are not interrelated. Whether or not the imaginary community of a feminized space can provide room for transnational solidarity remains open in the novel. In part, the reliance on traditionalist understandings of what constitutes Indian culture and how it needs to be preserved make such transnational solidarity difficult. This aspect in *Motherland* is analogous to Natarajan's contestation that nationalist discourse is always accompanied by or results in fundamentalist ideology. In specific relation to gender images, so Natarajan further proposes, women become "a site for countering the challenge posed by 'Westernization'" (79). Such is also the case in *Motherland*, however not so much in relation to Ammamma's role as embodiment of traditional Hindu culture, but in the fact that the reliance on traditional female roleship within the diasporic Indian community. In other words, it is the Indian American and British Indian young women, as the example of Maya and Madhu respectively illustrate, that most consciously encounter the convergence of gender and nationality in Indian modern culture. Madhu is aware of the restrictions on female social behavior and sexuality because her grandmother taught her through the legend of Sita that a woman's moral reputation cannot be restored within the community even if she was falsely accused of deviance (111). And Maya experiences this issue firsthand when Suraj's family withdraws their initially rather aggressive marriage proposal after Maya loses her good reputation when they find Brindha's Tamil Tiger memorabilia and Madhu's birth control pills in Maya's suitcase. The birth control pills suggest to Suraj's family that Maya is probably already sexually active, and the Tamil Tiger memorabilia suggest that she is potentially linked to a Muslim fundamentalist group. Hence, both Maya's sexual and national identity are under scrutiny in this incident. But more importantly, it is the prevalence of fundamentalist ideology within the diaspora that governs Maya's identity. This becomes clear in Reema and Sanjay's suggestion that because Maya lives in the U.S., many "good" Indian families will believe in her ability to fulfill the role a "good" Indian woman. Such a role, as Manisha Roy's sociological case study among Indian American families suggests, requires that a young woman be "maternal, accommodating, gentle, self-effacing, serving, kind, and chaste. In India, a woman is brought up to be a 'good woman' for her family and for her community" (105).

While Maya's Indian relatives are more modern in other regards, such as in their consumption of fashion magazines to the point that characterize her mother Kamala's sense of Indian style old-fashioned (71), their aspirations for their American niece strictly conform to traditional gender roles. Her aunt Reema in particular wants to arrange for Maya a traditional Hindu marriage, which requires of Maya that she behave more in lines with traditional female gender roles. In contrast, Maya's mother Kamala understands that to raise her daughter in a more traditional Indian way would push her into more severe teenage rebellion. Kamala explains in the novel's last chapter, "Karma": "I spent years feeling like India had taken a daughter from me, and that was probably not fair. But I don't want India to take my only living daughter from me now. If I try to make Maya live in American the way we would have lived here [in India], I'll lose her" (231). This passage proposes a dialectics of communality that is missing from the large sub-canon of texts that portray the cultural and social differences between mothers and daughter as obstacle rather than as asset for the formation of a new, fundamentally transnational, feminist heuristic. It also differs strongly from Roy's assertion that Indian American mother-daughter relationships inevitably experience communication problems with regards to female gender norms. If anything, Kamala and Maya are able for the first time to empathize with each other. Kamala's awareness that the more she tries to mold her daughter after traditional Indian social codes, the more difficult it will be for Maya to embrace her roots, is also important for their creation of a mother-daughter community at large. The "sexual control of youth" is a prominent concern in Indian American families, as Sayantani DasGupta and Shamita das Dasgupta suggest in an essay in the form of an intergenerational critical dialogue, but it is even more so a concern because the issues of sexuality between Indian American mothers and daughters "created fearsome myths that effectively silence and divide the women in our community" (111).

Of Reterritorializations and Denationalizations

This moment of understanding between Maya and Kamala is thus indicative of a feminist ethics that recognizes the discursive constructedness of female communities along realities of power inequalities. Such recognition has shaped to a large extent to growing body of scholarship in transnational feminism in its dedication to counter premature assertions of global sisterhood within feminist theory and practice. And it displays the desire to open up, what Uma Narajan and Sandra Harding define in their book, *Decentering the Center: Philosophy for a Multicultural, Postcolonial, and Feminist World* (2000), as "democratic, nondogmatic, and open-ended dialogues" that can accommodate difference within the feminist community without adopting essentialist discourses and practices for the sake of drawing clear distinctions between the various groups or individuals (Narayan and Harding ix). I read *Motherland* in the context of transnational communities in the sense of Alison M. Jagger's suggestion that communities which treat difference as incentive to exclude members on the basis of their deviation from an established group normalcy reinforce dichotomous categories. Alison M. Jagger asserts that the individual is often not aware of the fact that her oppressed position within society is more than just her personal fate (6). In this light, community in *Motherland* exhibits its quintessential roles within feminist theory and practice as a catalyst for profound awareness of women's position within society / within the collective.

Much like Narayan and Harding's project, Chela Sandoval's discussion of a "coalitional consciousness" (78) in her book *Methodology of the Oppressed: Theory Out of Boundary* (2000) proposes a "both/and" space for feminist consciousness and poetics, one that occupies a "third space" equipped to accommodate difference in a productive and generative manner.[69] In this last section, I argue that Asian American critique has recently adopted such as space and discursive practice in its investigation of the performativity of community from multiple angles. As my discussion of Nora Okja Keller's *Comfort Woman* demonstrates, the interconnectedness of Asian studies, Asian American studies and American studies demands a reconceptualization of identity politics in order for this both/and rhetoric to materialize. Similalry, the question of translation and literary communities, as my discussion of Amy Tan's *The Bonesetter's Daughter* illustrates, shapes the bridging of East-West global encounters. In this last section, I therefore wish to locate *Motherland* in the larger conversation about space in Asian American critique. Space here refers to the politics of location that Asian American writers demonstrate through their works as well as the disciplinary space in which critical conversations about Asian American cultural productions take place. Analyzing the question of national community in *Motherland*, I wish to point out in the following section a shift in Asian American critique from "denationalization" to "reterritorialization."

Sau-ling C. Wong proposes the term "denaturalization" as a means of making sense of the shifting paradigms in Asian American critique with the beginning acknowledgment of transnational perspectives. Wong identifies three interrelated trends in Asian American studies that suggest that the concept of place has somewhat lost its importance in the conceptualization of Asian American identity. These trends are, first, "the easing of cultural nationalist concerns" (1) facilitated by the understanding of Asian American communities as inherently heterogeneous groups on the one hand and the shift in methodologies and heuristics, including the adoption of transnational frameworks, on the other hand; second, the growing "permeability" of the fields of Asian American and Asian studies, and, I would add also of American studies, as my discussion of Keller's novel in chapter five of this book proposes; and third, the shift away from a "domestic perspective" as Asian American experience within the U.S. nation-state to the "diasporic perspective" that considers Asian American experience as an example of Asian global diasporas (2). Through the concept of denaturalization, Wong offers a means of theorizing Asian American experience while foregrounding the U.S. nation-state as sole context in which the various discourses on Asian American cultural productions emerge.

---

[69] Adela C. Licona's discussion of zines, that is of self-published magazines, recovers the aspects of Sandoval's coalitional consciousness in a queered space of cultural productions and espouses in her analysis a rhetoric which "resists the delimitations of imposed relationships between ambiguous, oppositional, and even contradictory parts" (105).

A similar move can also be traced through transnational feminism. In her essay, "Deterritorializations: The Rewriting of Home and Exile in Western Feminist Discourse," Caren Kaplan proposes a means of liberating feminist literary theory from the center/margin division that does not apply to all woman writers of color in the U.S. Kaplan does so by offering an analysis of Michelle Cliff's *Claiming an Identity They Thought Me To Despise*, Gloria Anzaldúa's essay "Speaking in Tongues," and Minnie Bruce Pratt's essay "Identity: Skin, Blood, Heart," by means of examining aspects of "deterritorialization." Taking cues from Deleuze and Guattari's use of the term deterritorialization as in relation to language and literature, Kaplan redefines it as a "term of displacement of identities, persons, and meanings that is endemic to the post-modern world system" (188). Kaplan's emphasis on the space in-between center and margin of feminist theory as a "minor" space, in Deleuze and Guattari's terms, opens up the possibility of reading the literature of U.S. women of color without returning into the habit of claiming essentialist locations and identities in ways that the majority of second wave feminist scholarship proposed. Like Deleuze and Guattari do in their essay "What is a Minor Literature?," Kaplan considers deterritorialization not as a practice of loss and nostalgia but as a practice which allows the writer "to express another potential community, to force the means of another consciousness and another sensibility" (Deleuze and Guattari, 17). This understanding of the potential of discussing literature outside of the center/margin binary is central to Kaplan's project of "reterritorialization" because it suggests that there is room for the practice of "reinhabit[ing] a world of our own making" (195). While Deleuze and Guattari acknowledge the presence of community influence on the imposition or appropriation of the term minor in literature, Kaplan's project of reterritorialization in feminist theory and poetics emphasizes the imaginary: "it is a space in the imagination which allows for the inside, the outside, and the liminal elements of inbetween" (197).

Community in / through Literature

In his discussion of Hannah Arendt's *Lectures on Kant's Political Philosophy*, Alan Singer contends that "contemporary literary criticism has given new currency to the ideal of *sensus communis*, but at the expense of a credible social-political agency" (210). In Arendt's work he sees an exception to this general dilemma: "a common sense that is neither commonplace not ahistorically universal but constitutive-analytical of the idea of community itself" (208). In a similar light, Btihaj Ajana characterizes "literature as community" (105) due to its ability to bridge the binary oppositions that are at the basis of

Western concepts of community: "In general terms, and in the Western tradition at least, the entire edifice of community seems to have derived its foundations from the metaphysics of subjectivity in which demarcation lines are sharply traced between the dichotomies of self/other, sameness/difference, inside/outside, inclusion/exclusion, presence/absence" (100). Ajana goes on to argue that a sense of community can be established through literature in so far as "singular beings are, thus, in a continuous movement of actualisation[70] [sic], actualising [sic] themselves as well as belonging, and thereby moving toward their 'own taking place'" (101). Hence, so argues Ajana, the possibility of community established through literature emerges: "Literature instead reveals the limit of community. This limit is engendered by the finitude of singular beings and by the porous space of community where sharing and hence being-in-common takes place. So literature is an interruption of myth in that it 'communicates' precisely this limit, making singular beings (writers and readers) incline toward one another, while exposing them to their shared finitude, the finitude of their limit" (105). This inclination between author and reader which Ajana proposes is a complex business in itself in so far as the *sensus communis* that may arise from it manifests itself on various levels, thus underscoring the multiplicity of communities at play in literary interpretation. For instance, Roland McFarland identifies four different types of community that are related to literary interpretation: on an intra-textual level, the community of characters and their relationships to each other; and on an extra-textual level, the "interpretative communities" of the readers; the "real-life communities" of the readers; real-life communities of the authors (551-52).

In *Nation and Narration* (1990), Homi K. Bhabha argues the following: "Counter-narratives of the nation that continually evoke and erase its totalizing boundaries – both actual and conceptual – disturb those ideological manoeuvres through with 'imagined communities' are given essentialist identities" (300). If nations share with narratives, as Bhabha argues in his introduction to *Nation and Narration*, their dependency on "the mind's eye" in order to "fully realize their horizons" (1), how then do these multiple communities that McFarland categorizes determine the interaction between nation and narration in *Motherland*? Much in line with recent literature by diasporic and transnational authors, whose works "redefin[e] the terms of communal identity so that nationality is not the fixed or definitive basis" (Lehman 103), Vijayaraghavan's novel addresses the issue of community on the level of literary conceptualization. Still rather undiscovered by an American reading audience, *Motherland* does not have many telling Amazon book reviews whose rhetoric might lead to

[70] Ajana refers here to Deleuze's concept of "Actualisation" and Agamben's concept of "taking-place."

similar observations that Inderpal Grewal has made in her book *Transnational America* about the reception of Bharati Mukherjee's and Chitra Banerjee Divakaruni's works of fiction.[71] Instead, the novel forges an explicit link between the reception of literature and community in its intertextual reference to Mark Twain's *Huckleberry Finn*, Maya's assigned book for her summer reading. This book raises issues about literature and community not only through Sanjay's comment about Huck Finn "It is just like an American to try to have a friendship like that and think it can make a difference" (229), but also through the juxtaposition between the presence of American and British literature in India. While Sanjay's comment is a hidden criticism of Maya's naïve assumption that she could befriend Rupa against all social obstacles, it also adds to an earlier conversation Maja had with her uncle and aunt about the extensive presence of British literature in her uncle and aunt's home. Maya is puzzled by the fact that so many British authors are included in the literature curriculum in India. When she asks her uncle "Why look to England when you fought for independence against them," he argues that England and Indian have a lot in common, such as the acceptance of class as social institution, and that the prevalence of "race" in American literature remains inaccessible to an Indian reading audience (104). In the larger context of Maya's identity negotiation, this discussion speaks to the issue of community as established through literature, one of the key instruments that, so Benedict Anderson maintains, contribute to the circulation of nationalism (46).[72]

In *Reflection & Imagination*, Paul Ricoeur argues that "The meeting between text and reader is a meeting between the whole of the text's claims, the horizon which it opens onto, the possibilities which it displays, and another horizon, the reader's horizon of expectations" (492). While the reader's expectations are various, all of the texts that I discussed in this book resist a labeling of Asian American communities as homogenous entities. Not only do they illustrate the ways in which Chinese American, Korean American, and Indian American literatures contribute to and challenge negotiations of pan-Asian assumptions about Asian American communities, they also foreground the multiplicity of the individual strategies and contexts that mediate these negotiations. In the particular context of *Motherland*, the intertextual reference to *Huckleberry Finn* suggests a way in which to envision Ricoeur's concept of a horizon of expectations. Similar to Kingston's use of the story "No Name

[71] Grewal observes that most reviewers on amazon.com find the stories that are set in India "to be most compelling" (73).

[72] Capitalism is the other instrument, and it is precisely this one –"how to make money the way Americans do" - that Maya's uncle mentions as a possible point of identifications for Indians with American culture (105).

Woman" as a means of illustrating to the reader the necessity of dismantling the use value of a story as defined by the context in which the storytelling occurs, so, too, does *Motherland* offer cues about how to read matrilineage in transnational communities by evoking an intertextual relationship between the novel's treatment of national community and the establishing of community through literature. This intertextual connection and the emphasis on the protagonists' attempts to delineate this connection also indicates a way in which to read community critically by making these "horizons" become "tangible and verifiable" (Partridge 11) instead of leaving them unidentified and open to wild guesses.

This is also what brings together the six books that I have discussed in this project. Kingston, Tan, Ng, Keller and Vijayaraghavan embed the question about expectations in their depictions of complex mother-daughter relationships. Characterized through psychological and cultural complexity and often contradictions as far as the daughter's process of identification is concerned, the mother-daughter relationships in the works by these authors not only raise important questions about community in Asian American literature, but also perform narratives gestures that depict the daughters' expectations of and need to reshape their ideas about the possibility of community within Asian American identity. On the level of narrative structure, the emergence of a mother-daughter aesthetic and the prevalence of polyvocal narrative discourses, such as in Kingston's *The Woman Warrior*, Tan's *The Loy Luck Club* and *The Bonesetter's Daughter*, and Keller's *Comfort Woman*, for instance, preclude monolithic assumptions about Asian American representations of cultural issues through literature. And on the thematic level, the specific contexts in which the mother-daughter relationships are located and the various aspects that they encompass by evoking issues of home, memory, body, translation, and nationhood, emphasize the dynamics of the negotiations that characterize Asian American communities. These literary performances of identity and community, and the ways in which the two dialogue with each other, characterize the "counter-narratives" (Bhabha 1990, 300) that are always already implied in the intersubjective relationships that determine and textualize the mother-daughter relationship.

Moreover, the transnational conversations in which the daughters participate through their acts of negotiating their ancestral Asian heritages through their mothers challenge concepts of Asian American literary productions as representations of ethnic American national communities. Yunte Huang coins the term "transpacific displacement" to denote the "historical process of textual migration of cultural meanings, meanings that include linguistic traits, poetics, philosophical ideas, myths, stories, and so on" (3). This notion of transpacific displacement, I would argue based on my analysis of the depictions of mother-daughter relationships, applies to the negotiations of their matrilineage that the daughters undertake as well as to the literary prepresentations of these negotiations that the texts perform. This notion of negation, as I hope my study points out, lies at the heart of depictions of the mother-daughter relationship in Asian American literature and emphasizes the ulinear nature of the gestures towards a recovery of matrilineage that these texts perform. Reading along the transnational martilineages that these texts sketch liberates Asian American critique from essentialist propositions about the concept of identity and community.

BIBLIOGRAPHY

Abarca, Meredith E. "Authentic or Not, It's Original." *Food and Foodways* 12.1 (2004): 1-25.

Abdel-Messih, Marie-Thérèse. "Translating Silence / Traversing Death." *Ephemera: Critical Dialogues on Organization* 3.1 (2003): 7-25.

Abel, Elizabeth. "Race, Class, and Psychoanalysis?: Opening Questions." *Conflicts in Feminism*. Ed. Marianne Hirsch and Evelyn Fox Keller. New York and London: Routledge, 1990. 184-204.

Adams, Alice. "Maternal Bonds: Recent Literature on Mothering." *Signs* 20.2 (Winter 1995): 414-27.

Aguilar-San Juan, Karin. "Going Home: Enacting Justice in Queer Asian America." *Feminist Theory Reader: Local and Global Perspectives*. Ed. Carol R. McCann and Seung-Kyung Kim. New York: Routledge, 2002. 267-76.

Ajana, Btihaj. "Rethinking Community through Literature." *Journal for Cultural Research* 11.2 (April 2007): 99-110.

Amal, Amireh, and Lisa Suhair Majaj, eds. *Going Global: The Transnational Reception of Third World Women Writers*. New York and London: Garland, 2000.

Alarcón, Norma, Caren Kaplan, and Minoo Moallem. "Introduction: Between Woman and Nation." *Between Woman and Nation: Nationalisms, Transnational Feminisms, and the State.* Durham: Duke University Press, 1999. 1-16.

Alexander, M. Jacqui, and Chandra Talpade Mohanty, eds. *Feminist Genealogies, Colonial Legacies, Democratic Futures*. New York: Routledge, 1997.

Anderson, Wanni W., and Robert G. Lee, eds. *Displacements and Diasporas: Asians in the Americas*. New Brunswick, NJ: Rutgers University Press, 2005.

Ang, Ien. "On Not Speaking Chinese: Postmodern Ethnicity and the Politics of Diaspora." *New Formations* 24 (Winter 1994): 1-18.

Anderson, Benedict. *Imagined Communities*. 1983. London: Verso, 2006.

Anzaldúa, Gloria. *Borderlands/La Frontera: The New Mestiza*. 1987. 2nd Edition. San Francisco: Aunt Lute Press, 1999.

------. "Speaking in Tongues: A Letter to Third World Women Writers." *This Bridge Called My Back: Writings By Radical Women of Color*. Ed. Cherríe Moraga and Gloria Anzaldúa. Watertown, MA: Persephone Press, 1981. 165-74.

Appadurai, Arjun. *Modernity at Large: Cultural Dimensions of Globalization*. Minneapolis: University of Minnesota Press, 1996.

Arcana, Judith Pildes. *Our Mothers' Daughters*. Berkeley: Shameless Hussy Press, 1979.

Attridge, Derek, ed. *Jacques Derrida: Acts of Literature*. London: Routledge, 1992.

Bakhtin, M. M. "Discourse of the Novel." *The Dialogic Imagination: Four Essays by M. M. Bakhtin*. Ed. Michael Holquist. Trans. Caryl Emerson and Michael Holquist. Austin: University of Texas Press, 1981. 259-422.

Ball, David. *China Run*. New York: Simon and Schuster, 2002.

Bassnett, Susan and Harish Trivedi, ed. *Post-Colonial Translation: Theory and Practice*. London: Routledge, 1999.

Basu, Amrita. "Globalization of the Local/Localization of the Global: Mapping Transnational Women's Movements." *Feminist Theory Reader: Local and Global Perspectives*. Ed. Carole McCann and Seung Kyung-Kim. New York and London: Routledge, 2000. 68-77.

Baudrillard, Jean. *The Mirror of Production*. St. Lois, MO: Telos P, 1975.

Beauvoir, Simone de. *The Second Sex*. New York: Vintage, 1952.

Bedingfield, Agnieszka, "Trans-Memory and Diaspora: Memories of Europe and Asia in American Immigrant Narratives." *Sites of Ethnicity: Europe and the Americas*. Ed. William Boelhower, Rocío G. Davis and Carmen Birkle. Heidelberg: Universitätsverlag Winter, 2004. 333-46.

Benjamin, Jessica. *The Bonds of Love: Psychoanalysis, Feminism, and the Problem of Domination*. New York: Pantheon Books, 1988.

------. "Authority and the Family Revisited: or, A World Without Fathers?" *New German Critique* 13 (Winter 1978): 35-58.

Benjamin, Walter. "The Task of the Translator: An Introduction to the Translation of Baudelaire's Tableaux parisiens." Trans. Harry Zohn. *Illuminations*. Ed. Hannah Arendt. 1969. London: Pimlico, 1999. 70-82.

Bhabha, Homi K. "The Third Space: Interview with Homi Bhabha." *Identity: Community, Culture, Difference*. Ed. Jonathan Rutherford. London: Lawrence & Wishart, 1998. 207-21.

------. *The Location of Culture*. London and New York: Routledge, 1994.

------. "DissemiNation: Time, Narrative, and the Margins of the Modern Nation." *Nation and Narration*. New York: Routledge, 1990. 291-322.

------, ed. *Nation and Narration*. New York: Routledge, 1990.

Bloom, Lynn Z. "Heritages: Dimensions of Mother-Daughter Relationships in Women's Autobiographies." *The Lost Tradition: Mothers and Daughters in Literature*. Ed. Cathy N. Davidson and E. M. Broner. New York: Frederick Ungar, 1980. 291-303.

Bourdieu, Pierre. *The Field of Cultural Production: Essays on Art and Literature*. New York: Columbia University Press, 1993.

Bové, Paul A. "Discourse." *Critical Terms for Literary Study*. Ed. Frank Lentricchia and Thomas McLaughlin. Chicago: University of Chicago Press, 1990. 50-65.

Bow, Leslie. *Betrayal and Other Acts of Subversion: Feminism, Sexual Politics, Asian American Women's Literature*. Princeton: Princeton University Press, 2001.

Bulosan, Carlos. *America Is in the Heart*. 1943. Seattle: University of Washington Press, 1973.

Burlingame, Robert. "Sweet Smile of Success." *Star Bulletin*. April 1, 1997. http://starbelletin.com/97/04/01/features/story1.html (accessed March 5, 2007).

Butler, Judith. *Excitable Speech: A Politics of the Performative*. New York: Routledge, 1997.

------. *Bodies that Matter: On the Discursive Limits of "Sex."* New York and London: Routledge, 1993.

------. *Gender Trouble: Feminism and the Subversion of Identity*. New York: Routledge, 1990.

Butler, Pamela, and Jiqna Desai. "Manolos, Marriage, and Mantras: Chick-Lit Criticism and Transnational Feminism." *Meridians: Feminism, Race, Transnationalism* 8.2 (October 2008): 1-31.

Brown, Linda, and Kay Mussell, eds. *Ethnic and Regional Foodways in the United States: The Performance of Group Identity*. Knoxville: University of Tennessee Press, 1984.

Caruth, Cathy. *Unclaimed Experience: Trauma, Narrative, and History*. Baltimore: John Hopkins University Press, 1996.

Cha, Theresa Hak Kyung. *DICTEE*. 1982. Berkeley: University of California Press, 2001.

Chen, Tina. *Double Agency: Acts of Impersonation in Asian American Literature and Culture*. Stanford: Stanford University Press, 2005.

Chiu, Monica. "Trauma and Multiplicity in Nieh Hualing's *Mulberry and Peach*." *MOSAIC* 36.3 (September 2003): 19-35.

Cheung, King-kok, "Re-Viewing Asian American Literary Studies." *An Interethnic Companion to Asian American Literature*. Cambridge: Cambridge University Press, 1997. 1-36.

------. *Articulate Silences: Hisaye Yamamoto, Maxine Hong Kingston, Joy Kogawa*. Ithaca, NY: Cornell University Press, 1993.

------. ed. *An Interethnic Companion to Asian American Literature*. Cambridge: Cambridge University Press, 1997.

------. "'Don't Tell': Imposed Silences in *The Color Purple* and *The Woman Warrior*." *PMLA* 103.2 (March 1988): 162-74.

Chin, Frank. "Come All Ye Asian American Writers of the Real and the Fake." *The Big Aiiieeeee!: An Anthology of Chinese American and Japanese American Literature*. Ed. Jeffery Paul Chan, Lawson Fusao Inada, and Shawn Wong. New York: Meridian: 1991. 1-12.

Chow, Esther Ngan-Ling. "The Feminist Movement: Where Are All the Asian American Women?" *From Different Shores: Perspectives on Race and Ethnicity in America*. 1987. 2nd Edition. Ed. Ronald T. Takaki. New York and Oxford: Oxford University Press, 1994. 184-91.

------. "The Development of Feminist Consciousness Among Asian American Women." *Gender and Society* 1.3 (Spring 1987): 284-299.

Chow, Rey. "Where Have All The Natives Gone?" *Contemporary Postcolonial Theory: A Reader*. Ed. Padmini Mongia. New York: Arnold, 1996.122-46.

------. *Writing Diaspora: Tactics of Intervention in Contemporary Cultural Studies*. Bloomington: Indiana University Press, 1993.

------. "Violence in the Other Country: China as Crisis, Spectacle, and Woman." *Third World Women and the Politics of Feminism*. Ed. Chandra Talpade Mohanty, Ann Russo, and Lourdes Torres. Bloomington and Indianapolis: Indiana University Press, 1991. 81-100.

------. *Woman and Chinese Modernity: The Politics of Reading between West and East*. Minneapolis: University of Minnesota Press, 1991.

Chu, Patricia P. "'To Hide Her True Self': Sentimentality and the Search for an Intersubjective Self in Nora Okja Keller's *Comfort Woman*." *Beyond the Hyphen: Asian North American Identities*. Ed. Eleanor Ty and Donald C. Goellnicht. Bloomington: Indiana University Press, 2004. 61-83.

------. "*The Woman Warrior: Memoirs of a Girlhood Among Ghosts* by Maxine Hong Kingston." *A Resource Guide to Asian American Literature*. Ed. Sau-ling C. Wong and Stephen H. Sumida. New York: MLA, 2001. 86-96.

------. *Assimilating Asians: Gendered Strategies of Authorship in Asian America*. 2000. Durham: Duke University Press, 2000.

Chuh, Kandice. *Imagine Otherwise: On Asian Americanist Critique*. Durham: Duke University Press, 2003.

---. "Discomforting Knowledge, Or, Korean 'Comfort Women' and Asian American Critical Practice." *Journal of Asian American Studies* 6.1 (2003): 5-23.

Chuang, Hua. *Crossings*. 1968. Boston: Northeastern University Press, 1986.

Cisneros, Sandra. *The House on Mango Street*. New York: Vintage, 1984.

Cixous, Hélène. *La Jeune Née*. Paris: UEG, 1975.

Chodorow, Nancy. *The Reproduction of Mothering: Psychoanalysis and the Sociology of Gender*. Berkeley, Los Angeles and London: University of California Press, 1978.

Christian, Barbara, Gloria Hull, Patricia Bell Scott, and Barbara Smith, eds., *All The Women are White, All the Blacks are Men, But Some of Us Are Brave: Black Women's Studies*. New York: The Feminist Press, 1982.

Conboy, Katie, Medina, Nadia, and Sarah Stanbury, eds. *Writing on the Body: Female Embodiment and Feminist Theory*. New York: Columbia University Press, 1997.

Cosslett, Tess. "Matrilineal narratives revisited." *Feminism and Autobiography: Texts, Theories, Methods*. Ed. Tess Cosslett, Celia Lury and Penny Summerfield. New York: Routledge, 2000. 141-53.

Couser, G. Thomas. "Oppression and Repression: Personal and Collective Memory in Paule Marshall's *Praisesong for the Widow* and Leslie Marmon Silko's *Ceremony*." *Memory and Cultural Politics: New Approaches to Ethnic American Literatures*. Ed. Amritjit Singh, Joseph T. Skerret and Robert E. Hogan. Boston: Northeastern University Press, 1996. 106-20.

Cowie, Elizabeth. "Traumatic Memories of Remembering and Forgetting." In *Between the Psyche and the Polis: Refiguring History in Literature and Theory*. Ed. Michael Rossington and Anne Whitehead. Aldershot: Ashgate, 2000.

Cryer, Dan. Rev. of *Eating Chinese Food Naked*. *Newsday* (January 11, 1998): B11.

DasGupta, Sayantani, and Shamita Das Dasgupta. "Sex, Lies, and Women's Lives: An Intergenerational Dialogue." *A Patchwork Shawl: Chronicles of Sough Asian Women in America*. Ed. Shamita Das Dasgupta. New Brunswick, NJ: Rutgers University Press, 1998. 111-28.

Daswani, Kavita. *The Village Bride of Beverly Hills*. New York: Penguin Plume, 2005.

Davidson, Cathy N., and E. M. Broner, eds. *The Lost Tradition: Mothers and Daughters in Literature*. New York: Frederick Ungar, 1980.

Davis, Rocío G. *Begin Here: Reading Asian North American Autobiographies of Childhood*. Honolulu: University of Hawaii Press, 2007.

------, and Sue-Im Lee, eds. *Literary Gestures: The Aesthetic in Asian American Writing*. Philadelphia: Temple University Press, 2006.

de Lauretis, Teresa. *Feminist Studies/Critical Studies*. Bloomington and Indiana: Indiana University Press, 1986.

------. *Alice Doesn't: Feminism, Semiotics, Cinema*. Bloomington and Indianapolis: University of Indiana Press, 1984.

Deleuze, Gilles, and Félix Guattari. *Kafka: Towards a Minor Literature*. Trans. Dana Polan. Minneapolis: University of Minnesota Press, 1986.

DeHay, Terry. "Narrating Memory." *Memory, Narrative, and Identity: New Essays in Ethnic American Literatures*. Ed. Amritjit Singh, Joseph T. Skerrett, Jr. and Robert E. Hogan. Boston: Northeastern University Press, 1994. 26-44.

Delucchi, Michael. "Self and Identity Among Aging Immigrants in *The Joy Luck Club*." *Journal of Aging and Identity* 3.2 (1998): 59-66.

Dinnerstein, Dorothy. *The Mermaid and the Minotaur: Sexual Arrangements and Human Malaise*. New York: Harper and Row, 1976.

Dill, Bonnie Thornton. "Our Mothers' Grief: Racial Ethnic Women and the Maintenance of Families." *Journal of Family History* 13.4 (1988): 415-31.

Douglas, Mary. "Deciphering a Meal." *Deadalus* 101.1 (1972): 61-81.

Doyle, Jacqueline. "'A Love Letter to My Motherland': Maternal Discourses in Jessica Hagedorn's *Dogeaters*." *Hitting Critical Mass* 4.2 (Summer 1997): 1-25.

DuBois, W.E.B. *The Souls of Black Folk*. 1903. New York: New American Library, Signet Classics, 1982.

Duncan, Patti. *Tell This Silence: Asian American Women Writers and the Politics of Speech*. Iowa City: University of Iowa Press, 2004.

Dunick, Lisa M.S. "The Silencing Effect of Canonicity: Authorship and the Written Word in Amy Tan's Novels." *MELUS* 31.2 (Summer 2006): 3-20.

Eidelberg, Ludwig, ed. *Encyclopedia of Psychoanalysis*. New York: Free Press, 1968.

Eisenstein, Zillah, ed. *Capitalist Patriarchy and the Case for Socialist Feminism*. New York: Monthly Review Press, 1978.

Ellman, Mary. *Thinking About Women*. New York: Hartcourt, 1968.

Eng, David L., and Alice Y. Hom, eds. *Q & A: Queer in Asian America*. Philadelphia: Temple University Press, 1998.

Farquhar, Judith. *Appetites: Food and Sex in Post-Socialist China*. Durham: Duke University Press, 2002.

Ferraro, Thomas J. *Ethnic Passages: Literary Immigrants in Twentieth Century America*. Chicago: University of Chicago Press, 1993.

Firestone, Sulamith. *The Dialectic of Sex: The Case for Feminist Revolution.* 1970. New York: Farrar, Straus and Giroux, 2003.

Fischer, Michael M. J. "Ethnicity and the Post-Modern Arts of Memory." *Writing Culture: The Poetics and Politics of Ethnography.* Ed. James Clifford and George E. Marcus. Berkeley, Los Angeles and London: University of California Press, 1986. 194-233.

Fishkin, Shelley Fisher. "Crossroads of Cultures: The Transnational Turn in American Studies – Presidential Address to the American Studies Association, November 12, 2004." *American Quarterly* 57.1 (2005): 17-57.

Fuss, Diana. *Essentially Speaking: Feminism, Nature, and Difference.* New York: Routledge, 1989.

Flax, Jane. "The Conflict Between Nurturance and Autonomy in Mother-Daughter Relationships and Within Feminism." *Feminist Studies* 4.2 (June 1978): 177-91.

Fox-Keller, Elizabeth, and Marianne Hirsch, eds. *Conflicts in Feminism.* New York and London: Routledge, 1990.

Freud, Sigmund. *The Uncanny.* 1941. Trans. David McLintock. New York: Penguin, 2003.

Friday, Nancy. *My Mother/My Self: The Daughter's Search for Identity.* New York: Delacorte, 1977.

Friedan, Betty. *The Feminine Mystique.* New York: Norton, 1963.

Genette, Gerard. *Narrative Discourse: An Essay in Method.* Ithaca: Cornell University Press, 1980.

Gilbert, Sandra, and Susan Gubar. *The Madwoman in the Attic: The Woman Writer and the Nineteenth Century Literary Imagination.* New Haven, CT: Yale University Press, 1979.

Gilligan, Carol. *In a Different Voice: Psychological Theory and Women's Development.* Cambridge: Harvard University Press, 1982.

Gilroy, Paul. "Black Cultural Politics: An Interview with Paul Gilroy by Timmy Lott." *Found Object* 4 (1994): 46-81.

------. "'It Ain't Where You're From, It's Where You're At ...:' The Dialectics of Diasporic Identification." *Third Text* 13 (Winter 1990/91): 3-16.

Grewal, Inderpal. *Transnational America: Feminisms, Diasporas, Neoliberalisms.* Durham: Duke University Press, 2005.

------, and Caren Kaplan, eds. *An Introduction to Women's Studies: Gender in a Transnational World.* Boston: McGraw Hill, 2002.

------. *Scattered Hegemonies: Postmodernity and Transnational Feminist Practices.* 1994. Minneapolis: University of Minnesota Press, 1997.

Grice, Helena. *Negotiating Identities: An Introduction to Asian American Women's Writing*. Manchester and London: Manchester University Press, 2002.

Gunn Allen, Paula. *The Sacred Hoop: Recovering the Feminine in American Indian Traditions*. Boston: Beacon Press, 1986.

Hagedorn, Jessica Tarahata. *Dogeaters*. New York: Penguin, 1991.

------ ed. *Charlie Chan is Dead: An Anthology of Contemporary Asian American Fiction*. New York: Penguin, 1993.

Hall, Stuart. "Cultural Identity and Diaspora." *Identity: Community, Culture, Difference*. Ed. Jonathan Rutherford. London: Lawrence and Wishart, 1998. 222-37.

Hansen, Elaine Tuttle. *Mother Without Child: Contemporary Fiction and the Crisis of Motherhood*. Berkeley: University of California Press, 1997.

Har, Janie C. "Food, Sexuality, and the Pursuit of a Little Attention." *Hitting Critical Mass* 1.1 (Fall 1993): 83-92.

Hassan, Waïl S. "Agency and Translational Literature: Ahdaf Soueif's *The Map of Love*." *PMLA* 121.3 (2006): 753-68.

Hattori, Tomo. "Psycholinguistic Orientalism in Criticism of *The Woman Warrior* and *Obasan*." *Other Sisterhoods: Literary Theory and U.S. Women of Color*. Ed. Sandra Kumamoto Stanley. Urbana and Chicago: University of Illinois Press, 1998. 119-38.

Haynes, Rosetta R. "Intersections of Race, Gender, Society, and Experimentation in the Autobiographical Writings of Cherríe Moraga and Maxine Hong Kingston." *Women of Color: Defining the Issues: Hearing the Voices*. Ed. Diane Long Hoeveler and Janet K. Boles. Westport, CT: Greenwood Press, 2001. 133-45.

Heung, Marine. "Daughter-Text/Mother-Text: Matrilineage in Amy Tan's *Joy Luck Club*." *Feminist Studies* 19.3 (Fall 1993): 597-616.

Hicks, George. *The Comfort Women: Japan's Brutal Regime of Enforced Prostitution in the Second World War*. New York: W.W. Norton, 1994.

Hirsch, Marianne. *Family Frames: Photography, Narrative, and Postmemory*. Cambridge, MA: Harvard University Press, 1997.

------. *The Mother/Daughter Plot: Narrative, Psychoanalysis, Feminism*. Bloomington and Indianapolis: Indiana University Press, 1989.

------. "Mothers and Daughters." *Signs* 7.1 (Autumn 1981): 200-222.

------, and Evelyn Fox Keller, eds. *Conflicts in Feminism*. New York and London: Routledge, 1990.

Ho, Wendy. *In Her Mother's House: The Politics of Asian American Mother-Daughter Writing*. Walnut Creek: Alta Mira, 1999.

------. "Swan-Feather Mothers and Coca-Cola Daughters: Teaching Amy Tan's *The Joy Luck Club*." *Teaching American Ethnic Literatures*. Ed. John R. Maitino and David R. Peck. Albuquerque: University of New Mexico Press, 1996. 327-45.

Hoeveler, Diane Long and Janet K. Boles, eds. *Women of Color: Defining the Issues: Hearing the Voices*. Foreword Toni Michelle C. Travis. Westport, CT: Greenwood Press, 2001.

Hoffman, Eva. *Lost in Translation: A Life in a New Language*. New York: Penguin Books, 1989.

Hom, Alice Y. "Stories from the Homefront: Perspectives of Asian American Parents With Lesbian Daughters and Gay Sons." *Debating Diversity: Clashing Perspectives on Race and Ethnicity in America*. 3rd Ed. Ed. Ronald Takaki. New York and Oxford: Oxford University Press, 2002. 176-83.

Hong, Terry. "The Dual Life of Nora Okja Keller." *AsianWeek*. http://www.asianweek.com/2002_04_05/arts_keller.html (accessed October 8, 2006).

hooks, bell. "Conference Presentation." *Critical Fictions*. Ed. Philomena Mariani. Seattle: Bay Press, 1991. 53-61.

------. *Yearning: Race, Gender, and Cultural Politics*. Boston: South End Press, 1990.

------. *Talking Back: Thinking Feminist, Thinking Black*. Boston: South End Press, 1988.

------. *Ain't I a Woman: Black Women and Feminism*. Boston: South End Press, 1981.

------. *Feminist Theory: From Margin to Center*. Boston: South End Press, 1984.

Huang, Yunte. *Transpacific Displacement: Ethnography, Translation, and Intertextual Travel in Twentieth-Century American Literature*. Berkeley: University of California Press, 2002.

Irigaray, Luce. "And One Doesn't Stir Without the Other." Trans. Hélène Vivienne Wenzel. *Signs* 7.1 (1981): 60-67.

------. *Ce sexe qui n'est pas un*. Paris: Minuit, 1977.

------. *Spéculum de l'autre femme*. Paris: Minuit, 1974.

Jagger, Alison M. "Globalizing Feminist Ethics." *Decentering the Center: Philosophy for a Multicultural, Postcolonial, and Feminist World*. Ed. Uma Narayan and Sandra Harding. Bloomington: Indiana University Press, 2000. 1-25.

Jelinek, Estelle C., ed. *Women's Autobiography: Essays in Criticism*. Bloomington and Indianapolis: Indiana University Press, 1980.

Jen, Gish. *The Love Wife*. New York: Alfred Knopf, 2004.

------. *Mona in the Promised Land*. New York: Vintage, 1996.

------. *Typical American*. New York: Penguin, 1991.

Joseph, Betty. "Gendering Time in Globalization: The Belatedness of the Other Woman and Jamaica Kincaid's *Lucy*." *Tulsa Studies in Women's Literature* 21.1 (Spring 2002): 67-83.

Joseph, Gloria I., and Jill Lewis. *Common Differences: Conflicts in Black and White Feminist Perspectives*. Boston: South End Press, 1981.

Juan, E. San, Jr. "From Identity Politics to Strategies of Disruption: USA Self and / or Asian Alter?" *Asian Americans: Collages of Identities*. Ed. Lee C. Lee. Ithaca, NY: Cornell University Press, 1992. 123-39.

Kahodata, Cynthia. *Kira Kira*. New York: Simon and Schster, 2005.

Kalcik, Susan. "Ethnic Foodways in America: Symbol and the Performance of Identity." *Ethnic and Regional Foodways in the United States: The Performance of Group Identity*. Ed. Linda Brown and Kay Mussell. Knoxville: University of Tennessee Press, 1984. 37-65.

Kang, Laura Hyun Yi. "Conjuring 'Comfort Women": Mediated Affiliations and Disciplined Subjects in Korean/American Transnationality." *Journal of Asian American Studies* 6.1 (2003): 25-55.

------. *Compositional Subjects: Enfiguring Asian/American Women*. Durham and London: Duke University Press, 2002.

Kaplan, Caren. *Questions of Travel: Postmodern Discourses of Displacement*. Durham: Duke University Press, 1996.

------. "The Politics of Location as Transnational Feminist Critical Practice." *Scattered Hegemonies: Postmodernity and Transnational Feminist Practices*. 1994. Ed. Inderpal Grewal and Caren Kaplan. Minneapolis: University of Minnesota Press, 1997. 137-52.

------. "Resisting Autobiography: Out-Law Genres and Transnational Feminist Subjects." *De/Colonizing the Subject: The Politics of Gender in Women's Autobiography*. Ed. Sidonie Smith and Julia Watson. Minneapolis: University of Minnesota Press, 1992. 115-38.

------, Norma Alarcón, and Minoo Mallem, eds. *Between Woman and Nation: Nationalism, Transnational Feminisms, and the State*. Durham: Duke University Press, 1999.

Karpen, Lynn. Rev. of *Eating Chinese Food Naked*. *New York Times* (March 1, 1998): sec.7, 21.

Keating, AnaLouise. "(De)Centering the Margin? Identity Politics and Tactical (Re)Naming." *Other Sisterhoods: Literary Theory and U. S. Women of Color*. Ed. Sandra Kumamoto Stanley. Urbana: University of Illinois Press, 1998. 23-43.

------. *Women Reading Women Writing: Self-Invention in Paula Gunn Allen, Gloria Anzaldúa, and Audre Lorde*. Philadelphia: Temple University Press, 1996.

Keller, Nora Okja. *Comfort Woman*. New York: Penguin, 1997.

------. "My Mother's Food." *New Woman* (September 1997): 68-71.

------. *Fox Girl*. New York: Penguin, 2002

Kilby, Jane. "The Writing of Trauma: Trauma Theory and the Liberty of Reading." *New Formations* 47 (Summer 2002): 217-32.

Kim, Elaine H. "Home Is Where the *Han* Is: A Korean-American Perspective on the Los Angeles Upheavals." *Asian American Studies: A Reader*. Ed. Jean Yu-Wen Shen Wu and Min Song. New Brunswick, NJ: Rutgers University Press, 2000. 270-89.

------. "Dangerous Affinities: Korean American Feminisms (En)counter Gendered Korean and Racialized U.S. Nationalist Narratives." *Hitting Critical Mass* 6.1 (Fall 1999): 1-12.

------. "Poised on the In-Between: A Korean American's Reflections on Thesera Hak Kyung Cha's *DICTEE*." *Writing Self/Writing Nation: Selected Essay on Theresa Hak Kyung Cha's* DICTEE. Ed. Elaine H. Kim and Norma Alarcón. Berkeley: Third Woman Press, 1994. 3-30.

------. "Foreword." *Reading the Literatures of Asian America*. Ed. Shirley Geok-lin Lim and Amy Ling. Philadelphia: Temple University Press, 1992. xi-xvii.

------. "Defining Asian American Realities through Literature." *The Nature and Contexts of Minority Literature*. Ed. Abdul JanMohammed and David Lloyd. New York: Oxford University Press, 1990.146-70.

------. *Asian American Literature: An Introduction to the Writers and their Social Contexts*. Philadelphia: Temple University Press, 1982.

Kim, Jodi. "Haunting History: Violence, Trauma, and the Politics of Memory in Nora Okja Keller's *Comfort Woman*." *Hitting Critical Mass* 6.1 (Fall 1999): 61-78.

Kim, Ronyoung. *Clay Walls*. New York: The Permanent Press, 1987.

Kingston, Maxine Hong. *China Men*. New York: Alfred A. Knopf, 1980.

------. *The Woman Warrior: Memoirs of a Girlhood Among Ghosts*. 1976. New York: Vintage, 1989.

Koo, Eunsook. "Heterotopia on an Island: The Literary Representations of the American Military Camp Town in Korea." *Feminist Studies in English Literature* 10.2 (Winter 2002): 131-40.

Koshy, Susan. *Sexual Naturalization: Asian Americans and Miscegenation*. Stanford: Stanford University Press, 2004.

------. “The Fiction of Asian American Literature.” *Asian American Studies: A Reader*. Ed. Jean Yu-Wen Shen Wu and Min Song. New Brunswick, NJ: Rutgers University Press, 2000. 467-95.

------. “Category Crisis: South Asian Americans and Questions of Race and Ethnicity.” *Diaspora* 7.3 (1998): 285-320.

Kristeva, Julia. *Revolution in Poetic Language*. 1984. Trans. Margaret Waller. New York: Columbia University Press, 1974.

------. *About Chinese Women*. 1977. Trans. Anita Barrows. London: Marion Boyars, 1974.

------. “La femme, ce n’est jamais ça.” *Tel Quel* 59 (Automne 1974): 19-24.

Kwa, Lydia. *This Place Called Absence*. New York: Kensington Books, 2003.

Lahiri, Jhumpa. *The Namesake*. New York: Houghton Mifflin, 2003.

Lauter, Paul. "The Literatures of America: A Comparative Discipline." *Redefining American Literary History*. Ed. A. LaVonne Brown Ruoff and Jerry Ward. New York: MLA, 1990. 9-34.

Lee, Christopher. “Diaspora, Transnationalism, and Asian American Studies: Positions and Debates.” *Displacements and Diasporas: Asians in the Americas*. Ed. Wanni W. Anderson and Christopher Lee. New Brunswick, NJ: Rutgers Universiy Press, 2005. 23-38.

Lee, Ken-fan. “Cultural Translation and the Exorcist: A Reading of Kingston’s and Tan’s Ghost Stories.” *MELUS* 29.2 (2004): 105-27.

Lee, So-Hee. “A Study of the First-Person Narrative in *Comfort Woman*: From A Perspective of Women’s Speaking and Writing.” *Feminist Studies in English Literature* 10.2 (Winter 2002): 163-88.

Lee, Sue-Im. “Introduction: The Aesthetic in Asian American Literary Discourse.” *Literary Gestures: The Aesthetic in Asian American Writing*. Ed. Rocío G. Davis and Sue-Im Lee. Philadelphia: Temple Universiy Press, 2006. 1-14.

Lee, Young-Oak. “Nora Okja Keller and the Silenced Woman: An Interview.” *MELUS* 28.4 (Winter 2003): 145-65.

Lehman, Sophia. “In Search of a Mother Tongue: Locating Home in Diaspora.” *MELUS* 23.4 (1998): 101-118.

Levitt, Peggy, and Mary C. Waters, eds. *The Changing Face of Home: The Transnational Lives of the Second Generation*. New York: Russell Sage Foundation, 2002.

Levy, E. J. Introduction. *Tasting Life Twice: Literary Lesbian Fiction by New American Writers*. Ed. Levy. New York: Avon Books, 1995. 1-9.

Li, David Leiwei. *Imagining the Nation: Asian American Literature and Cultural Consent*. Stanford: University of Stanford P, 1998.

Licona, Adela C. "(B)orderlands' Rhetorics and Representations: The Transformative Potential of Feminist Third-Space Scholarship and Zines." *NWSA Journal* 17.2 (Summer 2005): 104-29.

Lim, Shirley Geok-lin. Lim. "Where in the World Is Transnational Feminism?" *Tulsa Studies in Women's Literature* 23.1 (2004): 7-12.

------. *Among the White Moon Faces*. New York: The Feminist Press, 1997.

------. "Assaying the Gold: Or, Contesting the Ground of Asian American Literature." *New Literary History* 24.1 (Winter 1993): 147-69.

------, John Blair, Stephen Hong Sohn, and Gina Valentino, eds. *Transnational Asian American Literatures: Sites and Transits*. Philadelphia: Temple University Press, 2006.

------, and Amy Ling. *Reading the Literatures of Asian America*. Philadelphia: Temple University Press, 1992.

Ling, Amy. "Chinese American Women Writers: The Tradition behind Maxine Hong Kingston." *Maxine Hong Kingston's* The Woman Warrior*: A Casebook*. Ed. Sau-ling Cynthia Wong. New York: Oxford University Press, 1999. 135-58.

------. *Between Worlds: Women Writers of Chinese Ancestry*. New York: Pergamon Press, 1990.

Lionnet, Françoise, and Shu-mei Shih, eds. *Minor Transnationalism*. Durham: Duke University Press, 2005.

Liu, Catherine. *Oriental Girls Desire Romance*. New York: Kaya, 1997.

Lowe, Lisa. "The Intimacies of Four Continents." *Haunted By Empire: Geographies of Intimacy in North American History*. Durham: Duke University Press, 2006. 192-212.

------. *Immigrant Acts: On Asian American Cultural Politics*. Durham: Duke University Press, 1996.

------. "Canon, Institutionalization, Identity: Contradictions for Asian American Studies." *The Ethnic Canon: Histories, Institutions, and Interventions*. Ed. David Palumbo-Liu. Minneapolis and London: University of Minnesota Press, 1995. 48-70.

------. "Heterogeneity, Hybridity, Multiplicity: Marking Asian American Differences." *Diaspora* 1.1 (1991): 24-44.

------. *Critical Terrains: French and British Orientalisms*. Ithaca, NY: Cornell University Press, 1991.

Lyotard, Jean-Francois. *The Postmodern Condition: A Report on Knowledge*. Trans. Geoff Bennington and Brian Massumi. Minneapolis: University of Minnesota Press, 1984.

Ma, Sheng-mei. *East-West Montage: Reflections on Asian Bodies in Diaspora*. Honolulu: University of Hawaii Press, 2007.

Madison, D. Soyini, ed. *The Woman That I Am: The Literature and Culture of Contemporary Women of Color*. 1994. New York: St. Martin's Griffin, 1997.

Maglin, Nan Bauer. "'Don't never forget the bridge you crossed over on': The Literature of Matrilineage. *The Lost Tradition: Mothers and Daughters in Literature*. Ed. Cathy N. Davidson and E. M. Broner. New York: Frederick Ungar, 1980. 257-67.

Magnus, Kathy Dow. "The Unaccountable Subject: Judith Butler and the Social Conditions of Intersubjective Agency." *Hypatia* 21.2 (Spring 2006): 81-103.

Mani, Lata. "Multiple Mediations: Feminist Scholarship in the Age of Multinational Reception." *Inscriptions* 5 (1989): 1-23.

Manual, Dolores de, and Rocío G. Davis, eds. *Asian American Children's Literature*. Special Issue of *Lion and the Unicorn: A Critical Journal of Children's Literature* 30.2 (2006).

Martin, Biddy, and Chandra Talpade Mohanty. "Feminist Politics: What's Home Got To Do With It?" *Feminist Studies/Critical Studies*. Ed. Teresa de Lauretis. Bloomington and Indianapolis: Indiana University Press, 1986. 191-212.

McAlister, Melani. "(Mis) Reading *The Joy Luck Club*." *Asian America: A Journal of Culture and the Arts* 1 (1992): 102-08.

McCann, Carol R., and Seung-Kyung Kim, eds. *Feminist Theory Reader: Local and Global Perspectives*. New York: Routledge, 2002.

McClintock, Anne, Aamir Mufti, and Ella Shohat, eds. *Dangerous Liaisons: Gender, Nation and Postcolonial Perspectives*. Minneapolis: University of Minnesota Press, 1997.

McFarland, Roland E. "Community and Interpretative Communties in Stories by Hawthorne, Kafka and García Márquez." *Studies in Short Fiction* 29.4 (1992): 511-59.

Mehrez, Samia. "Translation and the Postcolonial Experience: The Francophone North African Text." *Rethinking Translation: Discourse, Subjectivity, Ideology*. Ed. Lawrence Venuti. London: Routledge, 1992. 120-38.

Mendoza, Louis, and S. Shankar. *Crossing into America: The New Literature of Immigration*. New York: The New Press, 2003.

Miller, Jean Baker. *Toward a New Psychology of Women*. Boston: Beacon Press, 1976.

Millett, Kate. *Sexual Politics*. New York: Avon, 1970.

Moallem, Minoo. "Transnationalism, Feminism, Fundamentalism." *Between Woman and Nation: Nationalisms, Transnational Feminisms, and the State*. Durham: Duke University Press, 1999. 320 – 48.

Mohanty, Chandra Talpade. Introduction. *Feminism Without Borders: Decolonizing Theory, Practicing Solidarity*. Durham and London: Duke University Press, 2003. 1-13.

------. "'Under Western Eyes' Revisited: Feminist Solidarity through Anticapitalist Struggles." *Feminism Without Borders: Decolonizing Theory, Practicing Solidarity*. Durham and London: Duke University Press, 2003. 221-51.

------. "Under Western Eyes: Feminist Scholarship and Colonial Discourses." *Contemporary Postcolonial Theory: A Reader*. Ed. Padmini Mongia. London and New York: Arnold, 1996. 172-97.

------. "Introduction: Cartographies of Struggle: Third World Women and The Politics of Feminism." *Third World Women and the Politics of Feminism*. Ed. Chandra Talpade Mohanty, Ann Russo, and Lourdes Torres. Bloomington and Indianapolis: Indiana University Press, 1991. 1-47.

------, Russo, Ann, and Lourdes Torres, eds. *Third World Women and the Politics of Feminism*. Bloomington and Indianapolis: Indiana University Press, 1991.

Moi, Toril. *Sexual/Textual Politics: Feminist Literary Theory*. New York: Methuen, 1985.

Mongia, Padmini, ed. *Contemporary Postcolonial Theory: A Reader*. London and New York: Arnold, 1996.

Moraga, Cherríe, and Gloria Anzaldúa, eds. *This Bridge Called My Back: Writing by Radical Women of Color*. Foreword Toni Cade Bambara. Watertown, MA: Persephone Press, 1981.

Morin, Carol. Rev. of *Eating Chinese Food Naked*. *The Scotsman* (March 7, 1998): 14.

Morrison, Toni. *Beloved*. 1987. New York: Penguin, 1988.

------. *Sula*. 1982. New York: Penguin Books, 1982.

Mountain, Chandra Tyler. "'The Struggle of Memory Against Forgetting': Cultural Survival in Amy Tan's *The Joy Luck Club*." *Paintbrush* 22 (Autumn 1995): 39-50.

Mufti, Aamir, and Ella Shohat. "Introduction." *Dangerous Liaisons: Gender, Nation, and Postcolonial Perspectives*. Ed. Anne McClintock, Aamir Mufti and Ella Shohat. Minneapolis: University of Minnesota Press, 1997. 1-12.

Mukherjee, Bharati. *Desirable Daughters*. New York: Hyperion, 2003.

Mylan, Sheryl A. "The Mother as Other: Orientalism in Maxine Hong Kingston's *The Woman Warrior*." *Women of Color: Mother-Daughter Relationships in 20th Century Literature*. Ed. Elizabeth Brown-Guillory. Austin: University of Texas Press, 1996. 132-52.

Najmi, Samina. "Decolonizing the Bildungsroman: Narratives of War and Womanhood in Nora Okja Keller's *Comfort Woman*." *Form and Transformation in Asian American Literature.* Ed. Zhou Xiaojing and Samina Najmi. Seattle: University of Washington Press, 2005. 209-30.

Narayan, Uma, and Sandra Harding, eds. *Decentering the Center: Philosophy for a Multicultural, Postcolonial, and Feminist World.* Bloomington: Indiana University Press, 2000.

Natarajan, Nalini. "Woman, Nation, and Narration in Midnight's Children." *Scattered Hegemonies: Postmodernity and Transnational Feminist Practices.* Ed. Inderpal Grewal and Caren Kaplan. Minneapolis: University of Minnesota Press, 1997. 76-89.

Ng, Fae Myenne. *Bone.* 1993. New York: HarperPerennial, 1994.

Ng, Mei. *Eating Chinese Food Naked.* New York: Washington Square Press, 1998.

------. "This Early." *Tasting Life Twice: Literary Lesbian Fiction by New American Writers.* Ed. E. J. Levy. New York: Avon Books, 1995. 213-19.

Nguyen, Viet Thanh. *Race and Resistance: Literature and Politics in Asian American Literature.* New York: Oxford University Press, 2002.

Ong, Aihwa. *Flexible Citizenship: The Cultural Logics of Transnationality.* Durham: Duke University Press, 1999.

Ordóñez, Elizabeth J. "Narrative Texts By Ethnic Women: Rereading the Past, Reshaping the Future." *MELUS* 9.3 (Winter 1982): 19-28.

Palumbo-Liu, David, eds. *The Ethnic Canon: Histories, Institutions, and Interventions.* Minnesota: University of Minneapolis Press, 1995.

Partridge, Jeffrey F. L. *Beyond Literary Chinatown.* Seattle: Univerasity of Washington Press, 2007.

Paranjape, Makarand. "Displaced Relations: Diasporas, Empires, Homelands." *CRNLE Journal* (2000): 64-72.

------. "What About Those Who Stayed Back Home?: Interrogating the Privileging of Diasporic Writing." *Shifting Continents, Colliding Cultures: Diaspora Writing of the Indian Subcontinent.* Ed. Ralph J. Crane and Radhika Mohanram. Amsterdam: Rodopi, 2000. 225-45.

Park, Linda Sue. *Project Mulberry.* New York: Houghton Mifflin, 2005.

Perry, Ruth, and Martine Watson Brownley, eds. *Mothering the Mind: Twelve Studies of Writers and Their Silent Partners.* New York and London: Holmes and Meier, 1984.

Pettersson, Bo. "The Postcolonial Turn in Literary Translation Studies: Theoretical Frameworks Reviewed." *Canadian Aesthetics Journal* 4 (Summer 1999): n.p. http://www.uqtr.ca/AE/vol_4/petter.htm (accessed June 21, 2007).

Phan, Aimee. *We Should Never Meet*. New York: St. Martin's Press, 2004.

Quinby, Lee. "The Subject of Memoirs: *The Woman Warrior*'s Technology of Ideographic Selfhood." *De/Colonizing the Subject: The Politics of Gender in Women's Autobiography*. Ed. Sidonie Smith and Julia Watson. Minneapolis: University of Minnesota Press, 1992. 297-320.

Raussert, Wilfried. "Minority Discourses, Foodways, and Aspects of Gender: Contemporary Writings by Asian American Women." *Journal X* 7.2 (2003): 183-203.

Rich, Adrienne. *Blood, Bread and Poetry: Selected Prose, 1979-1985*. New York: W. W. Norton, 1986.

------. *Of Woman Born: Motherhood as Experience and Institution*. 1976. New York: Norton, 1986.

Ricoeur, Paul. *Reflection & Imagination: A Ricoeur Reader*. Ed. Mario J. Valdes. Toronto: University of Toronto Press, 1991.

Rodriguez, Richard. "Mexico's Children." *Crossing Into America: The New Literature of Immigration*. Ed. Louis Mendoza and S. Shankar. New York: The New Press, 2003. 197-219.

Romagnolo, Catherine. "Narrative Beginnings in Amy Tan's *The Joy Luck Club*: A Feminist Study." *Studies in the Novel* 35.1 (Spring 2003): 89-107.

Rony, Fatima Tobing. *The Third Eye: Race, Cinema, and Ethnographic Spectacle*. Durham and London: Duke University Press, 1996

Rosinsky, Natalie M. "Mothers and Daughters: Another Minority Group." *The Lost Tradition: Mothers and Daughters in Literature*. Ed. Cathy N. Davidson and E. M. Broner. New York: Frederick Ungar, 1980. 280-90.

Roy, Manisha. "Mothers and Daughters in Indian-American Families: A Failed Communication?" *A Patchwork Shawl: Chronicles of South Asian Women in America*. Ed. Shamita Das Dasgupta. New Brunswick, NJ: Rutgers University Press, 1998. 97-110.

Royal, Derek Parker. "Literary Genre as Ethnic Resistance in Maxine Hong Kingston's *Tripmaster Monkey: His Fake Book*." *MELUS* 29.2 (Summer 2004): 141-56.

Rubenstein, Roberta. *Boundaries of the Self: Gender, Culture, Fiction*. Chicago: University of Illinois Press, 1987.

Rumbaut, Rubén G. "The Agony of Exile: A Study of the Migration and Adaptation of Indochinese Refugee Adults and Children." *Refugee Children: Theory, Research, and Services*. Ed. Frederick L. Ahearn and Jean L. Athney. Baltimore: Johns Hopkins University Press, 19991. 53-91.

Rushdie, Salman. *Imaginary Homelands: Essays and Criticism 1981-1991*. London: Verso, 1991.

Sadoff, Dianne F. "Black Matrilineage: The Case of Alice Walker and Zora Neale Hurston." *Signs* 11.1 (Autumn 1985): 4-25.

Safran, William. "Diasporas in Modern Societies: Myths of Homeland and Return." *Diaspora* 1 (Spring 1991): 83-99.

Said, Edward W. *Culture and Imperialism*. New York: Vintage, 1993.

------. The World, the Text, and the Critic. Cambridge: Harvard University Press, 1983.

------. *Orientalism*. 1978. New York: Vintage, 2003.

------. *Beginnings: Intention and Method*. New York: Columbia UP, 1975.

Sandoval, Chela. *Methodology of the Oppressed: Theory out of Bounds*. Minneapolis: University of Minnesota Press, 2000.

------. "U.S. Third World Feminism: The Theory and Method of Oppositional Consciousness in the Postmodern World." *Genders* 10 (Spring 1991): 1-24.

Sangari, Kumkum, and Sudesh Vaid, eds. *Recasting Women: Essay in Indian Colonial History*. New Brunswick, NJ: Rutgers University Press, 1990.

Santiago, Esmeralda, and Joie Davidow, eds. *Las Mamis: Favorite Latino Authors Remember Their Mothers*. New York: Vintage, 2000.

Sato, Kumiko. "Differences That the Ethnic Autobiography Makes: Strategy of Maxine Hong Kingston's *The Woman Warrior*." *Studies in American Literature* 36 (February 2000): 73-90.

Schueller, Malinia Johar. "Theorizing Ethnicity and Subjectivity: Maxine Hong Kingston's *Tripmaster Monkey* and Amy Tan's *The Joy Luck Club*." *Genders* 15 (Winter 1992): 72-85.

Schultermandl, Silvia. "Hooked on the American Dream?: Transnational Sexual Labor in Nora Okja Keller's Fox Girl." *Feminist Studies in English Literature* 15.2 (Winter 2007): 159-83.

------. "Writing Against The Grain: The Cross-Over Genres of Maxine Hong Kingston's *The Woman Warrior, China Men, and The Fifth Book of Peace*." *Interactions* 16.2 (Fall 2007): 111-22.

------. "'What am I, anyhow?': Ethnic Consciousness and the Borderlands-Within in Maxine Hong Kingston's and Rebecca Walker's Autobiographies." *Close Encounters of An Other Kind: New Perspectives on Race, Ethnicity and American Studies*. Ed. Roy Goldblatt, Jopi Nyman, and John A. Stotesbury. Joensuu: Faculty of the Humanities: 2005. 3-17.

------, ed. *Contemporary Asian American and Asian British Literatures*. Special Issue of *Interactions* 15.2 (Fall 2006).

Shen, Gloria. "Born of a Stranger: Mother-Daughter Relationships and Storytelling in Amy Tan's *The Joy Luck Club*." *International Women's Writing: New Landscapes of Identity*. Ed. Anne E. Brown and Marjanne E. Goozé. Westport, CT: Greenwood Press, 1995. 233-44

Shigekuni, Julie. *A Bridge Between Us*. New York: Anchor Books, 1995.

Shohat, Ella, ed. *Talking Visions: Multicultural Feminism in a Transnational Age*. Boston: MIT Press, 2001.

Showalter, Elaine. "Feminist Criticism in the Wilderness." *Critical Inquiry* 8.2 (1981): 179-205.

Simmons, Diane. "Maxine Hong Kingston's Woman Warrior and Shaman: Fighting Women in the New World." *FEMSPEC* 2.1 (2000): 49-65.

Simon, Sherry. *Gender in Translation*. London: Routledge, 1996.

Singer, Alan. "Aesthetic Community: Recognition as an Other Sense of *Sensus Communis*." *boundary* 2 24.1 (1997): 205-36.

Singh, Amritjit, and Peter Schmidt, eds. *Postcolonial Theory and the United States: Race, Ethnicity, and Literature*. Jackson: University of Mississippi Press, 2000.

------, and Peter Schmidt. "On the Borders Between U.S. Studies and Postcolonial Theory." *Postcolonial Theory and the United States: Race, Ethnicity, and Literature*. Jackson: University of Mississippi Press, 2000. 3-69.

Singh, Amritjit, Skerrett, Joseph T., Jr., and Robert E. Hogan, eds. *Memory and Cultural Politics: New Approaches to Ethnic American Literatures*. Boston: Northeastern University Press, 1996.

------, eds. *Memory, Narrative, and Identity: New Essays in Ethnic American Literatures*. Boston: Northeastern University Press, 1994.

Singh, Sonja. *Goddess for Hire*. New York: Harper Collins, 2004.

Shear, Walter. "Generational Differences and the Diaspora in *The Joy Luck Club*." *Critique* 34.3 (Spring 1993): 193-99.

Shih, Shu-mei. "Towards an Ethics of Transnational Encounter, or 'when' does a 'Chinese' woman become a 'feminist'?" *Differences: A Journal of Feminist Cultural Studies* 13.2 (Summer 2002): 90-126.

Showalter, Elaine. "Feminist Criticism in the Wilderness." *Critical Inquiry* 8.2 (1981): 179-205.

Shu, Yuan. "Globalization and 'Asian Values': Teaching and Theorizing Asian American Literature." *College Literature* 32.1 (Winter 2005): 86-102.

Smith, Paul. "Julia Kristeva Et Al.: or, Take Three or More." *Feminism and Psychoanalysis*. Ed. Richard Feldstein and Judith Roof. Ithaca: Cornell University Press, 1989. 84-104.

Smith, Sidonie. "Filiality and Woman's Autobiographical Storytelling." *Maxine Hong Kingston's* The Woman Warrior*: A Casebook*. Ed. Sau-ling C. Wong. New York and Oxford: Oxford University Press, 1999. 57-83.

------. *A Poetics of Women's Autobiography: Marginality and the Fictions of Self-Representation*. Bloomington and Indianapolis: Indiana University Press, 1987.

------, and Julia Watson, eds. *De/Colonizing the Subject: The Politics of Gender in Women's Autobiography*. Minneapolis: University of Minnesota Press, 1992.

Smorada, Claudia Kovach. "Side-Stepping Death: Ethnic Identity, Contradiction, and the Mother(land) in Amy Tan's Novels." *Fu-Jen Studies* 24 (1991): 31-45.

Sollors, Werner. "Ethnicity." *Critical Terms for Literary Study*. Ed. Frank Lentricchia and Thomas McLaughlin. Chicago: University of Chicago Press, 1990. 288-305.

------. *Beyond Ethnicity: Consent and Descent in American Culture*. New York: Oxford University Press, 1986.

Sone, Monica. *Nisei Daughter*. Seattle: University of Washington Press, 1953.

Sophocles. *Electra*. Ed. Peter Burian and Alan Shapiro. Trans. Anne Carson. New York: Oxford University Press, 2001.

Souris, Stephen. "'Only Two Kinds of Daughters': Inter-Monologue Dialogicity in *The Joy Luck Club*." *MELUS* 19.2 (1994): 99-123.

Spelman, Elizabeth. *Inessential Women: Problems of Exclusion in Feminist Thought*. Boston: Beacon Press, 1988.

Spivak, Gayatri Chakravorty. *A Critique of Postcolonial Reason: Toward a History of the Vanishing Present*. Cambridge: Harvard University Press, 1999.

------. "Diasporas Old and New: Women in the Transnational World." *Textual Practice* 10.2 (1996): 245-69.

------. "The Politics of Translation." *Outside in the Teaching Machine*. New York: Routledge, 1993. 179-200.

------. "Can the Subaltern Speak?" *Marxism and the Interpretation of Culture*. Ed. Cary Nelson and Lawrence Grossberg. Urbana: University of Illinois Press, 1988. 271-313.

------. *In Other Worlds: Essays in Cultural Politics*. New York: Methuen, 1987.

------. "Three Women's Texts and a Critique of Imperialism." *Critical Inquiry* 12.1 (Autumn 1985): 243-61.

Srikanth, Rajini. *The World Next Door: South Asian American Literature and the Idea of America*. Philadelphia: Temple University Press, 2004.

------. "Gender and the Image of Home in the Asian American Diaspora: A Socio-Literary Reading of Some Asian American Works." *Critical Mass: A Journal of Asian American Cultural Criticism* 2.1 (Winter 1994): 147-81.

------, and Lavina Dhingra Shankar. "South Asian American Literature: 'Off the Turnpike' of Asian America." *Postcolonial Theory and the United*

States: Race, Ethnicity, and Literature. Ed. Amritjit Singh and Peter Schmidt. Jackson: University of Mississippi Press, 2000. 370-87.

------, and Esther Y. Iwanaga, eds. *Bold Words: A Century of Asian American Writing*. New Brunswick, NJ: Rutgers University Press, 2001.

Stanley, Sandra Kumamoto, ed. *Other Sisterhoods: Literary Theory and U.S. Women of Color*. Urbana and Chicago: University of Illinois Press, 1998.

Stetz, Margaret D. "Teaching 'Comfort Women' Issues in Women's Studies Courses." *Radical Teacher* 66 (Spring 2003): 17-21.

------. "Wartime Sexual Violence Against Women: A Feminist Response." *Feminist Theory Reader: Local and Global Perspectives*. Ed. Carole R. McCann and Seung-Kyung Kim. New York: Routledge, 2003. 138-45.

------, and Bonnie Oh, eds. *Legacies of the Comfort Women of World War II*. Armonk, NY: M. E. Sharpe, 2001.

Stoler, Ann Laura, ed. *Haunted By Empire: Geographies of Intimacy in North American History*. Durham and London: Duke University Press, 2006.

Stone-Mediatore, Shari. "Chandra Mohanty and the Revaluing of 'Experience.'" *Decentering the Center: Philosophy for a Multicultural, Postcolonial, and Feminist World*. Bloomington: Indianan University Press, 2000. 110-27.

Suleri, Sara. "Woman Skin Deep: Feminism and the Postcolonial Condition." *Critical Inquiry* 18 (1992): 756-69.

Takaki, Ronald T. *Strangers From a Different Shore: A History of Asian Americans*. New York: Penguin, 1990.

------, ed. *From Different Shores: Perspectives on Race and Ethnicity in America*. 1987. 2nd Edition. New York and Oxford: Oxford University Press, 1994.

Tal, Kali. *Worlds of Hurt: Reading the Literature of Trauma*. Cambridge: Cambridge University Press, 1996.

Tan, Amy. *The Bonesetter's Daughter*. New York: Ballantine, 2001.

------. *The Hundred Secret Senses*. New York: Ballantine, 1995.

------. *The Kitchen God's Wife*. New York: Ivy Books, 1991.

------. *The Joy Luck Club*. New York: Putnam, 1989.

Thiesmeyer, Lynn. "U.S. Comfort Women and the Silence of the American Other." *Hitting Critical Mass* 3.2 (Spring 1996): 47-67.

Thoma, Pamela. "Cultural Autobiography, Testimonial, and Asian American Transnational Feminist Coalition in the 'Comfort Women of World War II' Conference." *Frontiers* 21.1-2 (2000): 29-54.

Todorov, Tzvetan. "'Race,' Writing, and Culture." *Critical Inquiry* 13 (1986): 171-81.

Trinh, T. Minh-ha. *When the Moon Waxes Red: Representation, Gender and Cultural Politics*. New York: Routledge, 1991.

------. *Woman, Native, Other: Writing Postcoloniality and Feminism*. Bloomington and Indianapolis: Indiana University Press, 1989.

Ty, Eleanor. "Rethinking the Hyphen: Asian North American and European Ethnic Texts as Global Narratives." *Canadian Review of American Studies/Revue Canadienne d'etudes americaines* 32.3 (2002): 239-52.

------, and Donald C. Goellnicht. *Beyond the Hyphen: Asian North American Identities*. Bloomington: Indiana University Press, 2004.

Unali, Lina. "Americanization and Hybridity in *The Hundred Secret Senses*." *Hitting Critical Mass* 4.1 (Fall 1996): 135-44.

Venuti, Lawrence. *Scandals of Translation: Towards an Ethic of Difference*. London: Routledge, 1998.

------, ed. *Rethinking Translation: Discourse, Subjectivity, Ideology*. London: Routledge, 1992.

Vijayaraghavan, Vineeta. *Motherland*. New York: Soho, 2001.

Volpp, Leti. "'(Mis)Identifying Culture: Asian Women and the 'Cultural Defense.'" *Harvard Women's Law Journal* 17 (1994):57-80.

Wade-Gayles, Gloria. "The Truths of Our Mothers' Lives: Mother-Daughter Relationships in Black Women's Fiction." *Sage* 1.2 (Fall 1984): 8-12.

Wagner, Tamara S. "'After another round of tissues': 'Bad Time' Fiction and the Amy Tan-Syndrome in Recent Singaporean Novels." *Journal of Commonwealth Literature* 38.2 (2003): 19-39.

Walker, Alice. *In Search of Our Mothers' Gardens: Womanist Prose*. San Diego: Hartcourt Brace & Company, 1983.

------. "Everyday Use." *In Love and Trouble: Stories of Black Women*. New York: Harvest Books, 1974. 47-59.

Walters, Suzanna Danuta. *Lives Together/Worlds Apart: Mothers and Daughters in Popular Culture*. Berkeley, Los Angeles and London: University of California Press, 1992.

Washington, Mary Helen. "I Sign My Mother's Name: Alice Walker, Dorothy West, Paule Marshall." *Mothering the Mind: Twelve Studies of Writers and Their Silent Partners*. Ed. Ruth Perry and Martine Watson Brownley. New York and London: Holmes and Meier, 1984. 142-63.

White, E. Frances. "Listening to the Voices of Black Feminism." *Radical America* 18.2-3 (1984): 7-25.

Willard, Nancy. "Talking to Ghosts." *The New York Times* 18 February 2001. www.nytimes.com/books/01/0218/reviews/010218.18williard.html (accessed June 14, 2006).

Wong, Elizabeth. "The Struggle to Be An All American Girl." Rpt. *Crossing Cultures: Readings for Composition.* 3rd Edition. Ed. Henry and Myrna Knepler. New York: Macmillan, 1991. 21-23.

Wong, Jade Snow *Fifth Chinese Daughter.* 1945. Seattle: University of Washington Press, 1989.

Wong, Sau-ling Cynthia. "Autobiography as Guided Chinatown Tour? Maxine Hong Kingston's *The Woman Warrior* and the Chinese American Autobiographical Controversy." *Maxine Hong Kingston's* The Woman Warrior*: A Casebook.* New York and Oxford: Oxford University Press, 1999. 29-53.

------. "Deterritorialization Reconsidered: Asian American Cultural Criticism at a Theoretical Crossroads." *Amerasia Journal* 21.1 (1995): 1-27.

------."'Sugar Sisterhood': Situating the Amy Tan Phenomenon." *The Ethnic Canon: Histories, Institutions, and Interventions.* Ed. David Palumbo-Liu. Minneapolis and London: University of Minnesota Press, 1995. 174-210.

------. *Reading Asian American Literature: From Necessity to Extravagance.* Princeton: Princeton University Press, 1993.

------. "Ethnicizing Gender: An Exploration of Sexuality as Sign in Chinese Immigrant Literature." *Reading the Literatures of Asian America.* Ed. Shirley Geok-lin Lim and Amy Ling. Philadelphia: Temple University Press: 1992. 111-29.

------, and Jeffrey J. Santa Ana. "Gender and Sexuality in Asian American Literature." *Signs* 25.1 (Autumn 1999): 171-226.

------, and Stephen H. Sumida, eds. *A Resource Guide to Asian American Literature.* New York: MLA, 2001.

------, ed. *Maxine Hong Kingston's* The Woman Warrior*: A Casebook.* New York and Oxford: Oxford University Press, 1999.

Woo, Merle. "Letter to Ma." *This Bridge Called my Back: Writings By Radical Feminist of Color.* Ed. Cherríe Moraga and Gloria Anzaldúa. New York: Kitchen Table Press, 1981. 140-47.

Woolf, Virginia. *A Room of One's Own.* 1929. New York: Harcourt Brace Jovanovich, 1989.

Xu, Ben. "Memory and the Ethnic Self: Reading Amy Tan's *The Joy Luck Club.*" *MELUS* 19.1 (Spring 1994): 3-18.

Xu, Wenying. *Eating Identities: Reading Food in Asian American Literature.* Honolulu: University of Hawaii Press, 2008.

Yonayama, Lisa. "Traveling Memories, Contagious Justice: Americanization of Japanese War Crimes at the End of the Post-Cold War." *Journal of Asian American Studies* 6.1 (2003): 57-93.

------. *Hiroshima Traces: Time, Space, and the Dialectics of Memory.* Berkeley: University of California Press, 1999.

Yu, Yi-Lin. "Relocating Maternal Subjectivity: Storytelling and Mother-Daughter Voices in Amy Tan's The Joy Luck Club." *third space* 1.2 (March 2002): n.p. www. thirdspace.ca/articles/yu.htm (accessed July 14, 2008).

Yuan, Yuan. "The Semiotics of China Narratives in the Con/texts of Kingston and Tan." *Critique* 40.3 (Spring 1999): 292-303.

Zhou, Xiaojing. "Introduction: Critical Theories and Methodologies in Asian American Literary Studies." *Form and Transformation in Asian American Literature*. Ed. Zhou Xiaojing and Samina Najmi. Seattle: University of Washington Press, 2005. 3-29.

Zhou, Xiaojing, and Samina Najmi, eds. *Form and Transformation in Asian American Literature*. Seattle: University of Washington Press, 2005.

Zia, Helen. *Asian American Dreams: The Emergence of an American People*. New York: Farrar, Straus and Giroux, 2000.

INDEX

ABOUT THE AUTHOR

Silvia Schultermandl is assistant professor of American Studies at the University of Graz, where she teaches courses in American literature and culture studies. Her research interests lie in multi-ethnic American literatures and transnational feminism. Her publications include articles on contemporary authors such as Maxine Hong Kingston, Rebecca Walker, Linda Hogan, Julia Alvarez, Esmeralda Santiago, Nora Okja Keller, and Barbara Kingsolver. She recently put together a special issue for *Interactions* on Asian American and British Asian Culture, with a comprehensive critical introduction. She is currently at work on two collections of essays: *Growing Up Transnational: Family and Kinship in a Global Era* (co-edited with May Friedman, York University, Toronto); and *Transnational Identity Politics in Anglophone Literature* (co-edited with Sebnem Toplu).

FORECAAST

(Forum for European Contributions to African American Studies)
edited by Prof. Dr. Sabine Broeck, Prof. Dr. Maria I. Diedrich, and Prof. Dr. Christopher Mulvey

Michelle Wright;
Antje Schuhmann (Eds.)
Blackness and Sexualities
How queer is Black studies, how racialized is queer studies? In the West, racial fantasies are often sexualized, just as sexual fantasies often rely on notions of a racial Other. Bringing together the latest work by some of the foremost scholars in a variety of disciplines, Blackness and Sexualities offers analyses and critiques that span three continents and looks at topics such as: the secret marketing of black female pornography to white American men; the eroticization of colonial legacies in contemporary German media; the exoticization of African women in previously unpublished photos and diaries by America's first best-selling black novelist; the ways in which film captures how drag queens can claim agency and cooperate with all kinds of sexual communities across racial lines-or fail to do so with terrible consequences.
Bd. 16, 2007, 184 S., 19,90 €, br.,
ISBN 978-3-8258-9693-5

John Cullen Gruesser;
Hanna Wallinger (Eds.)
Loopholes and Retreats: African American Writers and the Nineteenth Century
Bd. 17, 2008, 232 S., 29,90 €, br.,
ISBN 978-3-8258-1892-0

Austria: Forschung und Wissenschaft – Literatur- und Sprachwissenschaft

Alwin Fill; Hermine Penz (Eds.)
Sustaining Language
Essays in Applied Ecolinguistics
Can language diversity be sustained on this earth? Can the resource language be used in a sustainable way? The essays in this volume address language loss in the age of globalization and discuss how language construes our view of Nature and Environment. The volume is also a plea for using an ecolinguistic perspective in school teaching. Kann die Sprachenvielfalt der Erde erhalten bleiben? Kann die Ressource Sprache nachhaltig genutzt werden? Dieser Band thematisiert den Sprachverlust im Zeitalter der Globalisierung und zugleich die Macht der Sprache bei der Konstruktion von Natur und Umwelt. Das Buch ist auch ein Plädoyer für die ökolinguistische Perspektive im Schulunterricht.
Bd. 5, 2007, 312 S., 19,90 €, br.,
ISBN 978-3-8258-9858-8

Werner Delanoy; Jörg Helbig;
Allan James
Towards a Dialogic Anglistics
When one looks at the history of English Studies there has been a noticeable proliferation of research interests since the 1970s. As a result of such development, attempts have been made to create a new basis for communication and cooperation inside Anglistics and across disciplines. Making a case for a Dialogic Anglistics is such an attempt. A Dialogic Anglistics is based on a normative concept of dialogue aiming for egalitarian forms of cooperation both inside, between and across disciplines leading to the redefinition of old and creation of manifold new directions for English Studies. In the nineteen articles presented in this volume dialogic encounters are encouraged both within and between different fields within Anglistics. Furthermore, dialogic links are created with colleagues from other academic disciplines.
Bd. 9, 2007, 320 S., 29,90 €, br.,
ISBN 978-3-8258-0549-4

Arno
Herberth; Thomas Niederkrotenthaler;
Benedikt Till (Hg../Eds.)
Suizidalität in den Medien. Suicidality in the Media
Interdisziplinäre Betrachtungen. Interdisciplinary Contributions
The portrayal of suicide in the media contributes to our understanding of the cultural

LIT Verlag GmbH & Co. KG Wien – Zürich
Auslieferung Österreich: Medienlogistik Pichler-ÖBZ GmbH & Co KG
IZ-NÖ Süd, Straße 1, Objekt 34, A-2355 Wiener Neudorf, Postfach 133
Tel. +43 (0) 2236 / 63 535 - 236, Fax +43 (0) 2236 / 63 535 - 243, e-Mail: bestellen@medien-logistik.at
Auslieferung Deutschland: Fresnostr. 2 48159 Münster
Tel.: 0251 / 620 32 22 – Fax 0251 / 922 60 99
e-Mail: vertrieb@lit-verlag.de – http://www.lit-verlag.de

phenomenon of suicide. The risk of inducing imitative effects, but also the possibility of a preventive impact on the recipients make this topic an important issue in suicide prevention. International contributions from psychology, medicine, sociology, media- and literary studies focus on semiotics of suicide portrayals in the media and their effects on the recipient. The analysis of daily press, literature, film genres and the new media gives an up-to-date insight into this interdisciplinary field of research.

Bd. 12, 2008, 288 S., 29,90 €, br.,
ISBN 978-3-8258-1641-4

Renate Hodab; Klaus-Dieter Ertler

Die Presse der spanischen Aufklärung:
El Corresponsal del Censor

Die vorliegende Untersuchung ist Teil eines auf mehrere Jahre angelegten Projektes, dessen vorrangiges Ziel die sozial- und kulturwissenschaftlich ausgerichtete Aufarbeitung und Beschreibung der moralischen Wochenschriften der Romania ist. Nach der Analyse der prominentesten spanischen Wochenschriften *El Pensador* (2003) und *El Censor* (2004) liegt nun auch die Studie zu *El Corresponsal del Censor* vor.

Bd. 11, 2008, 352 S., 29,90 €, br.,
ISBN 978-3-8258-1553-0

Repräsentation – Transformation
representation – transformation
représentation – transformation
Translating across Cultures and Societies

hrsg. von
Ao. Univ. Prof. Dr. Michaela Wolf
(Universität Graz)

Gisella M. Vorderobermeier; Michaela Wolf (Hg.)

„Meine Sprache grenzt mich ab ... “

Transkulturalität und kulturelle Übersetzung im Kontext von Migration

Derzeit wird „Übersetzung“ in erweiterter Betrachtungsweise als umfassendes transkulturelles Phänomen (Stichwort „kulturelle Übersetzung“) diskutiert. Damit kommen auch zentrale gesellschaftspolitische Fragen zu Exil, Diaspora oder Migration in den Blick. Im Zentrum dieses Bandes steht „Migration“ in der Perspektive der dafür konstitutiven Transferprozesse. Theoretisch gerahmt durch die Denkfigur „Migration als Übersetzung“ werden in interdisziplinärer Sicht die gesellschaftsverändernde Rolle von Translation thematisiert und durch Migration forcierte Umdenkprozesse in den Geistes- und Sozialwissenschaften erörtert („migrating theories“).

Bd. 3, 2008, 312 S., 24,90 €, br.,
ISBN 978-3-8258-1294-2

Michaela Wolf (ed.)

Übersetzen – Translating – Traduire

Towards a “Social Turn”?

Translating and interpreting as a social practice is now increasingly determining daily routines in a globalising world. This volume deals with the most significant questions of translation sociology as a new field of research in translation studies. The contributions show the social implications of translating and interpreting in various fields: translation trends between individual cultures, the social construction of images through translation, ideological restraints of translation production, the powerful relations between the actors in the translation process and finally the instances involved in the creation of translations.

Bd. 1, 2006, 368 S., 24,90 €, br.,
ISBN 3-8258-9552-1

LIT Verlag GmbH & Co. KG Wien – Zürich

Auslieferung Österreich: Medienlogistik Pichler-ÖBZ GmbH & Co KG
IZ-NÖ Süd, Straße 1, Objekt 34, A-2355 Wiener Neudorf, Postfach 133
Tel. +43 (0) 2236 / 63 535 - 236, Fax +43 (0) 2236 / 63 535 - 243, e-Mail: bestellen@medien-logistik.at

Auslieferung Deutschland: Fresnostr. 2 48159 Münster
Tel.: 0251 / 620 32 22 – Fax 0251 / 922 60 99
e-Mail: vertrieb@lit-verlag.de – http://www.lit-verlag.de